THE DYNAMICS OF HUMAN COMMUNICATION

A LABORATORY APPROACH

THE DYNAMICS
OF HUMAN
COMMUNICATION

A LABORATORY APPROACH

Gail E. Myers
Trinity University

Michele Tolela Myers
Communication Consultant

McGraw-Hill Book Company

New York St. Louis San Francisco Düsseldorf Johannesburg
Kuala Lumpur London Mexico Montreal New Delhi
Panama Rio de Janeiro Singapore Sydney Toronto

Library of Congress Cataloging in Publication Data

Myers, Gail E   1923–
  The dynamics of human communication.

  Includes bibliographies.
  1. Communications.   2. Interpersonal relations.
I. Myers, Michele Tolela, 1941–   joint author
II. Title.
BF637.C45M9   301.4   72-6718
ISBN 0-07-044205-3

THE DYNAMICS OF HUMAN COMMUNICATION
A Laboratory Approach

    34567890MUMU79876543

This book was set in Trade Gothic by Black Dot, Inc. The editors
were Walter Maytham, Alison Meersschaert, and James R.
Belser; the designer was Burke/Paccione Associates, Ltd.; and
the production supervisor was Ted Agrillo. The drawings were
done by Danmark & Michaels, Inc.
The printer and binder was The Murray Printing Company.

TO ERIKA

CONTENTS FOR TEXT

CONTENTS FOR TEXT

CONTENTS FOR LABORATORY MANUAL

CONTENTS FOR LABORATORY MANUAL

PREFACE

The Dynamics of Human Communication is part of a new wave of teaching speech-communication in which the focus is on human interaction or human behavior rather than on the skills of platform speaking. This book has also grown out of the need to combine information about communication and practice in communication. We believe that such an approach to the study of human communication is different from the approach used in most speech-communication textbooks. Ours is an approach which permits students to learn *about* communication as well as to learn *to* communicate more effectively.

Basic to our approach in *The Dynamics of Human Communication* are two premises which should be highlighted here. The first premise is that we approach communication as a behavioral science. What happens between people and among people is a human relations function, a dynamic system of interactions. There is nothing static about human communication—it comes from somewhere in the past history of the participants and will go on affecting their future relationships. Even when we attempt to stop the process to study it, we can pick up only fragments of the ongoing process and must treat our studies of the parts and pieces of communication as what they are: the stop-motion analyses, or the instant replays, of what is essentially an interrelated chain of behaviors.

The second premise, essential to understanding this textbook's approach, is that the laboratory method of learning provides an excellent system for learning *about* communication and for learning *to* communicate more effectively. Laboratories have been primarily used in the physical and natural sciences while the social sciences have used the laboratory method of learning more rarely. The laboratory approach helps students learn from interacting with the data about the course—the textbook material and lectures. Perhaps more significantly, the laboratory helps students learn a great deal from interacting with one another, and in this way the effect of one instructor is multiplied over and over by the interaction among the students working on their lab projects. Students have a great ability to learn from one another. In education we have hardly begun to tap this remarkable source of learning energy. Our Laboratory Manual in *The Dynamics of Human Communication* makes full use of this educational advantage by providing situations and activities in which students can and will have a vital effect on the learning of other students.

The style of *The Dynamics of Human Communication* is straightforward and will be understood by any student of human communication.

We have deliberately kept communication jargon to a minimum. No previous exposure to the field of communication is necessary to read and understand this book. We felt very strongly that our main task was to communicate simply and clearly to reduce as much as possible the chances for misunderstanding.

We also felt that some of our readers might wish to explore more deeply into the intricacies of human communication. For this reason, we have included at the end of each chapter an extensive list of bibliographic material. The student interested in more readings in communication will find ample scholarly sources cited there. For those students simply interested in finding out what human communication is about and in discovering some ways to improve their communication, *The Dynamics of Human Communication* provides the information and activities they need.

What we have chosen to write in this book has been influenced so directly by one person that a special tribute must be paid here. The behavioral approach which we have used is a reflection of the earliest pioneering efforts of Elwood Murray at the University of Denver. Three decades or more ahead of his colleagues, Elwood Murray wrote of the human element of the communicative act when much of the speech discipline was still involved with declamatory elocution and the first beginnings of rhetorical innovations.

In other ways, many people have contributed to this book and we must only generalize their names or provide a list of so many professional people and friends we would not have room for text. Our colleagues at the University of Denver led by Alvin Goldberg gave support and encouragement for this manuscript. Much of the material for the laboratory manual was assembled with the help of Martha Herl and Cyndy Ulevitch, former students at Monticello College. Alison Meersschaert, our editor with McGraw-Hill, pulled things together for us in a most sympathetic and efficient way. The Tolelas gave us bed and board at Portet de Moraira while we put the manuscript together on many tiring siesta-less afternoons. And finally, it was Erika Lynn Myers whose arrival in January 1972 prevented outside employment for Michele and thus made us finish the text on time.

GAIL E. MYERS
MICHELE TOLELA MYERS

THE DYNAMICS OF INTRAPERSONAL COMMUNICATION

PART ONE

YOU AND YOUR COMMUNICATION   Chapter 1

A textbook like this usually starts with a definition, in this case of communication. However, in this chapter, we will first discuss some characteristics of communication before providing a definition. In fact, the process of communication is so all inclusive in our lives that it is difficult to formulate a brief definition, that is, communication is so important to our daily living that it is hard to compress all these considerations into a few words which will define communication for everyone.

COMMUNICATION IS EVERYWHERE

Man may be only vaguely aware of those things which are closest to him in his life and often pays very little attention to familiar things. Just as a fish takes for granted the water around him, man living in a communication world takes his communication for granted. The fish might miss the water when he is taken from the lake or stream, and man will miss communication if he is suddenly cut off from it.

The universal human characteristic of symbol using is highly developed in some societies, less well developed in others. But whether you are in the heart of our greatest cities or in a small village in some primitive area of the world, the use of symbols is what will tie you to the people and activities around you. Most human behavior involves the use of a system of symbols. We speak in oral symbols, we write in written symbols, and we make use of a highly structured and rich system of nonverbal signs, gestures, moves, and actions to express much of what we want to convey to another person.

Anthropologists tell us that any society will develop a symbol system necessary for that society to survive. If the needs for symbols only involve the necessities of gaining food and shelter, that society will develop these. It is important here to note that we should not feel superior to a culture which does not have our mechanical devices for communication, nor feel that our language system is better because it may have some words or symbols which another culture lacks. It has, in fact, been argued that there is no such thing as a "primitive" language, because whatever language a society uses will meet the needs of that society and cannot therefore be called primitive. Many spoken languages have the ability to express concepts which are not normally found in English or which we may take many different words to express. Symbol systems, and hence communication, arise in relation to man's need to express himself for that place he occupies in the world.

Not only do all humans need and use communication, but we find it all around us. When you start your day by waking up, it may be to the sound of an alarm clock, a radio, or someone calling you. At least the message gets across that you should get up.

Getting dressed and cleaned up are largely the product of previous communication. You were not born with a tremendous urge to brush your teeth, shower, or comb your hair. If these have become part of your behavior patterns it is because you learned them and because someone at some age in your life conditioned you with rewards and punishments through an effective communication system called child-rearing.

You select some clothes to wear for the day. They will be part of your communication with others. You know through previous communication that some outfits are acceptable in certain situations and some in others; that you can give a pretty strong message by showing up in class too dressed up, or at a formal party in a T-shirt. Clothes you wear will communicate much about you: your tastes, your finances, the groups you want to be identified with. This will also influence the response of others to you. Jewelry you wear, style of your hair, and any articles you may carry will all tell something about you and will bring some kinds of predictable responses from others in your communication day.

By now you are ready for breakfast and whether or not you eat and what you eat will be influenced by previous communication. If you believe "it is not good to leave the house with an empty stomach," you may be listening to the voices of your parents or of a TV commercial. The cereal you eat, the brand of coffee you use, and the amount you eat have all been conditioned by your communication environment.

Going outdoors brings you into more communication, this time with your natural environment. Noisy, smoky, or quiet and clear, it may well influence you in what you do the rest of the day. Meeting another person lets you select your behavior—to speak to him or not. If you speak, you make a selection of tone of voice and message: hello, hi, nice day, (or a grunt) can all convey an important message.

If you walk to work or to class, you will communicate with others as you move past people and avoid running into them. In the city as we move rapidly down the street, we have a radar-like system of communication established to tell each other which way we will dodge when we come close to colliding. Sometimes we don't read these signals well and can end up in a kind of "dance" with a stranger as we try to move around him. Research in this field has clearly established the communicative nature of the simple act of walking on a crowded sidewalk even when we think we are not paying any attention to the moves of others. This hidden dimension of our communication is treated also by Edward T. Hall[1] and popu-

[1] *Edward T. Hall*, The Hidden Dimension, *Doubleday & Company, Inc., Garden City, N.Y., 1966.*

THE DYNAMICS OF INTRAPERSONAL COMMUNICATION

larized more recently by Julius Fast[2] in an interesting way. Our communication, then, can be silent and so automatic that we are not consciously aware we are communicating.

Another example occurs if you drive to work or class. After you have made the trip a few times, your responses to symbols and signals around you become almost automatic. You pull out into the street; watch for cross traffic at the corner, a "School Slow" sign in the next block, a blind intersection coming up next; wonder whether or not the light will change to green at the next corner; anticipate the 35-mile zone which is often patrolled by a radar car; turn into the parking lot; head for the only available place near your work or class and find it occupied by a sports car with the top down; and finally make a few turns around the lot and settle for a place far away from where you want to go. You were responding all this time to symbols and signals from other drivers; from your past experience; from the normal controls placed on drivers by authorities who communicate to us by setting up signs, lights, and lanes; and from uniformed representatives for them. Even though the authorities may be many miles away and doing something else at the moment, they still communicate to the drivers and pedestrians everywhere in the city.

When we get to class, we begin to see more clearly the communication process. You hear a lecture, you get assignments, you talk about the class with another student, and you agree to meet someone for lunch. We know these acts involve communication because they involve obvious verbal messages and it is our intention to communicate. But all the time these overt or open acts of communication are occurring, there is another level going on. What is happening inside us, our thoughts and our seeing and hearing many other kinds of data, are also communication. Writing on the blackboard, noises from the other room, or someone passing by the door all will attract us momentarily. The way a student next to us is dozing off or the way the professor fumbles in his notes are all part of our communication. The notes we take from the lecture and the items we leave out and decide not to write down are important communication decisions. Asking questions and listening to others bring us actively again into communication.

The rest of our day will broaden our communication. Do you listen to a radio, watch TV, talk on the telephone? These are extensions of your personal contact with people. An advertiser on radio will tell thousands of us at once where to get a bargain in short-term loans, hoping that some of us need money and will respond. At least an advertiser has paid *his* good money on the assumption that the communication will reach someone. You can find out from newspapers, magazines, and media news reports what has happened in Washington, Moscow, London, Chicago, or

[2]*Julius Fast,* Body Language, *M. Evans and Company, Philadelphia, 1970.*

Podunk, even though you were not there. Someone is ready to report to you every hour the big news stories of a world you may not even know and tell you about people you have never met. The mechanical and electronic means of communication have increased for us far beyond our ability to assimilate all the potential. We listen to only one radio station at a time, although there may be hundreds within reach of the instrument we tune in. We may read one or two newspapers out of the hundreds published every day. We see only a few selected programs on TV although the several stations available will broadcast all day and most of the night. A friend phones you, or you telephone someone to seek information or perhaps just to keep your personal contact with others.

During your day you will speak, will be spoken to, will write, will read, will respond to many symbols. You will be in touch with many people who will tell you things, ask you to remember some others, and ask you to do still others. You may feel satisfied with your day in relation to how successful you feel your communication has been: Did you ignore someone you wished you had spoken to? Did you miss seeing and talking with a friend or not get the phone call you expected? Did you get confused in class? Out of the entire day of communicating possibilities, you have selected certain things to do and not do. You are like your radio, in a way, as you tune in certain "stations" to pay attention to; you cannot listen to all of them at once. In later chapters we will develop this idea that *communication is everywhere,* and also that because we select and choose our communicative behaviors, *communication is not random.*

COMMUNICATION IS CONTINUOUS

Our communication comes from the past and goes into the future. It does not have a clear-cut beginning and end. It is part of our life which flows and changes as our environment changes, as we change and others change. Our communicative needs are never static and therefore require adjustment based on our previous experiences and our future expectations.

Any communicative behavior has roots in the past as pointed out earlier. We are conditioned to talk in a certain way about things and to think in ways our habits have shown us we should. In this same way, we plan what should happen and our communication affects the outcome. An example of a simple sounding statement such as "Will you marry me?" asked by a boy of a girl has a history of past association and many future implications. It is not merely a flow of words in the present. On very simple matters such as "Phone me tonight," or "Read the next chapter," or "What do you want to eat?" one can trace a history of past associations with the subject of the statement and can realize there will also be effects in the future if the friend does or does not phone, if you read or do not read the chapter, or if you eat something you don't like.

THE DYNAMICS OF INTRAPERSONAL COMMUNICATION

When you advise a friend about what kind of movie to see, or what clothes to buy, or whom to date, it will be on the basis of the values you have developed about movies, clothes, and members of the opposite sex. You will not usually tell a friend "that is your business" when the question of dating, or buying, or entertainment comes up. You will usually have an opinion based on your previous experience and be perfectly willing to share that opinion. Your values, then, make up part of your present communication and the long-range effects of this communication will be felt by the participants. We bring to any communication a lifetime of attitudes, values, experiences, and assumptions. We carry along with us, after the communication, the consequences of our behaviors.

"Feedback" is essential to the continuous process of communication. We guide our future communication by using a rear-view mirror of our own past. We direct our communication by finding out from others how things are working out. The term feedback refers to that part of our communication behavior which pays attention to the effect of a message so we can know what to do next.

The classic example of feedback in the physical world is the thermostat in a house. We set a certain temperature to be maintained, and the thermostat sends a signal to the furnace that more heat or less heat is needed. In this respect, the heating system is self-regulating because as more heat is needed in a room, the furnace responds accordingly. Comparable to the desire to heat a house is our goal in communication to achieve some specific purpose such as seeking information, socializing, giving directions, etc. In order to know whether or not the goal is being met, we need to watch for feedback. The other person involved in our communication may talk to us; respond with a shake of the head, smile, frown; or otherwise indicate how the message is being received. Just as we steer a car, bicycle, or boat to keep in a certain direction, we need to steer our communication. Mathematician Norbert Wiener wrote about feedback as an essential part of the system he called "cybernetics" which dealt with control of goal-seeking machines and human beings. "Cybernetics" comes from the Greek word for "steersman," and our physical world and our communicative behaviors can profit from this concept.

Examples of feedback in our communication would include tests by a professor who wants feedback on what his students are learning, and in turn provides feedback to the students when he grades them. This feedback is a report on what someone is doing in a course.

More specifically, feedback is an essential part of our contact with others. We ask questions and expect answers. We speak to someone and expect a response in the form of words or nonverbal signs that tell us we have been heard. On receiving a response we may adjust our next communication in relation to how we interpreted the feedback we received. "Would you like a cup of coffee?" may result in a yes, no, maybe, or some other kind of answer. What you do next will be determined by how you received the response. If the answer is "no," you may next offer tea or milk, but you have adjusted your communication.

The continuity of communication depends on giving and receiving feedback as well as storing data for future use. In this book we will refer often to feedback in an attempt to keep you aware that what you say or signal to another person has a consequence and that only by appropriate interpretation of the feedback received can you continue effective communication.

COMMUNICATION IS THE SHARING OF MEANING

In describing communication, it is important to emphasize that it has a purpose. While most communication scholars agree that communication is related to symbol manipulation, there is not always agreement on the aims of communication. Some view communication as designed to transmit information and transfer ideas. If we take this view we will concentrate on the messages, or the content of what is said. Effective communication is therefore related to the messages' internal quality or to whether the messages are well organized and well documented. In this view, the receiver of the message is viewed as a rather passive element in the process.

This approach neglects the fundamental aspect of man's communication with himself and his environment and does not do justice to the dynamic complexities of the process of communication. Thus others have developed the view that creation of meaning, rather than the transmission of information, is central to the study of communication.

Ours is a world of booming and buzzing confusion, from which we are assailed from all directions with messages and stimuli. Yet this world becomes understandable to us, full of beauty or ugliness, because we assign significance to what we perceive. It is like walking into a vast supermarket of noise and sights without any organization. From our experience we begin to sort things out—the vegetables are there, the canned goods over there, meats are back there, and so on—and we can find with the help of signs the order in the otherwise chaotic world or disorganized store.

In the supermarket we get help from a classification system known to us from our past experience and from the arrangement of signs and aisles. You don't expect to find the canned string beans next to the fresh string beans, just because they are beans. Would you expect to find milk with the other beverages such as colas, coffee, or tea? In fact, the classifications used by most supermarkets are not the only way things could be arranged, but they reflect some needs for displaying and preserving the goods, which is why fresh vegetables are not found with the canned ones of the same name and milk will be located in a cooler with dairy products rather than with other beverages.

As we communicate with our environment we try to make meanings out of the variety of words and messages around us. We use a classification system to organize these messages and probably have developed this system carefully over the years so that we understand our environment in this way. When we receive a message, it may call up a memory of a previous experience just as when we see an object, we attempt to identify it in terms of what we already know. As our experience increases, the relationships with things around us expand so our world acquires more meaning.

Meanings may not be the same in two individuals because they have different classification systems and because they have had different experiences. Communication therefore is an attempt to call up inside ourselves a meaning which is appropriate and has a close relationship to what is going on around us. Communication with others involves an attempt to share our meanings with them by calling up inside another person a classification and experience reaction similar to ours.

COMMUNICATION IS A MULTILEVEL ACTIVITY

We have used examples of communicative behavior which do not all have the same elements in them. Waking up to an alarm clock is not the same as listening to a lecture or hearing the professor give you an assignment. In the first instance the communication is between you and your environment and the factors which affect the communication are primarily inside you. We say primarily, because factors within you are colored by your past experiences with other people and events. You get up when an alarm clock rings because it is familiar to you to respond to a ringing bell for getting up. In a society where no one normally has alarm clocks, the people might laugh, run, or be amazed at the alarm, but they would not use it to remind them to get up. Someone taught you about alarm clocks, and they have become part of your cognitive world, part of what you recognize in your environment, part of what communicates to you.

Other activities during your day—such as driving or walking to class or to work—are dictated by what you know about your world or can find out by communication. Think what power there is in a red signal light to cause all those highpowered automobiles and anxious drivers to come to a stop until a green light tells them to go on. Communication with our environment responds to the classification and recognition systems we have mentioned before.

When the response is primarily inside us—internal to the person—we call it "intrapersonal" communication. This is where the communication process begins with our perceptions of new messages and our organization of them with our assumptions and attitudes.

Our communication with others, whether it is by writing and speaking or by gestures and signs, we will call interpersonal. In this category is most of what we commonly think of as communication. The professor lecturing or giving an assignment, your advising a friend about movies or dates, etc. By involving another person, the process becomes even more complex because you have to consider his set of assumptions, his classification system, and his perceptions as well as your own.

When we say that communication is multilevel we are noting that it can go on (a) inside us as intrapersonal communication, (b) with others as interpersonal communication, and (c) in both cases involving not only the actual words or symbols but also the inside workings of all the speakers and listeners as well. Communication involves the content of the message and a whole host of unseen and unheard reactions which go on at the same time in all of us.

COMMUNICATION IS PREDICTABLE

In this text we will attempt to provide you with the means of understanding more about your communication, and hence to help you better predict the outcomes of your communication. For many years research has been conducted on the effects of communication on others, and more recently scholars have focused on what happens inside a person during a communicative act. Some results of these studies provide the basis for other chapters of this book. The experience of many years of research has led communication scholars to believe that what happens when a particular kind of message comes from a particular kind of source and reaches a particular kind of audience can generally be predicted.[3] With all the uncertainties of human association, we still can make our sending and receiving of messages consistently more accurate if we know more about the process of communication.

You are all familiar with the polls taken on the popularity of political candidates and on social issues. This guidance offered our leaders gives them some advance information on how a candidate may come out in an election or how a political move may be accepted. In a smaller way we tend to conduct our own "poll" when we talk with others and when we are sensitive to the feedback from our messages. We continually adjust our communication in relation to what we find out.

By further study of the factors involved in communication behavior, we can become more adept at this adjustment. For that reason, this book will deal with those factors which seem to affect communication—our own perceptions and assumptions, the way we deal with facts and infer-

[3]See Carl I. Hovland, Irving Janis, and Harold H. Kelley, Communication and Persuasion, *Yale University Press, New Haven, Conn., 1953. See also Edwin Bettinghaus,* Persuasive Communication, *Holt, Rinehart and Winston, Inc., New York, 1968.*

THE DYNAMICS OF INTRAPERSONAL COMMUNICATION

ences, language itself and the classification systems it provides, as well as other ways we may use to set up barriers to communication. The following chapters will provide information about communication and what we should expect from it, and the laboratory manual exercises will give you a chance to find out for yourself how these ideas come out in our everyday experiences. By understanding the material in this book, you may become better at predicting the outcome of your communication.

Let us emphasize here that communication begins inside us and for that reason this first part will deal primarily with intrapersonal communication. This is based on the belief that *no one but you can do anything to improve your own communication.* People do not learn by being told; they learn by discovering for themselves. If you can discover how your own communication behaviors work, you can understand the communication inside others and your communication with them.

Because we learned to communicate in an informal way beginning by imitating our parents and older children, we have picked up some unhealthy habits. Very little formal training has ever been offered us on how to perceive, or how language affects our behavior, or how our habits of thinking can make us more or less successful in communicating. We manage to erect barriers in our communication inside ourselves and with others which may not be necessary. We get confused and may confuse others when we really don't have to. Hopefully, by being aware of the barriers and the confusions and how they happen, we can avoid many of them. At the end of this first part we will summarize how our relations with our language and thinking may make our communication unsatisfactory and will give you some possible ways to avoid pitfalls of communication.

COMMUNICATION—ONE WORKING DEFINITION

As we wrote at the beginning of this chapter, a textbook on communication should probably include a definition of communication. In this chapter we have developed some characteristics of communication which set the scene for the following chapters. Keeping in mind our suggestions of some possible places you encounter communication in your daily lives, perhaps you now have a better understanding of its all-pervading influence.

As a process and not a static, unrelated act, communication is continuous. We are focusing in the early part of this text on what happens inside the communicator and showing that communication goes on at several levels.

Because it happens inside us, and not as an exchange of physical objects, we have said communication is a sharing of meaning. If we know more about our communicating, we can improve ourselves. There are certain things which are predictable about communication—one of the most important being that unless we know something about the process and want to make the effort ourselves, no one else can do it for us.

There are many definitions of communication offered, depending on the purposes of the definer and those parts of the communicative behaviors being emphasized. If we must have a definition, then, for this text, it might be: *Communication is a generally predictable, multilevel, continuous, and always-present process of the sharing of meaning through symbol interaction.*

BIBLIOGRAPHY

Berlo, D. K.: *The Process of Communication,* Holt, Rinehart and Winston, Inc., New York, 1960.

Campbell, J. H., and H. W. Hepler: *Dimensions in Communication,* rev. ed., Wadsworth Publishing Company, Inc., Belmont, Calif., 1971.

Deutsch, K. W.: "On Communication Models in the Social Sciences," *Public Opinion Quarterly,* vol. 16, 1952, pp. 356–380.

Miller, G. R.: *Speech Communication: A Behavioral Approach,* The Bobbs-Merrill Company, Inc., Indianapolis, 1966.

Miller, G. R.: "On Defining Communication: Another Stab," *Journal of Communication,* vol. 19, no. 2, 1966, pp. 88–98.

Newcomb, T. M.: "An Approach to the Study of Communicative Acts," *Psychological Review,* vol. 60, 1953, pp. 393–404.

Nilsen, T. R.: "On Defining Communication," *The Speech Teacher,* vol. 6, 1957, pp. 10–18.

Schramm, W. (ed.): *The Science of Human Communication,* Basic Books, Inc., Publishers, New York, 1963.

Shannon, C. E., and W. Weaver: *The Mathematical Theory of Communication,* The University of Illinois Press, Urbana, 1949.

Watzlawick, P., J. H. Beavin, and D. Jackson: *Pragmatics of Human Communication,* W. W. Norton & Company, Inc., New York, 1967.

Wiener, N.: *Cybernetics,* John Wiley & Sons, Inc., New York, 1948.

Wiener, N.: *The Human Use of Human Beings,* Doubleday-Anchor, Garden City, N.Y., 1956.

We rely on our senses to tell us what is happening in the world around us. We see things, people, situations, happenings. We hear noises and words. We taste food and drink. We smell odors and scents. We feel and touch objects and surfaces. We are generally excited by something outside our skin, and react to this stimulation by becoming aware of something we were not aware of before. Then we say, we perceived something—a sound, a taste, a sight, a touch. Because we do not live in a vacuum, we are constantly being bombarded by sensations. We are surrounded by things, people, odors, tastes, and happenings. There are sights to be seen, words to be heard. Asleep or awake, we are in the center of noises, smells, and a multitude of stimulations.

We have a great tendency to consider ourselves only passive receivers of all this stimulation coming to us from the world "out there," "the empirical world" as we will call it. We think these things "just happen" to us. We have a sort of resigned "I can't help it" attitude. We act as if we were being hit randomly by all the marvelous and not-so-marvelous things of the world, as if we were helpless victims. This is the "I am a camera" attitude—the film simply grinds away taking in the events around it; or the "tape-recorder" attitude—the recorder turns and turns, slowly accumulating recorded bits of sound with no selectivity or discrimination.

Human perception is much more complicated than such passive attitudes, as can be seen in the following conversations:

"Hey, did you see that John Wayne movie? Man, was it good, I really liked it. . . ."

"Yeah, I saw it. Hated it. Can't stand John Wayne. . . ."

"Beautiful, absolutely beautiful. Now that's the kind of art I really dig. . . ."

"Art? You call that art? That's trash, man, trash."

"See, I talked to him and he said I could leave early. He's really a great teacher. . . ."

"You mean Jones? Not Jones? Jones is a great teacher? He's a creep. Couldn't teach even if he tried. . . ."

"I know it happened like that. I was there. I saw it."

"My friend was there and he said it was different."

Conversations like those above are familiar to most of us. They sound like the kinds of remarks you've heard someplace before. All of them show that the same thing, person, or event may not have been perceived the same way by different people. You look at a painting and it's art; I look at it and it's trash. You like Professor Jones, I despise him. You like John Wayne movies and I don't. Why is it that two people looking at the same things may not see the same things? Who is right about the painting? Is there a right or wrong? What makes you so sure that, just because you were there and saw it happen, the report you give on it is accurate? Are our senses always reliable? Do we see things *as they are* or perhaps as we want them to be, or perhaps as *we* are? Is beauty in the eye of the beholder? If so, what are we really communicating about when we tell someone about the merits of Professor Jones, or a painting, or a movie?

To answer these questions, we need to look into the process of perception. We need to understand how perception works. In this chapter we will take the view that perception is not something that happens to us randomly. We are not the passive receivers of information through our senses. We are not the nonparticipating zombie-like recipients of unselected stimulations.

We are, in fact, the major actors in the perceiving process. We are active partners in what's going on "out there."

We actually *select,* choose, what we perceive, what we look at; we *organize* sensory stimulations and we *interpret* them into a meaningful picture of the world.[1] We do all this very rapidly, usually automatically, and unconsciously, but we do it nevertheless. We create what we see. This may sound exaggerated. You will say, "Come on now, we don't create what we see, we don't make it up. If we see it, it's there."

Not necessarily. There may or may not be something there. And even when there is, we may do something to it—distort it or mold it to our convenience. Let's take a look at the conscious and subconscious ways we do this.

[1] *Bernard Berelson and Gary Steiner,* Human Behavior, an Inventory of Scientific Findings, *Harcourt, Brace & World, Inc., New York, 1964.*

THE BLIND MEN AND THE ELEPHANT, BY JOHN GODFREY SAXE

> It was six men of Indostan
> To learning much inclined,
> Who went to see the Elephant
> (Though all of them were blind),
> That each by observation
> Might satisfy his mind.
> The First approached the Elephant,

THE DYNAMICS OF INTRAPERSONAL COMMUNICATION

And happening to fall
Against his broad and sturdy side,
At once began to bawl:
"God bless me! but the Elephant
Is very like a wall!"
The Second, feeling of the tusk,
Cried, "Ho! what have we here
So very round and smooth and sharp?
To me 'tis mighty clear
This wonder of an Elephant
Is very like a spear!"
The Third approached the animal,
And happening to take
The squirming trunk within his hands,
Thus boldly up he spake:
"I see," quoth he, "the Elephant
Is very like a snake!"
The Fourth reached out an eager hand,
And felt about the knee
"What most this wondrous beast is like
Is mighty plain," quoth he;
"'Tis clear enough the Elephant
Is very like a tree!"
The Fifth who chanced to touch the ear,
Said: "E'en the blindest man
Can tell what this resembles most;
Deny the fact who can,
This marvel of an Elephant
Is very like a fan!"
The Sixth no sooner had begun
About the beast to grope,
Than, seizing on the swinging tail
That fell within his scope,
"I see," quoth he, "the Elephant
Is very like a rope!"
And so these men of Indostan
Disputed loud and long,
Each in his own opinion
Exceeding stiff and strong,
Though each was partly in the right,
And all were in the wrong!

WE SELECT

At any given moment we pay attention, notice, are aware of, perceive only very little of what is going on around us. When we pay attention to something it means we are not paying attention to something else. There are many reasons for selective perception. Some of these reasons are physiological, some are psychological.

Physiological Factors in Selective Perception —How We Are Built

As you probably know, we are stimulated by what is going on outside of us through our five senses. We see, hear, smell, taste, and feel. However, these five senses are not all powerful. Human beings are built in such a way that there are sights we cannot see, sounds we cannot hear, tastes we cannot distinguish, smells we do not sense. Our sense of touch does not give us much information if we do not use our eyes to help us determine what we are touching. Many animals have much sharper senses which enable them to see better, hear better, and smell better than we do. Most other animals, of course, rely more on their senses than we do and have thus developed them more so than we have. It's a little bit like the blind man who cannot rely on his eyes to find out what's going on and will develop his sense of touch and of hearing to compensate for his lack of sight.

The human nervous system is built in such a way that we cannot register with our senses much of what is going on around us. We cannot hear certain sounds—those below 20 cycles per second and those above 20,000 cycles per second. Dog whistles are great to call a dog from a distance although, to us, they sound silent. We do not hear the sound because it is at a frequency higher than the ones we can perceive. We can only see one-seventieth of the total light spectrum. We do not see x-rays, infrared, ultraviolet rays. Most of us cannot distinguish between fine differences in delicate taste sensations. Part of the selection is thus made for us. We do not pay attention to certain things simply because we are not built to perceive them.

There also are individual differences. Parts of our environment are never experienced as stimuli or are experienced differently because our sensory "equipment" varies. Not everyone has 20/20 vision. Not everyone hears perfectly well. These physiological differences will affect the way each of us will select what we will pay attention to in our environment at any given time.

Position in Space— Where We Are

Your location in space, where you sit or stand, has a great deal to do with what you will perceive or pay attention to. If you choose to be outdoors you will be exposed to a whole set of sensory stimulations that are different from those you would be exposed to had you chosen to remain inside. Your field of vision and your range of hearing are largely dependent upon

THE DYNAMICS OF INTRAPERSONAL COMMUNICATION

your position in space. Much of the time you have a choice of where you will sit or stand.

Take for example a classroom. Many of you tend to sit at the same place time after time. When you do this, you tend to maintain the same field of vision and to see what's going on always at the same angle. Sometime, things look different when you look at them at a different angle. If the fellow sitting next to you also sits at the same place every time, you will then be in each other's field all the time, and you will be aware of each other's presence. This would not have happened had you chosen to sit somewhere else.

Psychological Factors in Selective Perception —What Interests Us

All of us differ in terms of our needs, motives, interests, desires, etc. All of us tend to perceive what is in accord with our needs, motives, and interests. For example, two friends will go shopping at the local shopping center. If one is hungry he may notice the food shops, delicatessens, etc., while the other will be attracted to shoe stores, hardwares, or pharmacies. The attention of these two people was directed to what interested them most. If a person wants to buy a little sports car, he may not notice how comfortable or uncomfortable the car is, but pay more attention to the engine performance. If a person needs a car for long distance driving, the comfort of the interior is a factor that will likely be noticed.

We tend to pay attention to what interests us. Sometimes we distort things so they will fit what we want. You see what you want to see, and sometimes you hear what you want to hear. If a person feels very threatened or insecure, everything around him will appear to be a potential source of danger. If you ever have been in a house alone at night and suddenly you feel uncomfortable or nervous, every little noise will reinforce your fear while the same noises in broad daylight would sound perfectly normal and harmless.

Past Experience and Past Learning—What We Are Like

People are more likely to pay attention to aspects of their environment they anticipate or expect rather than those they do not anticipate or expect. And people tend to expect or anticipate what they are familiar with. You may for example vaguely hear people talking behind you without really identifying anything they are saying until they mention your name. You will usually hear your name distinctly. That word will stand out from all other words they were saying because you are familiar with it.

When you have followed the directions under Figure 2–1 and Figure 2–2 the following comments will be of interest. If you counted three F's and read "Paris in the spring time," "once in a lifetime," and "bird in the hand," you are wrong. There are six F's in Figure 2–1. Because the F in "of" sounds like a "V," it seems to disappear and most people will count

FINISHED FILES ARE THE RE-
SULT OF YEARS OF SCIENTIF-
IC STUDY COMBINED WITH THE
EXPERIENCE OF MANY YEARS

Figure 2–1 Count the F's in the statement in the box.

only three F's in the sentence. Read again the sentences in the three triangles. Perhaps you will need to read them aloud to realize that in two of
them, the word "the" was repeated, and in one of them the word "a" was
repeated. Conditioned habits make us fail to perceive things as they actually are. Have you ever bought a car only to find out that the whole world
seems to be driving the same kind of car you just got? If you bought a
Mustang, all of a sudden it seems everybody is driving a Mustang. Of
course, the sale of Mustangs did not increase dramatically overnight. You
were simply more cued to noticing Mustangs because you had been looking at them closely before you bought one.

Your particular kind of training affects what you perceive. Take for
example a doctor, a mechanic, and a policeman who saw an automobile
accident happen right in front of them. Because of his particular field of
expertise, each one will probably notice certain things about the accident—things that will stand out for each. The doctor will see the condition of the people involved in the accident, whether they need medical
help, an ambulance. The mechanic will notice the condition of the cars,
how much damage was done. The policeman might have seen who vio-
lated a traffic law, who was responsible for the accident. Each selected
from the total event the aspects he thought were significant. Our famil-
iarity with something helps us perceive it more readily than some other
things. We recognize things by what experiences we have had with them
and we take to any perception a lifetime of past learnings.

Figure 2–2 Read aloud the phrases in the triangles.

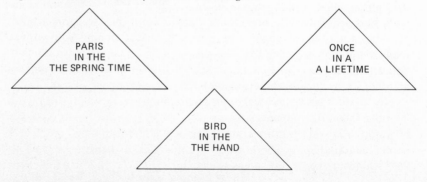

PARIS
IN THE
THE SPRING TIME

ONCE
IN A
A LIFETIME

BIRD
IN THE
THE HAND

THE DYNAMICS OF INTRAPERSONAL COMMUNICATION

Let's make an analogy here. Imagine you are given the task to find out the size of the fish in Lake Michigan. So you get yourself a net and you go to the lake to gather a sample of the fish. Maybe your net has 4-inch mesh. After you gather some fish you write a report in which you say "The fish in Lake Michigan are 4 inches in diameter or bigger." Let's say a friend of yours is given the same assignment, but his net has 2-inch mesh. His report reads, "The fish in Lake Michigan are 2 inches in diameter or bigger." Now, which report is right? Both? What are you and your friend reporting on? The size of the fish? *No.* Each of you is reporting on the size of the net you used. The size of the net you use determines the size of the fish you can collect.

We have nets in our heads. These nets are not made of threads, but of past learning, past experiences, motives, fears, desires, and interests. These nets act as a filter so the stimuli from our environment go through that filter to be perceived. Of course, each one of us has his own little net, his own little personal, individual filter. Even though we may be placed in the same environment we will not see it in the same way since we will filter different aspects. Most of us are not even aware that this filtering process is happening. Many of us have defective filters. Filters that are so clogged up that we see very little of what's going on. Some of us have filters that distort the stimuli that come to us from the environment. The important thing to remember, though, is that *whenever we make a comment about something we are not describing the something but rather our net, our filter.* When I say that the painting is beautiful, I am not commenting on the painting as much as I am commenting on myself, my taste, my value system.

Drove up a newcomer in a covered wagon: "What kind of folks live around here?" "Well, stranger, what kind of folks was there in the country you come from?" "Well, they was mostly a lowdown, lying, gossiping, backbiting lot of people." "Well, I guess, stranger, that's about the kind of folks you'll find around here." And the dusty grey stranger had just about blended into the dusty grey cottonwoods in a clump on the horizon when another newcomer drove up. "What kind of folks live around here?" "Well, stranger, what kind of folks was there in the country you come from?" "Well, they was mostly a decent, hardworking, law abiding, friendly lot of people." "Well, I guess, stranger, that's about the kind of people you'll find around here." And the second wagon moved off and blended with the dusty grey. . . . From The People, Yes, *by Carl Sandburg, copyright, 1936, by Harcourt Brace Jovanovich, Inc.; renewed, 1964, by Carl Sandburg. Reprinted by permission of Harcourt Brace Jovanovich, Inc.*

Figure 2–3 Which do you see? The goblet or the famous twins?

Figure 2–4 Describe the lady you see in this drawing. How old is she, how attractive, what kind of covering on her head, etc.?

Figure 2–5 In these patches of black and white, do you see the face of Christ?

Once we have "selected" what to perceive, we usually organize it in some fashion. Look at Figures 2-3, 2-4, and 2-5.

What do you see? Perhaps at first just some white and black shapes. Perhaps one shape will stand out. In that case you have organized the shapes into a picture by putting visually some of the shapes in the background and some in the foreground. Of course, we may not organize shapes in the same way everyone else does. Some of us fail to organize certain visual stimuli into some coherent picture. Many people do not see the face of Christ in Figure 2-5. Some cannot see the old lady or the young lady in Figure 2-4. Yet every line and shape you need to organize the particular configurations is in the picture. The *organization* of the lines and shapes into a specific design depends solely on the perceiver.

We also tend to organize what we perceive into whole figures. If what we look at is incomplete, we fill in the gaps. This is called "closure." Look at the figures on page 22. You see a dog, not twenty different spots. Look at the other picture. You see a completed square even though the lines do not touch.

What we look at or hear is often ambiguous. Sometimes we may not see distinctly because a room is dimly lighted or we look at something that goes by very quickly. "Now you see it, now you don't," says the magician who capitalizes on distraction and the speed of his movements to create

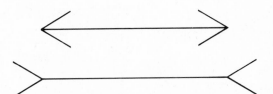

Figure 2-6 Are both of these lines the same length?

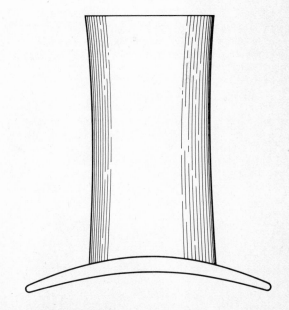

Figure 2-7 Is the hat higher than it is wide?

Figure 2-8 Are the long lines in this sketch parallel?

Figure 2-9 This collection of twenty discrete blotches is a picture of a dog.

Figure 2-10 Even though the corners of this square are missing, we can fill them in with our imagination and make a square.

THE DYNAMICS OF INTRAPERSONAL COMMUNICATION

visual illusions. But even when what we look at is very clearly delineated, there is no automatic conclusion about what the object is. Because even the simplest objects can produce a variety of visual stimuli (for example, a cup and saucer seen at different angles), and different objects can produce the same stimuli (for example, an orchestra and a 12-inch hi-fi speaker). Consequently we have to decide, to interpret what object the thing we are looking at actually represents. This interpretation is not always easy, and it is rarely conscious. The greater the ambiguity of the object, the more room there is for interpretation. This is the theory behind what psychologists call "projective tests"—the ink-blot-type test where you look at an ink blot like the one in Figure 2–11 and tell what you see. Usually what you see in it reveals what you project into it, and this comes from your personal experiences, motives, needs, interests, etc.

We usually interpret what we see by looking at the context in which the object we are looking at is. For example the shape "13" will be read as the letter "B" if it is preceded by the letter "A." However, if it is preceded by the number "12," then it will be perceived as the number "13."

What we all communicate about is our perception of what the world is like. Having created for ourselves a perception of people and events, we

IMPLICATIONS FOR COMMUNICATION

Figure 2–11 The Rorsach ink-blot assists our mind to shape meaning.

A B C

12 13 14

Figure 2-12 An example of the effect of context. The middle figure can either be a letter "B" or a number "13" depending on what kind of sequence it is surrounded by.

then go on to *re-create* for others, through the medium of language—oral, written, or nonverbal—what we perceive.

We always hope that the people we communicate with will translate our language into something similar to what we originally perceived. To the extent they end up with about the same conclusions we make, we say we have communicated successfully.

The process of communication among people can be said to include two phases: First it consists of the perceptions someone (maybe us) has of something, and second it consists of descriptions through symbols (language) so that someone may re-create in the other person's mind the original perception.

Let's examine the first phase and ask some important questions: How do we evaluate our perceptions or someone else's? How do we know if we perceive something as it "really is"? Do we know if we distorted what we saw or heard, and how much we distorted it? On what basis can we trust our perceptions or someone else's? How reliable are the conclusions we draw from our observations by our senses or the reports we get from someone else's senses?

Any perception or observation involves some distortion. We can never be absolutely certain that we have perceived something the way it is. Reports from others are most likely to contain additional distortions.

Checking Perceptions

In practice, then, how do we go about checking perceptions to try to get along better in the world? One way is by finding out that others seem to have perceived something the way we do. If we get support from others, we feel confident that what we perceive is accurate. We depend on others

THE DYNAMICS OF INTRAPERSONAL COMMUNICATION

to help us sort out what is real and what is not. There is some danger in this dependence on others. For one thing, if we only check our perceptions with those whose distortions may agree with ours, we may not get any nearer to the actual "truth" of an event or object. For another thing, we can be tricked by others who may want to fool us. If everyone around you said they saw a book on the table and you did not, but they insisted it was there and appeared to be quite serious about it, you might begin to doubt your own sanity. If all those around you swear that Communists have infiltrated the leadership of the Presbyterian Church and act very serious about it, you may begin to wonder.

Here we begin to get a clue for figuring out how we normally check our perceptions. If enough people agree with us about a given perception, we tend to trust that perception. This process is known as "consensual validation" which simply means other people agree with us that they perceive what we say we perceive.

We also tend to trust a perception we have repeatedly. If it happens over and over again, it builds confidence. If, for example, you see a tree in the front yard once, then look again and don't see it any more, you may think you had a vision. But if you look and see the tree time and again, you are pretty confident that it's there.

Another way we check our perception is to use more than one sense to determine what it is we perceive. If you saw that tree in the front yard and then walked toward it and went right through it, you might question your eyesight. If, on the other hand, you see the tree and touch it, you get a confirmation from the sense of touch that your sense of vision was not playing a trick on you.

Still another way we check our perceptions is by comparisons. If we see something that is a lot like something we saw before, we tend to believe in what we saw. This is related in some ways to the "repeated perception" idea but with a small difference. The new experience (or person, or thing) may not be in the same place, or may have some differences. That's where we can get into trouble—by treating the new event as if it were exactly like the other ones. As Wendell Johnson[2] wrote: "To a mouse, cheese is cheese. That's why mousetraps work." A warning here is to make sure that the similarities are genuine, and that the differences are not more important than the similarities we have perceived.

In summary then, we usually validate our perceptions in these ways:

Validation Type	Method
1. Consensual	by checking with other people
2. Repetitive	by checking with ourselves by repeating the observations

[2]Wendell Johnson, People in Quandaries, *Harper & Row, Publishers, Incorporated, New York, 1946.*

3. Multisensory   by checking with ourselves by using other senses
4. Comparative   by checking with ourselves and our past experiences with similar but not necessarily identical perceptions

When we get the same results from these check points, we have something solid to communicate about. We see the tree, we touch it, we look at it several times, we touch it several times again, we get others to agree that a tree is indeed there and that it is endowed with a kind of treeness that other trees in our experience have all had. Now we can be pretty sure the tree is really there. For all practical purposes, the tree is in our field of communication with ourselves and others.

Checking Communication

This is the second phase in the process of communication and deserves some special attention. Once we have established a perception inside us about something, we may say something about it. How do we know we have communicated successfully, or to put it another way, how do we know the other person has re-created the same perception we had? Did we manage to "get across" enough so the other person could translate our message about our perceptions?

Our communication may be written, oral, or nonverbal. We may write something, say something, or act out by gestures and signs. Then we watch and listen to see what happens. We may get a written message in return, we may hear a response in words or grunts, or we may simply observe something happen. When we do that, we are getting *feedback*.

To find out what part of our message was translated accurately by the other person, we make use of our senses to perceive again. At this point it is impossible not to communicate, because if the other person does absolutely nothing we still learn something about our communication. Being ignored is a very clear kind of feedback that the other person didn't hear, or see, or want to somehow make a response.

I feel cold and ask you to close the window. If you do nothing, there is a possibility that you don't want to do it or that you did not hear. If you go to the window and open it wider, the feedback of that behavior tells me you missed something in my message. If you turn to me and ask what I said, it means that you were at least hearing my voice if not listening to the message. Each of these responses then will give feedback to me which I will use for further communication. At the same time, I have been able to check my communication by feedback from you.

I may look at a tree and say to you, "That's a beautiful oak tree, isn't it!" Then you come back with a comment, "It is beautiful, but it is a maple tree." My prediction that you would agree about the tree's beauty brought a mixed response. You saw qualities of the beauty we could agree on, but you perceived qualities which made it a maple tree, and I perceived qual-

THE DYNAMICS OF INTRAPERSONAL COMMUNICATION

ities which made it an oak tree. This feedback meant that maybe both of us should check our perceptions. If we pursue the argument about what kind of tree it is, we continue to check our communication with each other. It is unlikely that the tree is both a maple and an oak. It is more likely that there are differences in perception which make us call things by different names.

We can name things by any name we want when we talk to ourselves, but when we communicate with others our perceptions become public and therefore subject to review by the other person.

Whenever we communicate with others we are making public reports of our private perceptions. The reactions of others to what we say (feedback, again) not only tell us something about our own perceptions and the perceptions of others but actually let us know how the communication is going. We can get agreement, disagreement, doubt, and even get tuned out. Each of these responses tells us something about the way we are heard by others, as well as something about our perceptions.

BIBLIOGRAPHY

Allport, F.: *Theories of Perception,* John Wiley & Sons, Inc., New York, 1955.

Ames, A., Jr.: "Visual Perception and the Rotating Trapezoidal Window," *Psychological Monographs,* vol. 65, 1951, pp. 1–31.

Berelson, B., and G. A. Steiner: *Human Behavior, an Inventory of Scientific Findings,* Harcourt, Brace & World, Inc., New York, 1964.

Broadbent, D. E.: *Perception and Communication,* Pergamon Press, New York, 1958.

Cantril, H.: "Perception and Interpersonal Relations," *American Journal of Psychiatry,* vol. 114, 1957, pp. 119–126.

Haney, W.: *Communication and Organizational Behavior,* rev. ed., Richard D. Irwin, Inc., Homewood, Ill., 1967.

Hastorf, A. H., and H. Cantril: "They Saw a Game: A Case Study," *Journal of Abnormal and Social Psychology,* vol. 49, 1954, pp. 129–134.

Ittelson, W. H., and F. P. Kilpatrick: "Experiments in Perception," *Scientific American,* August 1951.

Kilpatrick, F. P.: "Perception Theory and General Semantics," *ETC,* vol. 12, 1955, pp. 257–264.

Kilpatrick, F. P. (ed.): *Explorations in Transactional Psychology,* University Press, New York, 1961.

Segall, M. H., D. T. Campbell, and M. J. Herskovits: *The Influence of Culture On Visual Perception,* The Bobbs-Merrill Company, Inc., Indianapolis, 1966.

Tech, H., and M. S. MacLean, Jr.: "Perception and Communication: A Transactional View," *Audio Visual Communication Review,* vol. 10, 1967, pp. 55–77.

Vernon, M. D.: "Perception, Attention, and Consciousness," *Advancement of Science,* 1960, pp. 111–123.

Wittreich, W. J.: "The Honi Phenomenon: A Case of Selective Perceptual Distortion," *The Journal of Abnormal and Social Psychology,* vol. 47, 1952, pp. 705–712.

LANGUAGE AND REALITY— Chapter 3
THE TWO WORLDS WE LIVE IN

We live in two worlds: an empirical world and a symbolic world. The "empirical" world is the world of our actual living. It is the world of our firsthand experiences, our personal observations. It is the world which we get to know directly from our own senses, the one we can personally see, hear, touch, taste, and smell. It is the world of objects, persons, events, and situations, which we can observe outside our skin. It is also the world of sensations and feelings, which we can experience inside our skin.

Then, there is the "symbolic" world, the world of language, the world of the words we use to name and refer to the objects, persons, events, and situations we observe outside our skins, and the sensations and feelings we experience inside our skins—the world of "symbols".

SYMBOLS

A "symbol" is anything that stands for something else. Things can be symbols (a ring is a symbol for marriage; a uniform, a symbol for an occupation; the flag, the symbol of a country). A person may be a symbol (the minister stands for religion or the church, the President stands for his country). A picture is a symbol. A gesture—like a clenched fist—or an expression—like a smile—are symbols. A word, spoken or written, is a symbol. The word "chair" stands for or refers to the actual real object which we can observe outside our skins. The name Albert Einstein refers to the actual person who wrote about the theory of relativity.

Symbols in a way are shortcuts. Imagine what it would be like if we did not have convenient shortcuts like words to communicate with one another. If I wanted to tell you something, anything at all, about an object and did not have words to name it, I would have to point at it so you would know what exactly I had in mind. Our conversation would be limited necessarily to the objects or persons or events actually present to our senses at the moment of the conversation. If we did not have words at our disposal we would be extremely limited indeed. Actually, we would not be much different from animals whose survival depends mostly on being able to move around to get food, and whose communication is limited to some groans and grunts. Fortunately, our ancestors have very conveniently developed, little by little, a symbolic code in which certain sounds or sequences of sounds have come to be accepted by those living together to refer to certain objects, persons, events, situations, feelings, and sensations.

These sounds and sequences of sounds were given "meaning" by the members of these human groups, and these meanings were shared by the group members. This was the beginning of oral language, and this was our first step into humanity because oral language made communication step out of the boundaries of the immediate present. It became possible through the symbolic world, through the use of words, to talk not only about the empirical food to eat, present at the moment to the senses of the communicators, but also to talk about the food eaten yesterday and the food needed for tomorrow.

Words have become our link with the past and the future. It has become possible to store up experiences in our mind, to record them in our memory, and then *later* to recall them to ourselves or to others. If this sounds quite insignificant, don't be misled. The ability to communicate to others one's experiences is essentially what made human civilization possible. When man became able to transmit orally his knowledge— the sum of his stored up experience—to his children, and his children to their children, and so on, human civilization had begun.

Late twentieth century man is indeed the product of all the generations of those men who existed before him. As a late twentieth century man or woman you did not need to start your education completely from scratch when you were born. You could benefit from all the past discoveries and all the accumulated knowledge of your ancestors, which was recorded and preserved through the symbol system. You learned to read, write, and count, yet you did not need to invent the alphabet nor the number system. We all have inherited this knowledge from earlier men in the chain of humanity who were able to transmit through spoken words (or written, when mankind became a little more sophisticated) the products of their experiences and of their knowledge.

SYMBOLS AND OUR COMMUNICATION

What symbols accomplish, then, is to enable us to translate our firsthand experiences from the empirical world into a communicable version of these experiences. What we communicate to one another is *not* the experience itself, but a symbolic representation, a symbolic picture, of the experience. The symbolic picture of an experience is *not* the experience itself: the words we use to refer to the objects, persons, events, situations, sensations, and feelings from our empirical world are *not* the actual objects, persons, events, situations, sensations, and feelings. It is one thing to experience a toothache and quite another to say "I have a toothache." The words are not the pain itself. The words merely describe or refer to the pain and are a symbolic picture of the personal sensation you are experiencing.

THE DYNAMICS OF INTRAPERSONAL COMMUNICATION

This distinction is not as obvious as it sounds. Let's pursue it a little further.

We said that we communicate to ourselves (we call this thinking) and with others by using symbolic pictures of the experiences we seek to convey. When we communicate to ourselves, the process is extremely fast, of course. We feel something that is hot or cold, and as we feel it we label our feeling, we name it, and almost simultaneously we tell ourselves, "I am hot" or "I am cold." It is quite difficult to feel something and not immediately name it. Much of the time this labeling process is unconscious. When we communicate to others, the process of using symbolic pictures—using symbols to refer to a felt experience—is necessary and conscious because there seems to be no other known way to communicate a felt experience to someone else. *To be communicated at all, the experience must be translated into a symbolic picture of some kind, oral, written, or nonverbal.* Communication is oral when we speak words with one another; written when we write words to one another; nonverbal when we use gestures, facial expressions, and other symbols instead of words. The three kinds are symbolic pictures, for all three refer to and are not the experience felt.

Communication performs two vital and related functions: (1) it enables us to organize the sensations we get from our environment into an understandable picture of what that environment is like so we can adapt to it—intrapersonal communication and (2) it enables us to share our pictures of what the environment is like with other people—interpersonal communication.

WHAT COMMUNICATION DOES

In the case of intrapersonal communication, the process can break down when we organize our sensations in such a way as to get a distorted picture of what the environment is like. This of course raises the fundamental question of how do we know when we have a "correct" picture of the environment and when we do not. As we pointed out in the chapter on perception, there is no absolute way of knowing. In the case of empirical matters we rely on interpersonal communication to find out what others perceive our world to be like. For matters of values and opinion we do the same thing but probably should put less stock in it since we should realize that there may be many different answers.

In the case of interpersonal communication, the process can break down when the meanings we try to elicit in another person by using certain symbols are not elicited. This raises the question of how do we know when the meaning intended is elicited or is not. The answer again is through more communication. Usually through observations of the other person's behavior, that is, through feedback.

MAP AND TERRITORY

To make this a little clearer, let's use the familiar analogy of the map and the territory.[1] If you are planning a car trip in a territory you are not too familiar with, what do you usually do? You get hold of a road map to become acquainted with the area so that when you actually drive through the territory you will hopefully not get lost.

Well, what is a map? It is a picture of a specific piece of land drawn by experts. It is not a free picture as an artist might draw it. It is a picture very carefully drawn so that the actual measurements of the territory are accurately scaled down and, the crucial point, the spatial relationships between different points in the territory are maintained within the map. The advantages are great: we get a picture manageable in size yet accurate; a picture which shows us, in miniature, what the territory is like; a picture which helps us predict or anticipate what we will find in the actual territory when we take our actual trip.

Maps and Accuracy

A map should not lie. If it lies, it misleads. If we are misled, our predictons don't materialize, and we get lost and confused.

If maps are to be useful, that is help us make valid predictions, *they must present as accurately as possible the territory they describe.* In the case of communication, words are like maps. Words are symbolic maps. Words refer to, describe the empirical world just as a map refers to and describes an empirical territory. If you tell your little brother that "Columbus discovered America," you are making a symbolic map which describes an empirical territory which existed five hundred years ago. If you tell a friend that you're going to quit smoking tomorrow, you are making a symbolic map of a future territory. When you say "I have a headache," you are making a symbolic map of a territory you alone are able to survey.

Just like a map, words can describe the empirical world more or less accurately, more or less precisely. Just as inaccurate maps mislead, words that do not describe accurately the empirical world mislead.

If we use inaccurate symbolic pictures, or inaccurate symbolic maps, in our communication with ourselves or with others, we mislead ourselves, mislead others, and hence are unable to anticipate successfully events in the empirical world.

Let's look at some examples of inaccurate symbolic maps which often lead to difficulties. Take a young boy whose parents think he would make a good engineer. They tell him constantly how good an engineer he would be and how much he would like it. They have built around the boy a symbolic world in which the boy has to be an engineer and has to like it. The boy is pushed into conforming to this symbolic world. He thus takes

[1]*Alfred Korzybski,* Science and Sanity, 4th ed., *The International Non-Aristotelian Library Publishing Company, Lakeville, Conn., 1958, p. 58.*

THE DYNAMICS OF INTRAPERSONAL COMMUNICATION

courses to actually become an engineer and does very poorly in school. In reality, he passionately hates math and physics, really loves music, and he experiences a deep conflict between what his own feelings are, how he actually performs in class (empirical world), and what his parents' dream is (symbolic world).

The parents have an inaccurate picture of their son. The map they have about him is distorted. They see him as dedicated to math and physics, while he is actually more inclined toward music. The inaccurate symbolic map leads them to push him toward a career for which he is unfit and which will probably make him quite unhappy.

This is not an unusual example of symbolic maps that don't fit the real world, and of the conflicts and grief that are thus generated. Ask any vocational counselor. Their offices are full of students, like our young boy, who are pushed one way while their real talents and inclinations lead them a different way.

Take another common example. Friends of yours tell you about a great film they've just seen that you absolutely must not miss. It is *the* beautiful film of the year. So you go, and it's a flop. You can't see what's so great about the inane movie.

What happened in terms of our map-territory analogy? The film itself is the empirical world, the territory. Your friends' description of the film is the symbolic world, the map. Different people can draw different maps of the same events; film reviewers prove this every week. Which map is accurate? There is no answer to that question since it is a value question. However, if you know *how* your friends came to draw the map they drew, you might be in a better position to evaluate what they are telling you about the film and thus not blindly follow a statement which may be valid for them (they did have a good time at the movie) but may not be valid for you.

One final example. If you make a mistake in your checkbook and your balance reads $150 when you really only have $100 in your checking account, some of your checks will bounce. In this instance it is quite important for your map to fit the territory. Repeated errors might lead the bank to question your integrity.

We are making two important points here. First, there may be many different ways to experience reality. As we pointed out in the chapter on perception, we do not perceive alike. Perceptions are not necessarily right or wrong. They are private and may or may not be shared with others. There is no absolute way to know what reality is really like. Some guesses may be better than others in some circumstances, but that is the extent of our certainty. Second, the symbolic world—that is, what we say about what we perceive—must be treated with extreme caution. Maps are not territories. Words are not the things they represent. One person's verbal map about something may be useful for you, not useful to someone else.

Verbal maps must be evaluated carefully. Short of firsthand experiences they are all we've got to adapt to our environment. That's why you must examine carefully the ones you make for others and the ones others make for you.

A Common Barrier to Communication—the Allness Attitude

Maps don't say all. A map of some territory is, by definition, only a partial representation of the territory. It would be silly to make a map the size of and as detailed as the original area to be mapped.

In this respect, we are sometimes guilty of assuming that our words— as verbal maps—can do the impossible and say all there is to say about a topic. You have probably met a person who acted as though he knew all about automobiles, or politics, or what not. We may know that we don't say all about an event when we describe it, but we frequently act *as if* we had said all. This may be particularly true when we describe another person.

Two reasons why we cannot say all about something are: first, we cannot know all there is to know and second, we don't have the time to tell all. In these days of expanding knowledge and fast-changing events, it is presumptuous to believe that anyone can know all there is to know about even the most simple matters. Yet we find commentators on politics or national policy sounding off as if they knew all. We tend to do the same thing when we talk about a friend—we mention how tall, how dark, how smart, how rich, or what this person owns, such as a car, a stereo, a guitar, or some item of interest. For cursory description, these items may serve to identify some features of your friend, but they do not tell all, and you may omit some items which to another person may be of considerable importance. Add to that the fact that your friend is known to you only partially, no matter how much time you may spend together or how much you may feel you can predict about the friend's taste or behaviors.

Education is a process of finding out what you do not know and trying to fill in some of those gaps. The more you learn, the more you will tend to be tentative in asserting that you know all. The competent scientist is less sure of most things in his field of study than the person who is half informed. Alfred Korzybski (see the bibliography at the end of this chapter) coined the expression "allness" to refer to this attitude of pretending we can know all or say all.

An "allness" attitude can get in the way of learning. It can also mislead us into thinking that what we have heard or observed is all that is needed to know. The danger of allness in our communication behaviors occurs when we treat people or events as if we know all or can say all such as: all Texans are rich and loud, all students are rioters, all Mexicans are lazy, all blacks have a sense of rhythm, all Chicagoans are gangsters, all politicians are crooked, all automobiles are unsafe, everybody cheats on his income tax, everybody knows beetles are harmless, or nobody wears hats any more.

One of the most difficult things to say is "I don't know"—when we do sound dogmatically sure of something, can we for a moment entertain the possibility that we may be wrong, that we may not know a facet of the problem which could cause us to change our mind.

Unless we are willing to leave that door open—there is more to know about it—we shut ourselves off from learning and from satisfactory relationships with others.

To summarize the ideas in this chapter, let us say once again: **SUMMARY**

1. We live in two worlds:
   A. The *empirical world.* The world of direct experience, of firsthand observations; the world of our living.
   B. The *symbolic world.* The world of the symbolic pictures we draw of the empirical world; the world of the symbols we use to describe and refer to the empirical world; the world of language (oral, written, and nonverbal).
2. The symbolic world *is not* the empirical world.
3. The symbolic world only describes, represents, refers to the empirical world. It is like a map which gives us a picture of the empirical world.
4. We live our lives by constantly making maps about the empirical world which consequently help us decide how to act.
5. Verbal maps about the same event vary from person to person and are not equally useful to all.
6. Verbal maps must be evaluated carefully before we act on them.
7. Maps don't say all about what they describe.

In this chapter we have used many words which essentially refer to the same idea. These words have been grouped under two titles: *empirical world* and *symbolic world.*

Under each title follows a list of the words which all refer to the idea expressed by the title.

Empirical World	Symbolic World
Territory	Symbols
Direct experiences	Pictures or symbolic pictures
Firsthand observations	Maps, symbolic maps, or verbal maps
Objects	Symbolic representations

Persons	Words
Events	Language
Situations	1. Oral language—spoken words
Feelings	2. Written language—written words
Sensations	3. Nonverbal language—gestures, facial expressions, postures, etc.

BIBLIOGRAPHY

Berman, S. I.: *Understanding and Being Understood,* The International Communication Institute, San Diego, Calif., 1965.

Bois, S. J.: *Exploration in Awareness,* Harper & Brothers, New York, 1957.

Bois, S. J.: *The Art of Awareness,* Wm. C. Brown Company Publishers, Dubuque, Iowa, 1966.

Boulding, K.: *The Image,* The University of Michigan Press, Ann Arbor, 1956.

Brown, C. T., and C. Van Riper: *Speech and Man,* Prentice-Hall, Inc., Englewood Cliffs, N.J., 1966.

Brown, R.: *Words and Things,* The Free Press, New York, 1958.

Church, J.: *Language and the Discovery of Reality,* Random House, Inc., New York, 1961.

Condon, J.: *Semantics and Communication,* The Macmillan Company, New York, 1966.

Duncan, H. D.: *Symbols in Society,* Oxford University Press, Fair Lawn, N.J., 1968.

Hayakawa, S. I.: *Language in Thought and Action,* rev. ed., Harcourt, Brace and Company, Inc., New York, 1964.

Johnson, W.: *People in Quandaries,* Harper & Row, Publishers, Incorporated, New York, 1946.

Keller, H.: *The Story of My Life,* Doubleday & Company, Inc., Garden City, N.Y., 1954.

Keyes, K. S., Jr.: *How To Develop Your Thinking Ability,* McGraw-Hill Book Company, New York, 1950.

Korzybski, A.: *Science and Sanity,* 4th ed., The International Non-Aristotelian Library Publishing Co., Lakeville, Conn., 1958.

Lee, I. J.: *Language Habits in Human Affairs,* Harper & Brothers, New York, 1941.

Lee, I., and L. L. Lee: *Handling Barriers in Communication,* Harper & Brothers, New York, 1956.

Sondel, B.: *The Humanity of Words: A Primer of Semantics,* The World Publishing Company, New York, 1958.

Weinberg, H. L.: *Levels of Knowing and Existence,* Harper & Brothers, New York, 1960.

THE DYNAMICS OF INTRAPERSONAL COMMUNICATION

FACTS AND INFERENCES— Chapter 4
LOOK BEFORE YOU LEAP

Whenever we do anything, our behavior is the product of a complicated system of assumptions. We assume all the time and act on the basis of our assumptions. We sit in a room assuming the ceiling will not cave in. If we assumed otherwise, we probably would not sit and relax in the room with the same unquestioned feeling of confidence and security. Yet, ceilings have been known to collapse in earthquakes, during a tornado, or when a building simply gives in if it was not built well. Our feeling of security, then, is not based on the absolutely certain knowledge that ceilings do not fall. Our security comes from our assumption that they will not. When you sit on a chair, you assume it will hold you. You enrolled in your communication class and assumed it would provide something—give you credits, help you improve your interpersonal communication, or meet a requirement.

EVERYTHING WE SAY AND DO INVOLVES SOME ASSUMPTIONS

When you went to your class you made certain assumptions that the class would meet in its usual meeting room, that the instructor would be there, that most of your classmates would be there, and that the instructor would say something in a language you would understand about the subject of communication, and not geography, math, or French. These assumptions influenced your behavior.

Would you sit and put all your weight on the chair if you thought it were not going to hold you? Would you take the course if you knew the instructor rarely came to class? Would you go to class if you knew for certain the instructor was not going to be there or the rest of the class was not going to show up? Probably not. Your behavior in these instances is based on certain assumptions you make about the chair, the course, and the class.

Assumptions are a system of guesses you make about the nature of the environment in which you live. If you make the right kinds of guesses, you win. That is, your behavior is satisfactory—the chair does not collapse, the instructor and the classmates come to class. Sometimes, however, your guesses don't check out. You arrive at the usual classroom and wait there for ten minutes, only to notice a note on the board saying that the class is meeting elsewhere today. Or a chair breaks.

If we behave on the basis of guesses or assumptions, then we should take a look at how we arrived at the guesses we make, at the assumptions we have, and find out whether they are appropriate or misleading.

Where did your assumptions about ceilings, chairs, and courses come from? From two areas: *the empirical world, and the symbolic world.*

From the Empirical World

Consider the ceiling, the chair, and the class. Your assumptions about them come from your firsthand experience with these things. The ceiling—you have not had many ceilings fall on you lately. The chair—you may even have checked before you sat in it to see if it was sturdy, but your assumptions come from a number of years of experience with chairs, and they normally don't collapse under people. The class—you have come to class many times and found it repeatedly true that the instructor is present regularly, that your classmates are too, that the instructor speaks English and not Chinese, and that the instructor speaks about communication and not mathematics. You have observed all this in the past, and you feel it is pretty reasonable and logical to think it will go on like this in the future.

From the Symbolic World

What about your assumptions about the course? They don't come from the empirical world entirely. They come largely from the symbolic world. The course was listed in the catalogue so you assume it is a legitimate course to take. It is listed among certain requirements so you assume that you will get credit for it and thus meet these requirements. You further assume that the information you found in the catalogue was accurate and valid, that whoever wrote it knew what he was writing about and described the course accurately, that whoever printed it did not make printing errors, and that whoever was responsible for its production checked the final proofs to make sure there were no mistakes.

Yet, can we be certain that these assumptions are always absolutely accurate? Perhaps you took the course because your friends told you it was a good course. You assumed they were telling you the truth, and further that your taste and theirs were similar.

All these assumptions seem to be at a rather basic level with ceilings, chairs, etc. Let's take this a step further. You assume that as a result of several years of course work you will graduate, you will find a job, and you will reap certain benefits for having put in the time. Do you *know* that? How did you arrive at that idea? Did you analyze data on college courses and what they actually do for people? Or did you operate within a framework of assumptions that say college is "good"? The pattern of assumptions that govern going to college is a somewhat complex pattern. It is often hidden, unconscious. It is something we might do well to take out and inspect when we are faced with putting down cash, time, energy, and often hard work for this education. The decision to go or not to go, however, is often made on the basis of unidentified and complex assumptions.

Implications for Communication

What has this got to do with communication? Are we suggesting that you check the ceiling structures or the chairs before you go into a room and sit down? No. There are some kinds of things going on in our lives which we have to assume or we will never move—never go into a room, never sit in a chair, never sign up for a course. We are asking that people *become conscious of their assumptions.*

Being conscious of our assumptions is particularly important in the relations we have with our symbolic world. That is because of two things: first, that we have so much going on in our symbolic world and second, that wrong assumptions in the symbolic world can be as disastrous to our communicative function as a broken chair can be to our sitting functions.

In the rest of this chapter we will develop further reasons for being conscious of our assumptions—to help us know better where our faulty assumptions may lead us. But first, let's put the business of assumptions into some kind of order.

We begin our communicative lives by picking up *assumptions* and these become often the hidden, inside-us, base for *inferences* about what is happening. In turn, the inferences lead us to *actions.* Assumptions to inferences to actions. There is a payoff when we actually do something like talking, listening, reacting, reporting, dodging, moving, agreeing, disagreeing, hating, or loving.

We start with a whole system of assumptions about our world, usually gained from the symbolic world around us. These assumptions operate silently and usually unconsciously. When something is going on around us and we hear or observe, then we make inferences (or judgments) about what we see and hear. We make these inferences on the basis of how our assumptive system says to us the world goes around. Combine the old, comfortable, seldom-seen assumption system with the new information and we develop our inferences. This sequence is much weaker when we depend on our symbolic world—our world of words—to dictate our final actions.

We obtain most of our assumptions from the symbolic world—from the words we hear and read, from language. Relatively few of our assumptions come from empirically testing our environment. Most assumptions we hold come from the symbolic processes going on in our communication. Often we do not understand the assumptions which underlie the other person's language habits, and we also do not understand the assumptions which underlie our thinking and acting about other people.

Scientific American[1] published an article some time ago on the Black

ASSUMPTIONS ARE PRIMARILY SYMBOLIC

[1]*William L. Langer, "The Black Death,"* Scientific American, *vol. 210, no. 2, 1964, pp. 114–121.*

Plague in Europe. The article investigated the mass mood established by the plague. Of course, at the time (1348–1350) people did not know that the plague was caused by fleas on a particular type of rat. Because the cause of the disease was unknown and its effects disastrous (hundreds of thousands of people died as a result of the disease), considerable fear accompanied the pandemic. And people acted according to certain assumptions: (1) The very religious considered it a trial sent by God, a punishment visited on the human race, and they sought out the Jonahs whom they thought were responsible for this punishment. They found them and massacred them—a consequence of assumptions. (2) Many others assumed the plague was caused by the people living in the slums, and they reacted violently against them by burning down entire districts in some cities—a consequence of assumptions. (3) Some others fled to presumably safe places and, relying on the assumption there would be no tomorrow, ate, drank, and were merry—a consequence of assumptions.

Now, why would anyone worry about how people acted way back during the years of the plague? The answer, of course, is to attempt to find some parallels to the kinds of assumptions which are *today* influencing our society, our culture. Implicit in this kind of study is an attempt to understand what kind of assumptions people operate with. *Understanding people's assumptions will help us understand their behavior.* If we want to behave intelligently, we need to know how to make intelligent assumptions.

For example, if you assume that you can fly, and, on the basis of this assumption, jump without a parachute from the tenth floor of a building, you will probably end up in the hospital, or worse, in a cemetery. The assumption was not very good. Therefore your behavior was damaging to yourself and other people. Before jumping, it would have been wise to check the validity of the assumption and then decide whether to jump or not. Checking the validity of any of your assumptions requires first that you be aware that you are indeed making an assumption.

Belief and Disbelief Systems

According to the social psychologist Milton Rokeach,[2] we all have inside us a system composed of all the things we "know" that we agree with—all the information, biases, prejudices, and beliefs—that we have accumulated in ourselves since the time we were born. This, Rokeach calls the "belief system." We also have inside of us a "disbelief system," composed of all the things we disagree with.

Based on a whole complex system of assumptions, we go through life fortifying our belief system and attempting to overcome those things in

[2]*Milton Rokeach,* The Open and Closed Mind, *Basic Books, Inc., Publishers, New York, 1960.*

THE DYNAMICS OF INTRAPERSONAL COMMUNICATION

our disbelief system. For example, you may believe in God, you may belong to a specific church, and you may have a certain faith. This is your belief system in regard to religion. It is based on many assumptions about life, death, God, man's relation to man, and organized religion, which have become often an *unstated, unarticulated* part of your symbolic world. Your disbelief system includes religions other than your own, atheism, etc. These beliefs and disbeliefs usually come from the symbolic world. We get them from our parents, our schools, our churches, our governments, our friends, the books we read, the movies we see, and the place of our birth. If you are born in America, you will probably share many assumptions with other people born in this country—assumptions about freedom, civil rights, democracy, and races.

Rokeach further explains that we can be more or less "open-minded" or more or less "close-minded." To be "open-minded," according to Rokeach, is simply to be open to information about one's disbelief system. In other words, if you believe that pot is good and disagree with the present narcotics laws, yet are willing to listen to information regarding the opposite position, you have begun to open your mind. If you can listen to those who have views different from yours, if you are willing to subject yourself to information contrary to what you believe in, then you have begun to open your mind. How many people regularly read newspapers or magazines that reflect a political and social orientation drastically different from their own? How many Democrats will attend a Republican rally, not to heckle or boo, but to listen to what the other man has to say?

If we are able to admit that we *all* operate from a system of assumptions that we may not even be able to identify, and to admit further that someone else's assumptions may have a good deal of validity *for him,* then we have begun to open our minds.

Bruno Bettelheim, the child psychiatrist, wrote an article for *Life* magazine[3] about the fearmongers and the hatemongers. Read the following quote, keeping in mind our discussion on assumptions and their influence on behavior.

> They hate because they feel life has cheated them, has passed them by. Here in America, the *assumption* is that everybody, theoretically, can become president, or at least that everybody can make good in life. If we *assume* that we can all go to the top, it follows if we do not there must be something wrong with us.
>
> This is a painful conclusion. It attacks the very roots of our self-respect and leaves us open to the developing of some degree of self-hatred. And because all hate is basically retaliatory—a backlash at a seemingly hostile world—we grow to hate others. . . .

[3]Bruno Bettelheim, "Why Does a Man become a Hater?" Life, February 7, 1964, p. 78. Reprinted by permission of the author.

But the prevalence of hate in America is essentially related to tremendous demands the individual American makes on himself that he cannot live up to.[4]

Idealization, Frustration, Demoralization—the IFD Disease[5]

Very often the feelings we develop about ourselves, other people, and the world around us stem from the assumptions we have about ourselves, others, and the world. We plan a party, we plan a career, we plan to go see a movie, and in most cases we build up expectations about these events. We hope that the party will be successful, fun, and that we will have a "good time," whatever our definition of "good time" may be. We expect to "succeed" in whatever career we choose. We go to the movie, expecting to be entertained and spend a pleasant evening. This is the stage of *idealization.* We dream because we are human beings and we can use language to talk to ourselves and make all kinds of predictions. We can tell ourselves that we will have a good time with the blind date we were just matched with. We can start making all kinds of dreams about what he or she looks like, how we are going to get along, and how successful we are going to be. We may even see a diamond ring dangling in the future. At the idealization stage, our imagination goes free, and we get involved in making maps about the territory to come. Then the time arrives when we do go out with the blind date, we do go see the movie, we expect a promotion, or we are at the party we anticipated so much. And it just isn't what we expected. The party or movie is a real flop. The date is not a candidate for Miss or Mister America. We are not promoted in our job as we expected.

When this happens we are usually ready for the *frustration* stage. We may get upset at whatever we perceive to be the cause of our frustration—the people who arranged the blind date or the unfeeling, insensitive boss who does not appreciate us. We may even feel that we have failed, that somehow we are not as good as we should be.

We are then ripe for the *demoralization* stage, when we feel that there is just no hope and that we are definitely a failure. We can't ever get a decent date, everyone rejects us. We can even look around at the people in our world and find evidence that they really dislike us.

How many of you have never been depressed? Depression is a common feeling and usually stems from a comparison between our idealization (assumptions about the future and about ourselves) and the perceived reality of a given situation, what we perceive really happens to us. The larger the gap between our idealizations and what happens to us, the more depressed we tend to become.

[4]*Italics ours.*
[5]*Wendell Johnson,* People in Quandaries, *Harper & Row, Publishers, Incorporated, New York, 1946, pp. 3–20.*

THE DYNAMICS OF INTRAPERSONAL COMMUNICATION

Read the Bettelheim quote again. If we make demands on ourselves that we cannot live up to, we are in for frustration, perhaps hate, and certainly demoralization. If we set unrealistic verbal goals for ourselves, we are bound to be disappointed.

But where do you suppose these goals come from? Where do you get the idea that you will get A's or B's or C's in college? Where do you get the idea that your social life will be a roaring success? Here again, from assumptions you make that come perhaps from your past experiences in the empirical world, but also from the symbolic world, from what you read and hear, from the TV shows and the movies. Buy this brand of toothpaste and be a social success. Use this kind of mouthwash and get married the next day. Propaganda. Slogans. Words. We often believe them. We often act on claims without really inspecting them to find whether or not they have any validity.

The IFD disease is essentially a word disease. If what we experience does not fit what we expect, we can do two things. We can change what we experience or change our expectations. If we want to be the basketball star on the team and don't make the team, we can practice and practice and practice to improve our performance, or we can lower our expectations and decide we just want to play basketball for fun. If we are only 5 feet 4 inches tall, it might be better to lower our expectations, since our performance is not likely to improve that much to the point of making the team. The problem here is one of assessing the validity of our assumptions again. Where does the assumption come from that we can make the team? Is it just a totally unfounded dream, based merely on wishful thinking? Does it come from people in our environment who are able to assess accurately our capabilities and are encouraging us in this direction, or from people who are blind to the fact that we may not be good at all playing basketball but who still encourage us to wish for it? Have people told us that it was "easy" to make the team? Do these people know what they are talking about?

What we are talking about here is the need to be aware that we do operate on the basis of assumptions. We need to uncover these assumptions and where they come from in order to assess their validity. Assumptions that once were valid may be useless now. Unless they are consciously reevaluated, we may keep doing things that are no longer useful to us and to others.

Reports on what is going on around us are affected by what we see and what we think we see. We observe things and then begin making those observations fit what we know about our world. Inferences are what we add to our observations. They are the imagining and "certainties" we believe in.

OBSERVATIONS AND INFERENCES

THE KISS AND THE SLAP

> *In a railroad compartment, an American grandmother with her young and attractive granddaughter, a Romanian officer and a Nazi officer were the only occupants. The train was passing through a dark tunnel, and what was heard was a loud kiss and a vigorous slap. After the train emerged from the tunnel nobody spoke, but the grandmother was saying to herself: "What a fine girl I have raised. She will take care of herself. I am proud of her." The granddaughter was saying to herself: "Well, grandmother is old enough not to mind a little kiss. Besides, the fellows are nice, I am surprised what a hard wallop grandmother has." The Nazi officer was meditating, "How clever those Romanians are! They steal a kiss and have the other fellow slapped." The Romanian officer was chuckling to himself: "How smart I am! I kissed my own hand and slapped the Nazi!" (Alfred Korzybski, "The Role of Language on Perceptual Processes," in* Perception—An Approach to Personality, *edited by Robert R. Blake and Glenn V. Ramsey, copyright 1951, The Ronald Press Company, New York, pp. 170–171.)*

If you saw a friend driving a new car, what would you think? He bought it? He borrowed it? He was trying it out? He was driving it somewhere for someone? You observed his driving a new car and began immediately to make inferences that would explain the situation.

You see two people standing in the hall arguing. You begin to make some inferences on what is happening and what is going to happen.

A teacher asks one of the students to stay after class. The first-level observation includes the student and teacher talking, while the many-leveled inferences can make all kinds of stories about it.

A secretary shows up late for work at the office. Can the boss infer that she missed her bus, she overslept, she doesn't care, she has bad attitudes about being on time, or she got trapped fifteen minutes in the elevator?

We can mislead ourselves when we let our inferences go beyond what we can observe. We begin to mislead others when we tell them what we saw (observed) and what we thought about it (inferred).

Statements of Fact and Statements of Inference

In English we can make two kinds of declarative statements. We can look at a man and say, "He wears glasses." This is a *statement of fact* because it corresponds closely to what we observed. Or we can say, "He bought the glasses." This is a statement of inference which we make because the

THE DYNAMICS OF INTRAPERSONAL COMMUNICATION

man is wearing the glasses, he looks honest, and few people would steal prescription glasses and wear them.

A statement of inference is a guess about the unknown based on the known. The "known" may be an observation or a series of observations (the man is wearing glasses). Or sometimes the "known" may be only an inference or a series of inferences (the man looks honest, etc.).

Some guesses, of course, are more easily and quickly verifiable than others. Some are more probable than others. For example, if you go to the post office to mail a package at 10 A.M. on Tuesday, you are saying to yourself "the post office is open." This is a statement of inference. You do not know for a fact that it is open. You have not observed it to be open. It is an inference which is (1) easily verifiable through observation—all you need to do is get there and observe whether it is open or not, (2) quickly verified—right away if you wish, and (3) highly probable—post offices are usually open on work days at 10 A.M., you have seen a sign telling what the post office hours are, you went there yesterday at 10 A.M. and it was open, and you went there last Tuesday and it was open.

Your decision to go and mail your package is thus based on a pretty good inference. Of course, something might have happened today that resulted in an unexpected closing. But that's a chance or a risk you have to take. In this case, however, because you were aware that you were making an inference, you assessed its probability, you figured out the odds, so to speak. You ran a risk, but this was a *calculated risk.* You based it on information and experience.

If we look at facts and inferences on the basis of how certain or probable they are, we have a continuum such as the one below:

The Need to Distinguish between Statements of Facts and Statements of Inferences

Statements of Facts		Statements of Inferences
May approach certainty	Highly probable	Less probable

A fact, or an observation belongs to the "may approach certainty" end of the continuum. Why not absolutely certain? Because even observations cannot be fully trusted. Remember our discussion of perceptual distortions? However, if you observe something, time after time, if other people agree that they observe it too, you can approach certainty. But we never quite reach absolute certainty. We hope this does not come as a shock to you, for many people feel very certain about many things. Our feelings of certainty, however, come partly from the validity we attach to our senses and partly from the validation we get from other people. If you see something green, and everyone around tells you it's red and you know they are not joking, you begin to wonder. Inferences, on the other hand, never reach this "may approach certainty" level. Inferences are in the realm of probability. Some are more probable than others.

Why is it important to distinguish between fact and inferences? If we do not know that we are making an inference, then we do not know that we are operating in the realm of probability, in the realm of guesses. If we do not know it, then we are not likely to assess the probability of the inference. We are not likely to figure the odds. If we make an inference and treat it *as if it were* an observation, then we will feel it is almost certain and we don't need to do any checking. In this case we run an "uncalculated risk."

Automobile accidents often happen because of this confusion. You drive 65 miles per hour on the highway and a car comes out on your right at an intersection. There is a stop sign, on his side of the road. You see him, you see the stop sign, you "know" he will stop, and you proceed through the intersection at 65 miles per hour. In too many cases on record, the other car does not stop at the stop sign (he did not see it, or he did not see you, or he was going too fast to stop in time, or he thought he would have time to go through). Both of you end up in the hospital, or perhaps in the grave. When we treat an inference as if it were an observation, then we feel quite secure and sure instead of realizing that we should be dealing in terms of probability. If we think the other person may not stop, we will slow down.

William Haney gives the following suggestions to distinguish facts and observations from inferences:[6]

Statements of Observations or Statements of Facts	Statements of Inferences
A. Can be made only *after* observation	A. Can be made *anytime*
B. Must stay *within* what one observes and not go beyond	B. Can go *beyond.* Only limited by one's imagination
C. Can be made only by *observer*	C. Can be made by *anyone*
D. *Approaches certainty*	D. Deals only with *probability*
E. Can be made only to the extent of the observer's capabilities and *competency*	E. Can be made by the *incompetent*

It seems necessary to add this last qualification (not from Haney) be-

[6]*William Haney,* Communication and Organizational Behavior, *rev. ed., Richard D. Irwin, Inc., Homewood, Ill., 1967, p. 195. Reprinted by permission of the author and the publisher.*

cause some people are better-trained observers than others (and more honest) and therefore their statements about what they observe are more reliable. If a totally incompetent person looks at your car engine and makes a statement such as "Your carburetor is full of dirt" and gets agreement from several other mechanically incompetent people, we do not have a statement of observation because these people may not even know what a carburetor looks like.

When we hear statements of inference we should assess their probability. How can we do this? How do we figure out the odds? How do we calculate the risk? The first thing to do is to check the source of the inference. Is the inference based on one observation or many observations—observations made by one person or many people. What kind of people made the inference: competent, incompetent, trustworthy, biased, prejudiced, or deceitful?

How to Verify an Inference

You can make for yourself a scale of probability and place on the scale the different possible sources of your information. For example, when you want to determine whether the post office is open, and you are not in a position to find out for yourself through observation, you will have to take somebody's word for it. One person's word will be more reliable than another person's. If you call the post office and one of its employees tells you it's open, then your inference is pretty reliable (although it is conceivable the man could lie, or between the time of the phone call and the time you get there something happens to make the office close). If you ask someone who just went to the post office, it is also quite probable the post office is open. If you ask someone who read the sign that indicates the hours the post office is open, it's a little less probable, unless you can be pretty sure this person has a good memory. If you ask a stranger in town, then his answer is not too reliable unless you have evidence to the contrary. The important thing to remember is that when we make inferences, we may or may not be accurate. We should be cautious in evaluating inferences before we act on them. We should try not to jump to conclusions until we can be reasonably sure that we are taking a calculated risk.

Some statements are neither statements of facts nor of inferences. They are called "statements of judgment" because they reflect a value held by the person making the judgment.

STATEMENTS OF JUDGMENT

"The food in the cafeteria is terrible."
"The quarter system is better than the semester system."

"She is beautiful."
"He is real smart."

These statements are a reflection of personal values. They say very little about what is being talked about and a great deal about who does the talking. The man in love who says that his girl is the most beautiful girl in the world is not talking about the girl, not about the world, but about himself. When we say the food is bad, we are talking about *our* tastes in food. When we say someone is smart, we are talking about *our* criteria for smartness. Agreement among people on these statements proves very little about the validity of the statements. People are agreeing on values and not on observation.

We can operate better in life if we can distinguish between what is a statement about what's going on "out there" (statement of observation) and a statement about what's going on in somebody's insides (inferences or statement of judgment). Our communication will be helped if we can determine where any speaker or writer got his information: did he get it by observing and then stated only what he observed? Or did he think he saw something which was colored by his assumptions, then made some inferences, and then reported to us what he felt about the thing?

Example: The poet describes the beautiful sunset, and the scientist analyzes the wave lengths of the reds, yellows, and purples and gives us a report on the colors in Angstrom units. Maybe we feel the sunset is beautiful too, but we are dealing in judgments. The young lady's hair may be "flowing silken tresses entrapping my soul" to the poet, but to the advertiser trying to sell with a pseudoscientific message the hair is a protein extension of the myriad head follicles.

Statements of judgments come from somebody's insides and appeal to our own insides. It helps when we find others whose internal reactions seem to agree with ours, but it makes the judgment no more reliable— only more widely expressed.

It is true that standards of judgment or values are similar within a particular culture. Standards of beauty, right, wrong, good, bad, fashion, and pleasure are learned in the same way language is learned. To agree that long hair looks bad on men does not make it a fact. It simply means that those who agree have the same taste and value about hair. Agreement based on inferences should not be confused with the kind of agreement based on observations. It is important to recognize the difference in order to be more tolerant of other peoples' judgments particularly when they don't agree with ours. If we believe that, simply because other people agree with our judgments, we must be absolutely right, this will tend to reduce our tolerance of those people who do not agree with us. It will increase our need to convert everyone to our position since it is so "true and right." Both diminish the chances of successful communication.

One of the differences between a scientist and a layman lies in the kind of questions they ask. Most of us make the assumption that simply because a question has been asked there must be an answer, somewhere, waiting to be found. Sometimes we are so convinced of the validity of this assumption that we keep looking for an answer that eludes us, and we get ulcers in the process. Some questions are answerable, and some are not. Before we go frantically on the search for answers, we should know what was asked.

What is an "answerable question"? Essentially it is a question whose answer can be found in the empirical world through observations. A question whose answer is based on observations or on inferences that are capable of being verified by anyone in the position to make the observations. Scientists ask answerable questions, and then proceed to make observations in the empirical world to find answers. A question such as "How many pages are in this book?" is an answerable question. All you need do to answer it is count, and if you want to verify your answer, you may have someone else count also. If you both agree, your answer is very likely correct, but you found the answer by counting, in the empirical world, through personal observations. The question, "Is this book your textbook for your speech course?" is an answerable question because the answer can be checked in the empirical world through observations. You can go to the instructor and have him verify the answer. You can go to the bookstore where you bought it and check its list of textbooks for courses.

Questions which do not have answers in the empirical world—answers that cannot be obtained through observations—are "nonanswerable questions." It doesn't mean they don't have any answer at all. Actually these questions usually have many different answers, but these answers are not based on observations. The answers to these questions come from the symbolic world. They are usually of two kinds: (1) questions of values or of judgments whose answers are found in people's minds, in people's values and beliefs, and (2) questions of definitions whose answers are found in the verbal classifications we arbitrarily agree upon.

Questions of Values

For example, if someone asks you whether this book is good or not, no amount of observation of the book, no amount of looking at it, touching it, feeling it, or counting pages will give you the answer. Your answer will be based on your personal taste and value. The question "Does God exist?" is a nonanswerable question. It cannot be answered through observations. It is answered in many ways, however, but the answers come from the symbolic world. They come from the particular religious values people have agreed to share. Different people will arrive at different answers—thus we have hundreds of religions. "Is premarital sex wrong?"

is a nonanswerable question. Different people give it different answers. Total agreement is difficult because we are not dealing with an answerable question.

A great deal of controversy shook the Catholic Church in the Middle Ages when theologians battled fiercely over the question "How many angels can stand on the head of a pin?" Books were written. Doctoral theses were written. People called each other names, "proved" their viewpoints, and never did settle the question. A great deal of grief and energy could have been avoided had they realized this was a nonanswerable question. Speculations can be made, but the conclusion of these speculations should not be taken as Truth with a capital T, since the answers were only found in the mind or argument of those writing them. This did not just happen in the Middle Ages. Think of all the controversies we are a part of.

Some people are now arguing the existence of life on Mars. Until we have better data or observations than we have right now, the question as it is phrased is nonanswerable. It does not mean we should stop asking it. It means we should be very cautious of the supposed answers we get now, and we should not become angry at someone for arriving at an "answer" different from ours. It means we should try to find out what accounts for the differences in "answers." It means that in understanding what accounts for the differences, we can understand the phenomenon a little better and check the assumptions and inferences we have made that led us to believe in our answers. We need also to check what we mean by the word "life."

Questions of Definitions

Questions of definitions have to do with the *meaning* we attach to words. They have to do with the arbitrary agreement of how we classify something. Take the questions: "Is photography art?" and "Is bullfighting a sport?" Whether photography and bullfighting fall into the categories provided by your definitions, the answers are essentially verbal, for the definitions are verbal. No amount of staring at a photograph will yield an answer. Those who reject the classifications or reject the values implied in your definition will probably disagree with your answer.

Louis Salomon gives us some examples of classification questions in the legal world. The answers are important, although seemingly arbitrary, for the imposition of legal penalties or the granting of legal immunities hinge upon them.

1. Are peanuts nuts? (The Food and Drug Administration is responsible for enforcing accurate labeling of food products.)
2. Is an alligator farm a museum? (Liberal income tax deductions are allowed for contributions to museums.)

3. Is a coffeehouse a cabaret? (A cabaret license is expensive and often subject to special restrictions.)
4. Is a police slowdown in issuing parking summonses a strike? (There are laws penalizing public employees who strike.)
5. Is a ship that is registered in Panama but owned by a United States citizen or corporation an American vessel? (There is a legal minimum wage for crewmen on American vessels.)
6. Is a man who has lost his job and refuses to take a new one that has been offered unemployed? (At issue is not only his unemployment compensation but the reliability of official statistics of "unemployment.")[7]

The process by which we arrive at these definitions is relatively simple. Take a general category X. We say that to be classified as X, an object must have characteristics a, b, and c. Then we are confronted with the particular empirical object. We inspect it and find it has characteristics a, b, and c. We say that the object is an X. But what if we had decided initially that to be an X, an object should have characteristics a, b, c, *and d.* In that case, our particular object we inspected awhile ago would not be an X. The decision of what characteristics to include in the category is a verbal one, and the question of "what something is" is non-answerable.

Although scientists in the laboratories have operated on a useful system of dealing with assumptions, inferences, and conclusions, the process has not generally spilled over into our political, cultural, economic, or personal lives. Even scientists at times in history have gone beyond their observations to make statements more colored by judgment or inference than by fact. But the good scientist follows this general sequence when dealing with his world:

THE SCIENTIFIC METHOD

1. He makes his observations as carefully as possible, trying to stick to the issue at hand and not put his own personal bias into the job.
2. When he has observed things enough, he offers an explanation of what is probably happening in the form of
3. a tentative conclusion which doesn't go beyond what he was able to study, and which
4. remains tentative and temporary because he knows somebody else might find some more things that might make the conclusion inaccurate later.

[7]*Louis Salomon,* Semantics and Common Sense, *Holt, Rinehart and Winston, Inc., New York, 1966, p. 91. Reprinted by permission of the publisher.*

In our communication we sometimes follow this sequence; more often not. In the first place we begin with our assumption about how the world ought to work and what people ought to mean by what they say and write. Then we compound the error by:

1. making our observations in a sloppy way, introducing all kinds of other unrelated ideas, and trying hard to make sure the things happening in our world fit the way we think it ought to be
2. stopping short of enough observations, and moving too quickly to a
3. conclusion which generally covers more than the issue at hand
4. a conclusion which is the "final word"—a once-and-for-all totally true, unchangeable, engraved-in-stone, not-subject-to-any-argument kind of conclusion

SUMMARY

To improve our communication, then, we are recommending we operate on a kind of scientific method of seeing, speaking, writing, reading, and listening.

We need to check our assumptions. Where did we get them? Are they valid? Do they fit this particular case?

We need to know the difference between facts and inferences. What really happened? How do we know? What might be suspicious about our sources of information?

We need to ask answerable questions and not try to answer ones which have no answers. What is being asked? Where do we go to find the answers —to the world "out there" or to the symbolic world of our insides or the insides of others?

We need to be careful about our conclusions and our statements about them. Have we really arrived at the final word on the issue? Is the conclusion subject to change with additional time and additional data? Does our conclusion limit us to one course of action which might not be appropriate forevermore?

We need to know that our communication with others starts right inside ourselves. Communication gets even more complicated when we begin sharing our assumptions, inferences, judgments, and conclusions with others—and when they share theirs with us.

BIBLIOGRAPHY

Armstrong, C.: "The Enemy," in *14 of my Favorites in Suspense,* Alfred Hitchcock (ed.), Dell Publishing Co., Inc., New York, 1939.

Cantrill, H.: *The Invasion From Mars,* Princeton University Press, Princeton, N.J., 1940.

Haney, W.: *Communication and Organizational Behavior,* rev. ed., Richard D. Irwin, Inc., Homewood, Ill., 1967.

Rokeach, M.: *The Open and Closed Mind,* Basic Books, Inc., Publishers, New York, 1960.

Royce, J.: *The Encapsulated Man,* D. Van Nostrand Company, Inc., Princeton, N.J., 1964.

Chapter 5

MEANING AND COMMUNICATION— WORDS DON'T MEAN, PEOPLE MEAN

WHEN COMMUNICATION FAILS

A great deal of the misery we often experience in our daily communication comes from common but nevertheless irritating mix-ups with words. We say something, in words, which we think sounds quite simple, straightforward, and easy to understand. The other person does not understand. Someone uses a word which we think obviously means "such and such," and we get bawled out because that was not at all what the other man meant.

For example: You are invited to a party and you ask what you should wear. Your friend tells you "Oh, pretty casual." So you show up with your old jeans and boots only to find out that everyone else is (by your standards) "dressed up" in good-looking clothes. No one is wearing "grubbies." Or you ask someone for directions to get somewhere and you are told "It is not very far." As it turns out, you have to walk blocks and blocks, and it takes you half an hour to do it, and for you, that *is* quite far. And you wonder why that man lied to you.

In these examples, someone is talking and someone is listening. Communication takes place through the sending and receiving of some words, but somehow the people involved did not get through to each other. They missed each other. Neither understood exactly what the other meant.

MEANING

Meaning is the key to communication. Meaning is what communication is about. When we communicate with one another, we are attempting to translate into a symbolic system (language) a meaning we have in our head so that another person, upon seeing or hearing the symbolic system, will translate it back into a meaning similar to ours. The key here is that the function of the symbols we use is to make meanings appear in people's minds. If the symbols elicit similar meanings in different people, then these people understand the message.

THE FAULTY ASSUMPTIONS ABOUT MEANING

Meaning is often assumed to be a characteristic of words. Something that is contained in words, in a more or less permanent, natural, logical, and obvious way.

Words are not only assumed to have meaning, but they are assumed to have only *one* meaning.

The attitude which goes with these two faulty assumptions is pretty smug. We feel that when we use a word with a certain meaning, then obviously everybody else will use it in the same way. We assume quite confidently that other people have the same meanings for words that we have, that is, if these other people are not idiots, dishonest, or totally uneducated. The number of times we get into long arguments over the "real" and "proper" meaning of words still does not give us the clue that there is more to this business of meaning than meets the ear or the eye. Perhaps you know the story of the man who, when asked why a pig is called a "pig," replies, "Because it's so dirty."

In the next paragraphs we will take a close look at these two assumptions.

The Meaning of Meaning "Meaning" is the relationship which *we* make between a symbol and what the symbol stands for. Meaning is *not* in words. Words are *not* containers. They are merely scratches of ink on paper or sound vibrations wiggling through the air. Meaning is not some sort of physical attachment traveling in the word, with the word, from one person's mouth to another person's ear. Meaning is in people. We use words to *elicit* meaning in people, that is, to call up a particular relationship between a symbol and what the symbol represents.

The First Faulty Assumption: Words Have Meaning

Caution: There is no necessary, logical, God-given, or correct relationship between any symbol and what the symbol represents.

The relationship is man-made. It is arbitrary. It changes. Only to the extent it is agreed upon by more than one person can it have communicative value. We will come back to this later.

Ogden and Richards[1] refer to the indirectness of the relation between words and things. In our drawing (Figure 5–1) we have distorted the original Ogden and Richards diagram so we can compare meaning to a baseless triangle in which the three points are represented by an object, a symbol that stands for that object, and a human being. The relationship between the symbol and the object can only be made through the human being. The triangle has no base because there is no necessary connection between the word "chair" and the object on which we sit. That we call the object by this particular name, this particular set of letters, in that particular order reflects only the fact that people at some time have agreed to do so. Thus the symbol came to *mean* the object. Actually,

[1] C. K. Ogden and I. A. Richards, 8th ed., The Meaning of Meaning, *Harcourt, Brace & World, Inc., New York, 1946, pp. 10–11.*

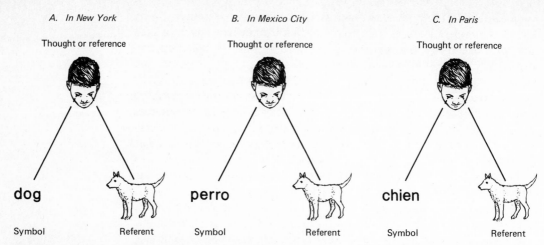

Thought or reference   Thought or reference   Thought or reference

dog   perro   chien

Symbol   Referent   Symbol   Referent   Symbol   Referent

Figure 5–1 There is no direct relationship between the "referent" (the thing we are talking or writing about) and the "symbol" (the words we use). Only as these referents and symbols are related through the thoughts of a person (reference) do they have meaning. Meaning is not in the object nor in the symbol but in the interaction of these through the human communicator.

the word does not mean the object. It is *we* who mean the object whenever we use the word.

If you feel this is linguistic nit-picking, bear with us some more.

Dictionaries Some of you might object to the statement that words do not mean anything at all. What about dictionaries, you say? Aren't they the supreme authority on matters of word meaning? Well, not really. Dictionaries do not set up authoritative statements about the "true" meaning of words but rather *record* what words have meant to certain authors, in certain contexts, at certain times. They also record the various *usages* of words at different times, in different parts of the country, in different contexts. Dictionaries provide us a historical record of how certain levels of society use words, but they can't predict how the next person you meet will use a word in a message to you. So dictionaries might be useful to settle a bet on spelling, or on the origin of a word, or as a guide in "Scrabble," but they will not provide us with the "true" or "correct" meaning for words.

Meanings Are in People Meanings are in people. They are the internal reactions of the human organism to its environment. Meanings are personal—our own private property. We add to them, change them. But we cannot find meanings in just unattached words. Meanings are in us, not in words. Words act as cues to elicit meanings in us and in others. To the extent the meanings elicited in different people are similar, successful

THE DYNAMICS OF INTRAPERSONAL COMMUNICATION

communication takes place. If there are no similarities of meaning, even if the words are identical, then communication goes awry. Meanings are not transmitted from person to person. They are elicited, called up, created internally.

How Do We Learn Meaning?[2]   Learning meanings is naturally associated with learning language since meaning is the relationship we agree to make between words and what the words will stand for. The process starts very early when a human baby starts imitating the sounds he hears around him. The sounds of a three- or four-month-old baby are the same all over the world. A Chinese baby sounds very much like an American baby or a French baby. However, after not too many months, the sounds will become more and more like the sounds made by the people the baby comes in contact with, simply because when the baby, for the first time, quite by accident, makes a sound that vaguely resembles something the parents can recognize, he is rewarded. The parents very likely reinforce him by laughing, talking to him, paying attention to him, and the baby learns that this particular sound seems to go over big in his family. Therefore he does it over and over again. With practice and rewards, the sound gets to be more and more like the parents' sound.

But how does the baby acquire meanings? How does he learn that this particular set of sounds refers to a particular object? Let's take the word "mother," or "mama," or "mommy" as an example. From the time a baby is born he will be fed, usually by his mother. Food will bring about a whole series of reactions in the baby. He will drool, he will make sucking motions with his mouth, he will feel the milk in his mouth, he will experience the warmth of another human being holding him while he is being fed, and he will get full and contented after he has been fed. The baby's reactions to food are quite natural, they are not learned, and they are quite instinctive. What we have here so far is (1) a baby, (2) food, and (3) the reactions the baby experiences in relation to the food.

However, every time the baby is in contact with the food, he is also in contact with another human being, his mother. So we also have (4) a person. Every time the baby experiences the food, he also experiences the mother. The two are simultaneous, and the baby learns that when there is food, there is mother. Because this happens over and over again, the baby learns to associate the two stimuli (food and mother) and to him they are inseparable. Finally, the baby *learns to respond to the mother as he responds to the food*. He will drool when his mother is around, even when there is no food. He will start sucking motions with his mouth when his mother comes close, even when she brings no food. The baby learned

[2]*This discussion of the learning of meaning is based on David Berlo,* The Process of Communication, *Holt, Rinehart and Winston, Inc., New York, 1960, pp. 180–185.*

to transfer his internal reactions from one stimulus to another. To him, food means mother. In addition, the baby will make another association. The mother usually talks to her baby when she feeds him, and she will make sounds such as "mommy," "mama," etc. Now we have (5) a word. The baby learns that every time there is food, there is the person, and every time there is the person, there is this particular sound. Since he has already associated the food with the person, he will associate the person with the sound.

At this point, the baby is ready for his third association: food and sound. The reactions he has to the food are now transferable to the person and to the sound that represents the person. To the baby, the word "mommy" means food. His internal meaning for the word "mommy" is thus associated with the experience he has had with his mother. This experience starts with food, and of course, as the baby grows up, becomes more diversified. As the experience with the person becomes more complex, so will his reactions to the person and thus to the word that represents that person. "Mommy" will come to mean other things besides food. It will come to mean love, play, cuddling, tickle, soft, warmth, spanking, etc.

The essential point here is that *the meanings we have for words grow out of our experiences we have had with whatever the words stand for.*

If our experiences with our mother have been generally pleasant, loving and warm, then our connotations, our meaning for the word, will evoke something pleasant, warm, and loving. If they have been unpleasant, the word will, most of the time, evoke unpleasant reactions.

Implications for Communication

This theory of meanings acquisition has some extremely important implications for communication.

People Can Only Have Similar Meanings to the Extent They Have Similar Experiences If your experiences about something are different than someone else's, your meanings will be different. Perhaps you and your friend will talk about dogs. Your experiences with dogs have always been pleasant. Man's-best-friend type of experiences. Your friend's experiences, however, were not so happy. He may have been bitten by a dog once and may have had to undergo painful rabies shots. His meaning for the word "dog" is going to include those bad memories, perhaps some degree of fear, and you may never convince him that dogs are fine to have around young children.

Unless we have had similar experiences with what a word stands for, we will not really understand each other, for we will not be talking about the same thing.

The word "telephone" would have been incomprehensible 200 years ago to anyone, for nobody had any experience to connect it to. Even in 1971, the word "telephone" does not quite mean the same thing to an American, who can usually use a telephone in America quite easily and inexpensively, and to a peasant in many underdeveloped countries who may never have seen, much less used, a telephone in his whole life.

The term "LSD" means something quite different to the scientist studying the effects of LSD on the chromosome structure in rats, to the parent afraid his child is experimenting with drugs, to the college student who has used LSD with no apparent bad effects, and to the student who had a really "bad trip" and ended up in a hospital after attempting suicide. This is not to say that any one of these people know more or less about LSD. This is to say that these people's experiences with LSD are of a different nature, and thus their meaning for the word will rather be different. So if they talk to each other, they may not be talking about the same thing.

Consider the word "car." To some who have never had any difficulties with cars, it may be a fairly neutral word referring generally to a means of transportation. To those living in crowded cities, it may mean those awful traffic jams and the pollution associated with car exhaust systems. To the person who has had a very serious accident and perhaps killed someone, or had a relative or close friend die as a result of a car accident, the word will never be neutral. It will bring up a whole series of painful associations.

People never have identical experiences, therefore, they never have identical meanings. 100 percent successful communication is not possible. Heraclitus, the Greek philosopher, said that a man never steps in the same river twice. The man changes, and the river changes. We are not the same from day to day. Our experiences with our environment change constantly even if slightly. As long as we live, we grow and change. If *we* do not even remain the same, how can we expect others to be like us? No two people are ever identical. No two people can ever live identical experiences. Even brothers and sisters in the same family are not raised in an identical environment. Parents act differently with one child than with another, with boys and with girls, with the first born and the last baby in the family. In addition, what we experience is the product of who we are and how we filter things from our environment. No one is identical psychologically and physically. Even if the environment were identical for different people, they would experience it differently because of their physical and psychological differences. Therefore, it is quite impossible to ever have totally identical meanings with anyone.

However, agreement on many basic kinds of nouns such as "chair," "table," "house," "car," can be substantially achieved. Our misunderstandings occur primarily in two ways:

(1) Over those abstract terms which have many connotations behind

them from our value system, such as "parents," "freedom," "love," "hate," "education," "teaching," etc.

(2) Overtreating any word as if the other person automatically uses the word in the same way; that is, when we are not aware of the possible differences in meaning each of us may have.

We should not, therefore, decide that because perfect communication cannot be achieved, we should become a hermit. Communication does go on more or less successfully, in spite of the limitations we have listed. We should not expect communication to be perfect, but strive for the maximum effect in relation to the limitations our language places on our communicative behaviors.

Having similar experiences facilitates communication. We know this because we find it easier to talk (and achieve understanding) with someone who has experienced things with us. A close friend will generally understand more easily what you are saying than a stranger. Not only is this a function of the similarity of language experiences, but it is also a function of role identification which we will discuss in a later chapter (see Chapter 8).

On a more optimistic note, it is likely that we can communicate at some levels because human beings have had enough similar experiences that there are sufficient universal kinds of experiences, in spite of the differences, if we are aware of the limits of our meanings.

Meanings Are Not Fixed; They Change as Experiences Change Our experiences with things, people, events, situations, are never static. They change constantly since our environment changes constantly. We change too. Even similar experiences are sometimes perceived differently at different times in our life. Our reactions and feelings to what is around us differ as we become different, as we see the world differently. Our meanings, thus, change.

The word "school" to the four-year-old, who cannot wait until he goes to this mysterious and exciting place, means this anticipation, getting to be a "big kid," all the nice stories his mother told him about what happens in school, etc. Two years later, after a year of kindergarten, the word "school" may call up the actual experiences accumulated with his classmates, teachers, the building, and the activities. Still a few years later, the word may refer to homework, having to read books, learning, social activities, grades, failing or passing, being pushed by his parents to improve his grades, or not being able to watch a particular TV program because he is told to go do his homework. When the boy gets to be in high school, his meaning for the word "school" will have taken still more connotations that will have grown out of his varied experiences in the course of his school career.

If he is a "big man on campus," school may come to mean the place

COCKLEBUR AND LINT THEORY OF MEANING

As a demonstration in a workshop, this "theory" was humorously developed by the authors to show how we acquire different meanings for words based on our personal experiences. It is a way of describing the difference between denotative meaning (the cocklebur) and connotative meaning (the lint).

We found a collection of cockleburs, those seed pods which a number of different plants produce and which were about half an inch long, were shaped like a small football, and had the usual number of sticky, thorny bristles on them.

Each participant in the workshop was given a cocklebur to carry for a week—in his pocket, purse, jacket, trousers—wherever there was a place for this prickly little seed pod. At the end of the week each person was supposed to check what had happened to his own cocklebur and compare it with those carried by others.

Cockleburs pick up lint from pockets the same way they attach themselves to the fur of animals, which is nature's way of distributing the seeds of the original plant. In a week's time the original cocklebur is nearly covered with bits of lint, threads, dust, and other collected debris, so one can barely make out the original bur.

As the workshop participants learned, everybody had some of his own special lint on the spines of the bur, just as we all pick up our own connotations for words. The original burs were very much alike —the denotative meaning—compared to the differences added to the original meaning by our association (lint)—the connotative meaning. The analogy was clear.

where he can exert some power and influence or the place to be popular. Or, it may be a place to satisfy intellectual curiosity or a place to be totally bored. If our hypothetical student goes on to college, here again, a whole new set of experiences, and thus meanings, will be added to his store of previously accumulated connotations. Graduate work, will still add some more, and if our student becomes a teacher he will develop more experiences and more meanings. What the word "school" meant to you when you were four is different from what it means to you when you are fifteen, eighteen, twenty-one, twenty-five, and fifty. The meanings we have for words really develop in us in a spiral fashion. We start with a very small association between a new sound and some kind of an experience and each time we have the experience again, a new layer of meaning will be added to the nucleus we started with.

We Always Respond to Our Environment in Light of Our Own Experiences   We think everybody reacts to things the way we do. It is difficult to think otherwise because we feel our own experiences must be somehow universal, but they are not. The ability to (1) recognize this fact, (2) figure out what the other person's experiences are like, and (3) try to see the environment as he does, through his eyes, is one key to effective communication. This ability is called many names: empathy, sensitivity, communication awareness, or psychological adaptation. Whatever the name, it refers to a conscious awareness of human differences and a genuine attempt to see the world through another person's eyes, as *he* might see it—even temporarily—in order to understand why another person feels the way he does about something and how he got to feel that way. This ability is premised on a great deal of curiosity about human behavior and a genuine interest in people. Communication often breaks down because of a lack of such efforts, because of the feeling that *my way* to see the world and understand it is the *only way* that makes sense—the right way.

The Second Faulty Assumption: the Fallacy of Single Usage

To complicate things further, we often are under the delusion that one word equals one usage. Take the word "run" as an example.

You can *run* a 50-yard sprint
   run a business
   run your hose
   have a *runny* nose
   have a *run* of cards
   run your husband (or wife) the way you like
   run out of time
   run out of cereal
   run out on somebody
   run over someone with your car

It has been shown that the 500 most common words in the English language have about 14,000 different meanings, an average of 28 different meanings per word. And we are not talking here about the infinite number of private meanings or private connotations each one of us will call up in our minds when we hear the word. We are talking about the public, or denotative, dimension of meaning. The agreed-upon relationship between a symbol and whatever the symbol stands for.

Summary   We tried to emphasize in the preceding section that words have no meaning of their own. Meanings exist in people, and it is people who ascribe meanings to words by labeling a specific experience in a particular way. If a given experience is labeled similarly by two different people, these people, then, are said to have communicated successfully since the label will call up in their respective minds a similar experience. But remember: We are saying *similar.* Experiences are *never* identical. Meanings therefore can never be identical.

The clues for figuring out what is meant by a given word come generally from the context in which the word is used, that is, come from the other words with which this particular word is used. A native of America will understand quickly the distinctions between the different usages of a word, say "run," by looking at the rest of the sentence in which the word "run" appears. However, foreigners might get very distressed when they hear someone is going to "pull their leg" for they understand the words in their literal usage. And perhaps an older grandfather will be surprised to meet a long-haired, bearded, and disheveled looking young man his granddaughter had previously described to him as "real neat."

Private Usages   Language may act like a code. If we know the key to the code, we can decipher the secret messages we receive. If we know the people who send the messages, we can decipher even better the private meanings they intended to share with us.

A code is a powerful tool. It makes us belong to the group which shares it. It also excludes anyone who does not know it. In a given society we manage to have codes within the main code, languages within the language, that only a few privileged members of special groups understand. English, as it is spoken in America, is many different languages. Do you use the same language—the same code—at home, with close friends, and in school?

Young people familiar with the latest slang can carry on a conversation which the adults nearby would not understand. Most scientific disciplines develop their own language in an effort to be more precise and narrow down the number of usages for a given word. To have gastroenteritis is more specific than a "tummy ache" or a "sore gut." However, the word "gastroenteritis" may be meaningful only to the medical specialist who has learned what it refers to.

Sometimes, the highly esoteric jargon of certain specialists can be an obstacle in communication, when the specialists are not talking to other specialists but to laymen. There is a story of a plumber of foreign extraction who wrote to the Bureau of Standards in Washington, D.C., that he had found hydrochloric acid was fine for cleaning drains, and was it harmless? Washington replied: "The efficacy of hydrochloric acid is indisputable, but the corrosive residue is incompatible with metallic permanence." The plumber wrote back that he was mighty glad the Bureau agreed with him. The Bureau replied with a note of alarm: "We cannot assume responsibility for the production of toxic and noxious residues with hydrochloric acid and suggest you use an alternative procedure." The plumber wrote he was happy to learn that the Bureau still agreed with him. Whereupon, Washington exploded: "Don't use hydrochloric acid, it eats hell out of pipes."

The Humpty-Dumpty Attitude   The following selection from Lewis Carroll underscores the importance of meaning and the effect it has on communication:

> "I don't know what you mean by 'glory,'" Alice said.
>
> Humpty Dumpty smiled contemptuously. "Of course you don't—till I tell you. I mean 'there is a nice knockdown argument for you.'"
>
> "But glory does not mean 'a nice knockdown argument,'" Alice objected.
>
> "When I use a word," Humpty Dumpty said in a rather scornful tone, "it means just what I choose it to mean—neither more nor less."
>
> "The question is," said Alice, "whether you *can* make words mean so many different things."
>
> "The question is," said Humpty Dumpty, "who is to be master, that's all."[3]

Can we make words mean what we want them to mean? After all, if the relationship between a symbol and what the symbol represents is an arbitrary one, if the fact that we call a chair a "chair" is just a convention agreed upon, then what prevents us from changing it and calling a chair a "strump"? Nothing prevents us from doing so, and much of the time we do call familiar objects by names known only to ourselves or to the people in our close circle of friends.

However, the value of language or any symbolic system rests in the fact that it is a *shared* system, that is, a system known to more than one or a few individuals. We can make words mean what we want them to mean and play Humpty Dumpty, but then we sacrifice our chances of being understood by other members of the human race. Language with shared symbols is what binds us all together. If we choose to invent our own personal language we are in a sense dropping out of human contact for no one will know what we mean. Unless, somehow, we have the power to impose our code (our language system) on other people and enforce it, we stay isolated. A schizophrenic may speak a language only known to himself. Its form may sound grammatically like English but the relationships between its symbols and what they represent is only known to that lonely and isolated human being.

Yes, we can invent our own private language, but unless we can be "masters," that is, unless we can make other people learn it and accept

[3]*Lewis Carroll,* Alice's Adventures in Wonderland, Through The Looking Glass, and The Hunting of the Snark, *Modern Library, Inc., New York, 1925, pp. 246–247.*

it and use it, we will not be able to communicate with anyone else but ourselves. The William Steig cartoon of the man huddled in a box saying "People are no damn good" is perhaps the cry of bitterness of those who understand the imperfections and limitations inherent in all human systems. Yet communication, however imperfect as it may be, is our only thread of sanity and humaneness.

BIBLIOGRAPHY

Barnlund, D.: "A Transactional Model of Communication," in Johnnye Akin, Alvin Goldberg, Gail E. Myers, and Joseph Stewart (eds.), *Language Behavior: A Book of Readings in Communication,* Mouton, The Hague, 1970.

Berlo, D. K.: *The Process of Communication,* Holt Rinehart and Winston, Inc., New York, 1960.

Brown, R.: *Words and Things,* The Free Press, New York, 1958.

Chase, S.: *The Power of Words,* Harcourt, Brace and Company, Inc., New York, 1954.

Cherry, C.: *On Human Communication,* The Technology Press of the Massachusetts Institute of Technology, Cambridge, Mass., 1957.

Davitz, J. R.: *The Communication of the Emotional Meaning,* McGraw-Hill Book Company, New York, 1964.

Hayakawa, S. I.: *The Use and Misuse of Language,* Premier Books, Greenwich, Conn., 1962.

Hayakawa, S. I.: *Language in Thought and Action,* rev. ed., Harcourt, Brace and Company, Inc., New York, 1964.

Lee, I.: *How to Talk with People,* Harper & Row, Publishers, Incorporated, New York, 1952.

Manis, J. G., and B. N. Meltzer, *Symbolic Interaction,* Allyn and Bacon, Inc., Boston, 1967.

Miller, G. A.: *Language and Communication,* McGraw-Hill Book Company, New York, 1951.

Ogden, C. K., and I. A. Richards: *The Meaning of Meaning,* 8th ed., Harcourt, Brace & World, Inc., New York, 1946.

Osgood, C., G. Suci, and P. Tannenbaum: *The Measurement of Meaning,* The University of Illinois Press, Urbana, 1957.

Salomon, I. B.: *Semantics and Common Sense,* Holt, Rinehart and Winston, Inc., New York, 1966.

Singh, J., and A. L. Zing: *Wolf Children and Feral Men,* Harper & Row, Publishers, Incorporated, New York, 1942.

Whorf, B. L.: *Language, Thought and Reality,* The Technology Press of the Massachusetts Institute of Technology, Cambridge, Mass., 1956.

Chapter 6   LANGUAGE AND COMMUNICATION — BEYOND OUR WILDEST DREAMS

Consider how many times the history of mankind has been drastically altered and shaped by new ideas. What happened to humanity when someone jiggled things and came up with the radical idea of the wheel? Or when some "nut" had the idea that the earth was revolving around the sun and not vice versa? Or when Darwin had the idea that biological man was somehow related to the ape through a long evolutionary line? Or when someone came up with the political idea that a man should only rule and govern by the consent of his fellow men? Or when a white man realized that a black man is as much a man and should thus have the rights of man?

Ideas such as these were, and are, not rapidly accepted because people intuitively realize that they will change the order of things. Yet these ideas slowly leave their mark in the history of our civilization. None of us is the same ever after, because of them.

Language is our medium to think about and talk about such ideas. What we call "knowledge" is language. What each one of us "knows" is the product of our language. Language, or symbolization, is more than a mere naming of the things we bump into in our environment. Language helps us dream of things that never were and perhaps never will be. Language is the major factor in producing our perceptions, our judgments, and our knowledge. Language is the medium through which we organize, talk about, and make sense out of reality. Unless we understand the relationship between language (symbolic world) and our environment (empirical world) we are blind to the relativity and uncertainty which govern our universe.

In this chapter, we want to increase your awareness of how language works and what language does to you. We are not concerned here with diagraming sentences, the parts of speech, the difference between *who* and *whom,* and Shakespeare. Our study will focus on the relationship between language and reality, between the symbolic world and the empirical world.

THE ABSTRACTING PROCESS[1]

The world around us is full of "stuff." There are sounds, smells, and sights —the noise of voices, cars, machines, and nature; the smells of cooking,

[1]*This material is adapted from Alfred Korzybski's* Science and Sanity, *4th ed., The International Non-Aristotelian Library Publishing Company, Lakeville, Conn., 1958.*

smoke, flowers, and exhausts; and the sights of people, animals, signs, and objects.

This empirical world, to use our expression, has things happening all around us. We pay attention to some, and we miss some. We don't hear or see everything. At least we consciously don't seem to know what is going on, and for a very good reason. We can't pay attention to everything at once. For that reason, we select those things we are interested in and pay attention to them.

In this respect we are like a radio. Think about all the different radio stations constantly transmitting music, news, and advertising, all day and night. All that stuff coming at us in wiggling little waves we neither see nor hear. Then we tune in the radio. It selects a station to pick up that frequency of waves, and we get a sound. Certainly the other stations don't stop broadcasting when we tune in only one of them. And when you change stations, what happens to the station you just tuned out? It goes on, beaming its messages of music or promotion in spite of the fact that you don't have it tuned in.

The world is like that. Things go on whether we tune them in or not. But when we decide to pay attention to something, we begin to take a part—but not all—of what is going on and listen to it. We select, that is we abstract, only some of the stimuli out of all that is available around us. If you recall our discussion of perception, you are already familiar with this idea. What we called *selective perception,* in Chapter 2, is what we now will refer to as the *abstracting process.*

It is impossible for any living organism to pay attention to all that is available at one time, so our responses are always selective. We usually abstract, or select, a very small part of what is going on around us. The abstraction process refers to this selection which takes place any time a living organism—including you—reacts to its environment. There is a sequence in this abstracting process we want to describe. Let us say, for example, that you go to the cafeteria and see hundreds of students moving in and out and sitting around. The cafeteria with its occupants, including a tall, skinny fellow walking with a cup of coffee in his hand, represents the total environment. Let's call that level one, the level of what is going on.

Level two is what *you* see of what is going on. As you know, you do not see all; you pay attention only to certain things and not to others, and you may also distort what you do pay attention to.

These two levels are silent. You haven't said anything yet. You haven't even put labels on the fellow with the cup of coffee, so words don't have to be involved. This fellow is, at level two, just someone that caught your eye whom you watched because he moved.

To go any further in abstracting, you'll have to use some kind of language or symbol system. You name the details of this tall, skinny fellow to yourself, and you begin to use language to think in, even if you don't speak to anyone else.

At level three, you begin to put labels on this moving creature—male, tall, skinny, carrying a cup of coffee. But you also leave out details when you put on the labels. You perhaps saw, but did not describe to yourself, his clothes, his eyes, or his hair. You chose the things to notice and to name.

At level four, you might say that the tall, skinny fellow carrying the cup of coffee is a student, thus generalizing from your previous observations.

At level five, you might say that he is a human being, thus generalizing even more.

To summarize our discussion about these levels, we can say that level one represents what is going on; level two, what we see of what is going on; level three, what we say about what we see, in a descriptive way; level four and all subsequent levels, the verbal generalizations we make which are based on the previous abstractions.

Our abstractions are personal. It is one thing to feel pain and quite another to say, "I have a toothache." This statement involves three different levels of our abstracting. The feeling of pain is at level two where we recognize something is happening that is painful out of all the things that are happening (level one). We tell ourself what it is at level three. The statement about the toothache is at level four, the level of interpretation and words about our silent experience at level two. Between the feeling of pain and the statement about it there is a reduction, a loss, a simplification, which the word "toothache" does not begin to represent. The throbbing, the heat, the dizziness, etc., somehow get lost in the translation.

Remember the map-territory analogy? The territory itself might be called level one. That's where things are going on, where the actual roads are, where the towns are located, etc. The map is what we abstract from that territory. The map becomes successive levels of abstracting.

When we begin to talk about what we perceive, we make a verbal map. Level three is a verbal map of level two. And what we say about what we perceive can be at various levels of abstraction depending on our degree of generalization. When we closely describe what we see—when we make reports of observations—we are quite close to level two, the level of our perceptions. The better we describe, the closer our maps are to the territory. When we start interpreting and generalizing with our language, we get farther and farther from the empirical world, from the territory. When we proceed along the levels of abstraction, we become more and more general and thus convey less information because we have lost more details from the territory.

Example: You want to find your way around your campus, so a campus map of all the buildings would be quite helpful. If you have only a map of the city the college is located in, it is likely you won't have a very good map of your campus and its buildings and sidewalks. The second map is a higher level of abstraction. It leaves out specific details you want. A map of the state will have your city in it; but not the campus roads (a still higher level of abstraction). A map of the United States will have your state and probably your city, but certainly not the campus (another level of abstraction). A map of the world will include the United States but maybe not your state, city, or certainly the campus.

What happens as you go from one level to the next? Essentially, the higher the level of abstraction, the more territory that level includes. If you cover more territory, you are bound to leave out smaller details. *You are saying less and less about more and more.*

Another example: I say I own a "means of transportation." That's a very general, high level term which covers a lot of territory such as airplanes, cars, bicycles, horses, trains, boats, buses, roller skates, or motorbikes. Those words, "means of transportation," don't give enough information, at that level of abstraction, to really tell what I am talking about. So you want to know what kind of "means." So I tell you, "a car." We eliminate the other things we listed, but even by restricting the territory you still don't have much of an idea of what we are talking about. We are closer to the territory, but maybe not yet close enough for communication purposes. Is it a new car, an old car, an American or foreign car, a station wagon, a sedan, a sports car; what make and model, what year?

The word "car" may be more specific than "means of transportation" but is still too high a level of abstraction to convey enough information to you. *To be the most descriptive possible, I would show you the car, and you could experience it at the lowest level of abstraction.* If there were no way to show you the car, then I could describe it in considerable detail, thus moving to a verbal level but still close to the territory with the verbal map I make.

A communication principle emerges from these examples. The lower the level of abstraction, that is, the more descriptive and specific we are, the more effective communication can be. On the other hand, the higher the level of abstraction, that is, the more abstract and general we are, the more chance there is for confusion—accidental or on purpose.

CLASSIFICATION

What happens when we talk? Whenever we use language, even at a very low level of abstraction, even at the descriptive level, we are essentially classifying. Language serves the purpose of organizing the confusion of the multitude of things we observe at a given time into some kind of an ordered sequence of stimuli. When you see a person or an object, you are really exposed simultaneously to a variety of different stimuli. You will experience many different reactions and feelings at the same time. Yet, whenever you start talking to yourself about what you are perceiving, your choice of characteristics to describe your perception forces you very subtly, but nonetheless effectively, to order the various sensations into something coherent.

SIMILARITIES AND DIFFERENCES

What does the word classification refer to? When we classify an object, or a person, or a situation, we are in essence saying that this object, person, or situation fits into a category which comprises objects, persons, and situations similar to the one we are talking about. We focus on *similarities*. Look at the book you are now reading. Take another book from your bookshelf. Look at these two objects. At the level of your perception, they are probably different. Different colors, different sizes, different type, paperback or hardback perhaps, different thicknesses, different weight, different words on the cover, different words inside, different uses, etc. Most everything about them is different at the level of perception, and even at the level of description. However, when you call both these objects "books," what you are doing is *neglecting* the numerous *differences* and focusing only on the one thing they have in common, "bookness," *however that may be defined.* The important thing here is that the classification process is *arbitrary.* You classify these objects as "books" because perhaps you subscribe to a definition of "books" as "printed pages bound together between covers." These objects you are looking at fit the definition; therefore they belong to the category and therefore they can be classified as books. The definition of the category is arbitrary. Your noticing the details that show they have the characteristics that put them in the category is a personal matter. In other words, the fact that you noticed the objects have printed pages and were bound between covers, comes out of your process of selection. Another person looking at these same two objects might notice only their weight and decide to classify them in the category "paperweight."

The same object can be classified in many different categories depending on the characteristics that you pay attention to.

As you know, we select what we see—the abstracting process—and thus will classify things a number of different ways. These classifications are not right or wrong. They simply reflect a different set of criteria on which the abstraction process was based. Classifications are not neutral, however. They do something to us and to the things that are classified. If a man were classified "guilty" by a jury, some consequences will follow that will be quite different had he been classified "not guilty." Something may be a piece of mail in your mailbox, thus protected by federal law—no one is free to tamper with it—yet it becomes trash when you throw it away, and it may be burned by the trash collector.

We must stress again that whenever we classify, we focus on similarities and neglect differences. "A rose is a rose . . ." may be a nice literary phrase. In reality all roses are not alike. They are different, even though we choose to focus on what they have in common when we put them all in the category "rose." At the empirical world level, at the first level of the abstracting process, everything is different, everything moves, everything changes, everything and everybody is unique. Whenever we choose to group things and people in neat little categories and pigeonholes, we are simply playing a verbal game, which of course can be very useful. We can talk about "houses" in general without referring to *a* particular house. Categories, at best, are shortcuts. When we say that a person is "a hippie," we are focusing only on certain traits or characteristics that we perceive in this individual. Perhaps his hair, his clothes, or his age. The same person can be classified as a father, a husband, a boy friend, a customer, a student, a citizen, an American, a taxpayer, a movie fan, etc. In each case we focus on certain characteristics that we perceive.

We tend to speak (and therefore to think) in terms of opposites in our language. Black is the opposite of white. Bad is the opposite of good. Stingy is the opposite of generous. Success is the opposite of failure. Our language is built by polar terms, or those items which can be on one side or another. We like to divide our world into competing opposites, into dichotomies. To give you an idea of how much this attitude of polarities is expressed in our language, try this test.

POLARIZATION: REAL OPPOSITES AND FALSE OPPOSITES

Fill in the middle point of this scale with *one word* which fits a middle point between the opposite pairs in the same way the first example fits:

black	gray	white
bad	_____	good
success	_____	failure
stingy	_____	generous
polite	_____	rude
honest	_____	dishonest

If we live in a world where the black hats of the Western movies are the guys who smoke and drink and shoot somebody in the back, then we expect the white hats to be clean-living, fast-drawing, honest cowboys who win the girl in the last reel. One is all bad and the other all good. Few people have these pure qualities in real life. But these polarizing terms give us a shortcut in our thinking, so we do not have to evaluate more than a few characteristics to determine who is good or bad, right or wrong. Our language, then, tends to give us support for our dividing the world into these false opposites.

There are, of course, some real opposites in our world, and we should not confuse them. A light switch can be on or off. A friend may be here or somewhere else, and that same friend may be tall or short in relation to some kind of height comparison.

Where we may have difficulties in our language adjustment is by treating the false opposites as real ones—by having an either-or attitude about persons or events when there are additional alternatives. There are, therefore, more gradations in our empirical world than we may have language to talk about easily. It is important for us to recognize this limitation of our language system.

THE INFLUENCE OF LANGUAGE ON OUR BEHAVIOR

To talk is to classify. We cannot utter a word without categorizing. How does this affect our behavior? We use language to describe to ourselves and to others what the environment we live in is like. Language influences our very way of looking at this environment. Our perception of the world is filtered through and shaped by our language patterns.

Language and Perception

All we know of the world we live in is what we perceive of it, and this perception is colored by the language we use to describe what we see. Language is not just a mere tool which names what our eyes see and our ears hear. Language acts on our perceptual processes to shape these perceptions.

Erich Fromm, in *Beyond the Chains of Illusion,*[2] explains how our linguistic filter permits certain experiences to enter our awareness while others are stopped. Some experiences such as pain, hunger, sexual desire, and most experiences having to do with individual and group survival, have easy access to awareness. However, when it comes to more complex experiences like "seeing a rosebud in the early morning, a drop of dew on it while the air is still chilly, the sun coming up, a bird singing," cultural differences are noticeable. In Japan, this kind of experience lends itself easily to awareness. In our modern Western culture this same experience may not come so easily into awareness because it is considered too uneventful and too unimportant to be noticed. There are many experiences for which certain languages have no word while another language may be rich in words which express these feelings. In a language in which different emotions are not expressed by different words, it is even more difficult to be clearly aware of what one is feeling. It is difficult to express subtle differences of feelings and emotions with some English words. We can

[2]*Erich Fromm,* Beyond the Chains of Illusion, *Pocket Books, Inc., New York, 1962, p. 125.*

love spaghetti; we can love our mother; we can love a boy (or girl) friend; we can love a husband, a child, a dog, horseback riding, reading, or "pot." The same word, yet a variety of different feelings.

Language provides us with a way to cut up our environment into little categories that make it easier for us to cope with what is around us. But these categories in turn shape our perceptions because they make us more prone to notice the characteristics that make up these particular categories. When you call something a pen, you are subtly made to perceive the ability of that object to write. If you had labeled it a weapon, you would notice the fact that it is a pointed object. To call things or people a name forces us to focus on the characteristics which are supposed to belong to anything or any person which is a member of that category. The words we have in a language thus force us to notice certain things and not others.

In the Navajo Indian language, there are three different ways to say "It rains" by conjugating the verb "rains" differently. There is one form of the verb which means "It rains and I know it because I went outside and got wet." All that. Another form means "It rains and I know it because I am inside and I am looking outside and I see the rain falling." The third form means "It rains and I know it because someone told me." This Indian language makes a distinction between the sources of information utilized to find out about an event. In one case, the verb form which is used indicates, *in addition* to the information about the rain, that this information was gotten *firsthand,* through direct observations. The second form carries the information that it rains, and in addition, tells that the information was gotten through *indirect firsthand* observation. Finally, the third form tells that the information was gotten through *hearsay.* If you recall our discussion about the difference between inferences and observations, you will see that this Indian tribe has incorporated in its language a very nice distinction between observations and inferences. The distinction has to be made before you talk about the rain because you must know which of the three verb forms to use. These people are practically forced to make this distinction before they talk. In English, of course, there is no such need. We just say "It rains," and we do not need to know whether we know it firsthand or we just heard someone telling us. Perhaps, if we had to make the distinction to know which verb to use, we might not mix up observations and inferences as much as we do and take for certain what is at best only slightly probable.

Eskimos, who live in a snowy world, have eighteen different words to refer to snow. We have only three in English. Snow, ice, and slush. Even when we add an adjective or adverb in front of the word we get only a few more types of snow. Freshly fallen snow, powdered snow, packed snow, and icy snow. This gives us about seven different kinds of snow. Where do Eskimos get their additional eleven types of snow? Each of their words refers to a particular kind of snow, different from all other kinds. Of course, they live in snow most of the year around. Snow is a very important part of their lives, and they must know it well, for its consistency may warn them of changes in the weather, possible storms, etc. Therefore, they probably are quite aware of tiny differences in consistency that most of us would overlook. And if you have never seen snow, you might not even see the difference between icy snow and packed snow. A skier would. The Eskimos saw all the tiny differences in snow and made up words for them. However, and this is an important point, *the fact that they have all these words helps them see the differences.* Each of these different words calls their attention to one little facet of the snow. It is probable that at the beginning of their language, the words were coined because they saw differences in the snow, but after awhile, the words themselves became pointers, pointing to one particular aspect of the snow. The words made it easier to perceive that particular characteristic, to perceive differences rather than similarities.

In English, there are many different words to talk about "what we throw away because we don't want it anymore." We have words such as litter, garbage, trash, rubbish, refuse, junk, debris, and waste. As you know, our culture is one in which cleanliness is very important. So we know all the little differences between things that are usually dirty and that we want to get rid of. Of course, because we pay much attention to these things so that we can get rid of them, we learn to perceive all kinds of differences between them. Garbage is not trash. Trash is not litter, etc. The more familiar we are with something, the more likely we are to perceive differences and to have a name to call these differences. And the name that is used to refer to something will point to one of its characteristics. Of course, the object has many more characteristics not covered by this particular name, but these other characteristics may not be perceived at all since the name will not call attention to them. "I am reading a textbook" or "I am reading a book" will convey something quite different to the person you are talking to. In the first case you may be drawing attention to the fact that you are doing your homework. In the other, you may be pointing to a pastime—what you do to entertain yourself.

Language and Stereotyping

Our language is thus a very powerful instrument which, quite literally, shapes the world that we know. The symbolic world does more than just describe the empirical world. It draws attention to some aspects and not others of the real world which are available, and thus influences our behavior. We behave on the basis of what we know. The classifying function of language is so pervasive in our lives that any time we are exposed to a new stimulus, to something we are not familiar with, we ask "what is it?" or "who is he?"

THE DYNAMICS OF INTRAPERSONAL COMMUNICATION

The questions beg for classification. We want to know what category this new thing or person can be placed into so we know how to deal with it or him. If he is a "lawyer," or a "radical," or a "college president," we then "know" what pigeonhole we can put him in. If we know the attributes that people in that particular pigeonhole are supposed to possess, then we can immediately "know" something about this new individual. If he belongs to the category, then he too will possess these attributes. This is the easy way for us to find out things about new people. It saves us the trouble of finding out what the person is really like. We judge him on the similarities we infer he has with other members of the category. We tend to overlook what makes him different from anyone else. This is called stereotyping.

Stereotyping is a direct consequence of classifying and categorizing. It means that you judge someone not on the basis of what you know about him specifically and personally, but what you know about the category he belongs to. So people will stereotype students, teachers, blacks, whites, radicals, hippies, activists, Jews, Republicans, Democrats, Communists, etc. The implication is that if they belong to the category, then they are all alike. You've seen one, you've seen them all. The problem with stereotyping is that it provides a shortcut for thinking and deters people from finding out for themselves what the person is really like and what makes him unique and different from anyone else.

Stereotyping permits us to set up neat, well-ordered, oversimplified categories into which we can slip our evaluations of people, situations, and happenings. As we will see in the next chapter, this often has disastrous consequences for our communication with others.

Labeling and Action

Language affects our behavior in some other ways. You remember the old saying, "Sticks and stones may break my bones, but names can never hurt me." If this were true, why would name calling arouse so many violent feelings and reactions? You know that if someone calls you a name you don't like, it will provoke some kind of reaction in you, which you may not show but which nonetheless affects you. Few people really like to be called chicken, dummy, goody-goody, moron, cheater, or phony. Most of you can add your favorite insults to the list. Names do hurt us, words do affect us.

Most of us react to labels. A college transcript is a record of the various labels you have accumulated during your academic career. The "A" label somehow will bring you more positive responses from prospective employers or other schools' officials than the "D" and "F" labels. Letters of recommendation are nothing but verbal labels. "Mr. Joe Smith is competent, responsible, and honest." Three labels right there, and they will elicit a particular reaction from whoever reads the letter. The reaction would have been different had the letter read, "Mr. Joe Smith is incompetent, irresponsible, and dishonest."

Think of the language of advertising and its influence on our behavior. A department-store manager once tried the following experiment.[3] He had received a shipment of high-quality handkerchiefs and decided to place half of them on one counter bearing the sign, "Fine Irish Linen— 50 cents each." The other half was placed on another counter and bore the sign, "Nose Rags—3 for 25 cents." The Irish linens outsold the nose rags five to one. What were the customers reacting to, do you suppose? The empirical world? The real handkerchiefs they could actually observe? No. They reacted to the labels and did not bother to check the territory to see if there were differences in quality between the "Irish linens" and the "nose rags." We react to the words which things are called, and it affects the way we react to the things themselves. We judge the book by the cover, in a way, when the name something is called will affect how we react to it. Read the ads in a newspaper. People don't advertise "houses." They sell "cute," "adorable," "exquisite," "elegant," "dandy," "glamorous" homes. Look at restaurant menus. What something is called may well determine how much you will pay for it!

Would you prefer to read "steak" on a menu or "piece of dead cow"? Somehow words have a kind of power over us, and we react. Would men buy an after-shave lotion called "Desertflower," or "Caprice," or "Golden Lace"? More likely they would prefer a product called "Brut," "Karate," "English Leather," "Jade East," or "Nine Flags." Men might buy "men's cologne," but definitely not a "perfume." Ethnic and religious derogatory labels are deeply resented by most people. Police officers probably do not enjoy being called "pigs," and the very fact that this word is shouted by demonstrators in run-ins with the police is a good indication that name calling is a powerful tool to vent anger and frustration and to hurt the other fellow.

SYMBOLIC AND EMPIRICAL ATTITUDES

To conclude this chapter on language, we are going to describe two basic attitudes people have toward the relationship between words and what they stand for, between symbolic maps and empirical territories, between language and reality.

Symbolic and empirical attitudes are not clear-cut dichotomies in which the world can be conveniently divided. Let's look at these attitudes as the two ends of a long continuum, a wide spectrum of human behaviors and responses.

[3]*William Haney,* Communication and Organizational Behavior, *rev. ed., Richard D. Irwin, Inc., Homewood, Ill., 1967, p. 379.*

Symbolic Attitude

A symbolic attitude characterizes the person who becomes so absorbed in his verbal maps, in what is *said* about something that he does not check the territory, the empirical world, to see if the words describe it accurately. A person with a symbolic attitude is more concerned with his inferences, assumptions, thoughts, suppositions, and beliefs "inside his skin" than with the "reality outside." We behave symbolically when we rely on labels, on words, on verbal maps to guide our behavior *without checking in the empirical world to see whether these words, labels, or verbal maps have any validity and are accurate representations of the territory.* Imagine you wanted to buy a used car. You answer an ad in the paper that describes the car as: "Foreign sports car, excellent condition, top shape, a beauty." If you bought the car without looking at it, driving it, or inspecting its engine, simply because you relied on the words you read in the ad, you would be behaving symbolically and perhaps in this case, foolishly. You would behave on the basis of an unchecked verbal map, which in this particular case, is not likely very accurate. Have you ever read an ad that said the car for sale was lousy, beat up, in terrible shape, and a real lemon?

When we respond to a rumor without checking its accuracy, we behave symbolically. When we respond to what we hear and read as if the words we heard and read were the real thing, we behave symbolically. When we are swayed by speeches, slogans, advertisements, propaganda, we are behaving symbolically. When we respond to people on the basis of our stereotypes, we behave symbolically.

Empirical Attitude

The empirical attitude characterizes the person who checks in the empirical world the validity of what he hears and reads. An empirical attitude is a tendency to inspect the territory *first* and then to make verbal maps to describe it and to correspond with it. The empirical attitude is the scientific attitude. The scientist makes a hypothesis (symbolic) but checks its validity by making observations in the empirical world.

The person with an empirical attitude will not believe an ad and buy a car without looking at the car, without inspecting it or checking it. The person with an empirical attitude will estimate the degree of probability of his inferences and will try to verify them in the empirical world, when possible. Note here that we do not say that the empirically oriented person does not make inferences. We all make inferences. We could not live without making them. The empirically oriented person is *aware* that he makes inferences and is consciously trying to determine how valid they are by checking these inferences in the empirical world. The empirical attitude is awareness that the abstracting process takes place constantly and that one cannot see all and say all. Such a person is aware of the difference between the levels of abstraction and relies less on the higher levels (far from the territory) than he does on the lower levels (close to the territory).[4]

THE SYMBOLIC-EMPIRICAL CONTINUUM

So far, it sounds as if there were only two kinds of attitudes, symbolic and empirical. Actually, most of us have both. We behave symbolically some of the time, empirically some of the time—and we should. There are situations which require a symbolic attitude, and some which require an empirical attitude. Behaving with the appropriate attitude is what is important.

Symbolic behavior becomes creative when done on purpose with frequent pull back to reality. Great novelists, poets, composers, imaginative engineers, business leaders, statesmen, people who have visions and dreams operate symbolically in their creative moments. When we make a bold guess, we behave symbolically, and we must make bold guesses about our world. The nature of the abstracting process makes it inevitable for us to make guesses about our environment. If we only believed what we saw and were only willing to operate on the basis of what can be checked firsthand, our world, our reality, would be very limited indeed. A symbolic attitude is very useful and creative *as long as we do some checking in the territory to make sure we are not too far off base.*

A symbolic attitude is dangerous when it is self-generated—when verbal behavior and silent assumptions become split off from reality, from the empirical world. Unchecked, habitual daydreaming. Prejudices based on stereotypes and categories can be very misleading. When we react to someone, not on the basis of what he is like in the empirical world, in our real contact with him, but on the basis of what we "know about his kind," we lose the benefit of direct observations which may go counter to public folklore and widespread prejudices. The mentally unbalanced individual who thinks he is Napoleon and that the rest of the world is mad, is showing an extreme case of symbolic behavior. He believes the words he tells himself rather than evidence from the empirical world. The paranoid person is absolutely sure that everyone hates him and persecutes him and believes what he tells himself repeatedly rather than what people actually do to him. His symbolic attitude is so extreme that he probably distorts the data that come to him from the empirical world to fit his inaccurate verbal maps. When we act as if the things we say about the empirical world make it so, we act symbolically, and these delusions may sometimes be dangerous.

[4]*The formulations of symbolic-empirical attitudes are adapted from Alfred Korzybski's discussion of intensional-extensional attitudes in* Science and Sanity, *4th ed., The International Non-Aristotelian Library Publishing Company, Lakeville, Conn., 1958.*

However, most of us are not that extreme. Most of us float along the symbolic-empirical continuum, from day to day, from event to event. Being stuck at any point in the continuum is probably not very useful for our communicative behavior. We usually drift from one end to the other. When we talk about things like whether or not the post office is open, we can have a pretty empirical attitude and call the place up to find out. When we use words like "religion," "blacks," "freedom," "democracy," and "Texans," we may drift toward the symbolic end of the scale.

On the other end, in the empirical area is the proof-demanding soul. If you think it's 60° outside, he will run to get a thermometer and then report it's really 61°. He is the researcher, the literal minded person, the absolute doubter, perhaps the cynic who cannot accept anything.

There is a story about President Coolidge riding on a train through the Kansas plains. The train passed a flock of sheep. Coolidge's friend, who was riding with him, said, "Look at the sheep; they've just been sheared." Coolidge looked and replied, "Yes, at least on this side."

An empirical attitude is a fine trait in the laboratory, but it can also be carried too far, to an extreme of foolish and needless doubting of everything that cannot be touched or experienced directly. When such a person intrudes in your day-to-day social communication, this kind of precision becomes a bore. Some call him a "nit-picker." People like these can cut themselves off from many wonderful things in the world without some degree of symbolic attitude, some degree of inference-making. The important thing is to be aware of what is inferential and what is factual. If we cut ourselves off from the world of vicarious experiences and sensations, we may become hermits living only on first-hand contact with the world. This is pretty limited living.

How to Recognize Inappropriate Symbolic Behavior

When people seem to pay more attention to words than to the things the words represent, when people pay more attention to symbols than to what the symbols stand for, when we react solely to a person's clothes or personal appearance as a symbol of what he is and do not check any further in the territory to find out more about him, we act symbolically.

Sometimes we react to words as if they were more than the things themselves. If someone says the word "snake," and there is no snake around and you jump and scream, you are behaving symbolically.

When a person is exposed to a fact from the empirical world but refuses to abide by it and still clings to his verbal theory, he is behaving symbolically. Some people are very good at that. They much prefer to twist the facts to make them fit their theories and verbal maps, than to change the theories to fit the territory.

No amount of saying that the world is flat is going to make it so. Some people still believe it is flat and will tell you that the pictures of the earth taken by the astronauts are fakes. To a lesser degree, students do the same thing when they receive a low grade on a paper. It is not the paper which is mediocre. It is the teacher who is unfair or biased against them, or it is the assignment which was lousy. At any rate, it will be something outside of what *they* did.

It is often quite difficult for all of us to accept reality. It takes a very mature human being to cope with reality as it is and not as he wishes it to be. This ability is the essence of healthy and rewarding communication.

BIBLIOGRAPHY

Carroll, J. B.: *Language and Thought,* Foundations of Modern Psychology Series, Prentice-Hall, Inc., Englewood Cliffs, N.J., 1964.

Miller, G. A.: *Language and Communication,* McGraw-Hill Book Company, New York, 1963.

Sapir, E.: *Culture, Language and Personality,* University of California Press, Los Angeles, 1957.

Skinner, B. F.: *Verbal Behavior,* Appleton-Century-Crofts, Inc., New York, 1957.

Smith, A. G.: *Communication and Culture,* Holt, Rinehart and Winston, Inc., New York, 1956.

Whitehead, A. N.: *Modes of Thought,* Putnam-Capricorn, New York, 1958.

Whorf, B. L.: *Four Articles on Metalinguistics, 1940–41,* Foreign Service Institute, Department of State, Washington, D.C., 1949.

Whorf, B. L.: *Language, Thought and Reality,* John Wiley & Sons, Inc., New York, 1956.

REDUCING INTRAPERSONAL   Chapter 7
BARRIERS—NO EASY WAY

In review of the previous chapters, we have discussed some ways in which we may set up barriers to communication. Although our focus has been primarily on the happenings inside us, we have frequently made reference to the effect of communication on others around us as well as on ourselves.

Before we go into the second section of the text with its focus on interpersonal and group communication, let's see if we have established a few basic points about communication, and in this chapter suggest some methods by which we may reduce the barriers to communication.

Point 1: We learn by discovering for ourselves, not by being told. For that reason we have used a laboratory approach in providing you data about communication and some opportunities to discover what happens to you in your communication contacts with others.

Point 2: Communication is not random. It is deliberate and can generally be predicted if we understand sufficiently the factors involved. Particularly, we can predict those times when communication will not bring us the desired results because all human beings pay attention to things in a pattern which is the product of their own uniqueness and their cultural environment. We will later go into the "whys" of our communication, but for the moment we will concentrate on the "whats" of the use of symbols, perceptions, observations and inferences, meanings, and some of our bad verbal habits.

Point 3: Our communication can stand improvement. We spend too much of our time in confusion and misunderstanding which might not be necessary if we apply some simple checks and balances. We are misled too often by propagandists, advertisers, friends, and enemies who may know more about communication than we do, and who may put their knowledge of human behavior to use, often to our disadvantage.

Point 4: Nobody can do anything about our communication behavior except ourselves. Because communication begins inside us, we are the first organism affected by what is seen, heard, felt, smelled, or tasted. We must respond to whatever comes to us, and we do so by ignoring, attending to, rejecting, accepting, or somehow making use of the noises and sights and sensations around us. Understanding ourselves and our relations to these stimuli is the starting place for understanding our own communication behaviors and those of others; how much we may be interested in changing our behaviors is up to us.

If for that reason it becomes important to make some adjustments in our behaviors, the guidelines and suggestions in this chapter may be useful. They have proved useful to many people in many workshop and laboratory situations. Not all the suggestions will work for everyone, because we may feel differently about our needs to adjust our communication. We also respond differently to suggestions such as these, which will make sense to one person and seem silly to another. Some suggestions may excite you and others may turn you off completely. This is no "royal road" to communication success, or a magic key to open the door to communication effectiveness. You will notice that all these items which follow are based on Point 4, above, because they all require *your* efforts. *No one can give you a "communication improvement pill"* or feed you better communication as a fortified ingredient in your breakfast cereal. It takes effort on your part and only a charlatan could sell you a program in which you would suddenly emerge a great communicator without your own efforts and motivation.

A MORE SCIENTIFIC APPROACH

Here are some ways you may more critically inspect your own communication and that of others. They are based on the idea that a more scientific approach to our symbol using will bring us closer to the empirical world and help us avoid some of the traps of language which we have discussed in the preceding chapters.

Describe

A statement that "he drinks a lot" or "she is a lousy teacher" is not description, but an evaluation. To make these same statements more descriptive, you can show what the person did—"He had six drinks at that party" or "She failed me in her course"—which developed your evaluation. In scientific terms, this may be called an operational definition, as it describes what happened so another observer can also see it happen. It leaves out the experimenter's value judgments. The evaluative statement tells more about the speaker than it does about the subject. "He drinks a lot" says that I have a value system about drinking and that he exceeds my norms. Such a statement does not convey much information about the drinker but says something about me.

To describe, try to stick to those data which also can be seen by someone else who may not share your value system. As the good experimenter knows, there is always danger of bias in the experiment simply because there are observations being made. Werner K. Heisenberg, a renowned physicist, in 1925 articulated a principle in scientific experimentation that the results of any experiment could be distorted simply by the fact that the observations were being made. Let us be aware of the Heisenberg principle of language, that we tend to insert something of ourselves in every observation we make and hence into the statements we make about our observations.

Quantify

Think and speak in terms of quantities instead of highly abstract and ambiguous words. How far is "far" when you tell a friend the car is parked not far away? How hot is "hot" when you get ready to eat spicy food? How expensive is "expensive"?

You cannot follow a cooking recipe with only vague terms in it, and an engineer does not build a bridge to support "lots of cars." Yet we try to work together and understand each other with vague terms to describe our personal world—many, few, some, heavy, tall, fat, soon, or "I'll be home early." The vagueness of our language, in addition to the fact that each of us has his own personal yardstick, scale, clock, or thermometer, tends to lead us unnecessarily into confusion.

Personify

There is a great "to me" factor in our communication. Our language is a personal expression of the minority report we make on the world around us and the people in it. "It was a good movie" is a statement of the effect on you. Because you use some criteria which may not be shared by others, it is important to remember that this is a "to me" statement and you should at least think that way whether or not you actually say the words "to me" or "in my opinion." If you announce that dogs are better pets than cats or goldfish, you can probably get an argument from someone around you. Can you also diminish the dogmatism of your comment by inserting the "to me" factor?

When we use value terms in our statements, it is appropriate to remember that these may be only to us. Others may not agree with our evaluations of good, bad, hot, cold, sincere, smooth, fat, salty, honest, beautiful, or rich.

Clarify

Don't be afraid to ask another person what he means by a word he is using, and be prepared to clarify your own use of words to others. This does not mean only those polysyllabic words which you have never heard before. This means those many, many words which have several kinds of meanings and may be as common as tall, short, big, little, soon, late, honest, help, think, see, or heard. It is quite possible that the word being used by someone calls up an image in you which is far from that which the other person intended. If you will remember that words have many meanings, depending on who is using them, you may find yourself seeking clarification or providing clear definitions to others.

A JOURNALISTIC APPROACH—ASKING QUESTIONS

Another way of more critically examining our communication is to borrow from the journalist's traditional question technique by asking the questions which follow. While these are phrased as if you were the receiver of communication, you should also make these same tests when you send messages to others:

Who Is Speaking?

Is he someone who has had direct observation of the things he is talking about? Is he biased in his report to you? Does he have the ability to make the statements of fact or judgment, and how sound are his sources? In other words, who made the observations on which this information is based?

What Is He Saying?

Is he using the words or symbols as you would use them or do these words mean something else to him? What is the content of the message which is obvious, and what else is not obvious? It is important to look critically at the substance of what is being said in terms of the language used and the meanings you may attach to the language.

When Did He Observe These Facts He Is Reporting?

Was it recently or was it a long time ago; firsthand or by hearsay? When he is telling you about it, does the circumstance of that "when" have an important place in the communication?

Where Was He When He Saw the Thing Happen?

Is it a report of his own observations, or was he not involved? Again, where he chooses to tell you may be a significant factor in the total communication, whether he is in a group or alone, in a public statement or in private.

Why Is He Reporting This to You?

What will be achieved by your receiving this message? Are there actions required if you hear this message? Could this message have been left unsaid?

How Is He Telling You?

Is there more to the message than just the words being used? How does he know about it? Did he get his information from a good source such as direct observation? How do you know he is reporting accurately to you?

A GENERAL SEMANTICS APPROACH

In his development of the language-adjustment system called general semantics, Count Alfred Korzybski postulated an extensional-intensional continuum, which we have called the symbolic-empirical continuum.[1] Korzybski developed five "extensional devices" to assist people in making their language fit better the empirical world it describes. He recommended these be used either aloud or silently as we communicate with others, and in our thinking about our communicating.

Dating

Use dates mentally to indicate to yourself, and possibly to others, that you are aware that people and things change with time. If people and events are in process, then it is important to indicate our understanding of the changing nature of these supposedly static objects or occurrences. You *today* are not the same as you were in *1960,* and a recognition of that difference is important to our understanding one another. We tend to react to a person we have not seen for a while as if he had not changed, and as if we had not changed. The man with a prison record knows well what it feels like to be haunted by people who react as if lives were not in process, constantly changing. We recognize the process nature of our world when we get an up-to-date road map. We would not think of planning a car trip with a twenty-five-year-old map. Our verbal maps must likewise be kept current, so we may not be misled into thinking that things are just the way they used to be, that our ways of dealing with our environment never need revising. Being aware of the "dating" device may help us adjust to a changing world and make our language reflect this adjustment.

Indexing

Look for differences within some supposed similarities. We can avoid stereotypes, we can help distinguish between things which may seem alike, and we can soften our attitudes and reduce our dogmatisms by a conscious effort at not lumping together what looks alike on the surface. This practice is called "indexing." We must remember that differences are closer to the empirical world in which no two things are ever identical—similarities appear to us as a result of the abstraction process. We see similarities by disregarding differences. Our language should be similar in structure to our world of difference and uniqueness and represent the similarities we abstract. An index subscript attached to a generic noun can help maintain a healthy balance between the two aspects of our world. If the generic noun emphasizes similarities, the index shows the difference. $Professor_1$ ("Professor" is the generic noun; "1" is the index) is not the same as $professor_2$, and $student_1$, $student_2$, and $student_3$ may all have different qualities we need to recognize, and not treat all professors and students alike when we think and act about them.

[1]*Alfred Korzybski,* Science and Sanity, *4th ed., The International Non-Aristotelian Library Publishing Company, Lakeville, Conn., 1958.*

Etcetera

This mental device helps avoid the idea that we can say all. Although the use of "etc." in an English composition may be frowned on, it was suggested that we recognize our own limitations of observations and reporting by using this device to indicate there are things left out. "Education makes success" probably should have an "etc." after the word "Education" and after the word "success" as well. Education, with some other factors, will produce success and some other things.

Quotes

This device can remind us that words are used personally, and that all possible meanings are not covered. Highly abstract words are often put in quotes by authors when their meaning is specialized, and the author wants to call attention to that fact. Use of quotes in your thinking and speaking helps remind you that your meaning may not be the same as someone else's. It is not unusual to see someone wiggle his fingers in the air to indicate quotes when he uses a particular word usually in satire. We often will say something like "She said she would be there (quote) early (unquote)" to indicate a special use of the word out of its context, or placing a particular emphasis on a word with accompanying facial contortions may achieve the same goal.

"Truth" for you may not be "truth" for me. Words such as "reality," "fact," "crime," "God," "education," and "freedom" certainly evoke different meanings in each one of us. And the uses of these words may reflect different chronological meaning as well. "Truth" in science today is not the same as "truth" was for Newton.

Hyphens

The hyphen device indicates that our words often divide the world into two competing opposites, and that often this is not appropriate. This device helps us avoid the either-or orientation of our language and the polarizing thinking of dividing things into opposites. Good-bad, mind-body, and space-time are ways of indicating a relationship between the terms which may not make a dichotomy of them. Our language is burdened with outlooks from common dichotomies of competing and mutually exclusive categories. Our thinking tags along with our language, and we often fall into the linguistic trap of dividing the world into either-or, into impossible blacks and whites without grays in between.

LEARNING TO GIVE AND RECEIVE FEEDBACK

An integral part of reducing barriers in communication is making optimum use of feedback, both in giving and receiving it. We need to practice giving clear indications of how much of a message sent us is actually received, and also train our senses to observe clearly how our messages are responded to by others.

To start, let us say that all human beings need the contact of relationships and that all organizations and the people in them do not operate in a vacuum. Even a hermit, living alone in a cave in a mountainside has contacts with his environment which make it essential that he respond. When he is hungry, he must find food, responding to the message from his stomach that it is empty. When he feels the cold wind blow on him, he responds by seeking shelter or putting on protective clothing. While the hermit may have little verbal communication, he still must be involved in sensing feedback and adjusting his moves to what happens to him in his surroundings.

Because few of us are hermits in this same sense, we need to adjust not just to the cold or to hunger, but to the constant stream of messages we get from others in the course of a day. The number of messages we send or receive may vary, just as our ability to react appropriately may vary from one person to another. In this way we begin to identify those who can give clear instructions, those who can do what they are asked, those who can understand complex information, those who have difficulty in grasping new ideas. Much of the ability to perform well in assignments is related to the ability to give and receive feedback. The sensitive person can pick up the cues offered by another who does not understand some instructions—maybe it is the professor responding to a quizzical look on the face of a student, and then asking "What is not clear in what we have been saying?" The sensitive person also can predict what parts of a message may be subject to confusion, and restate or clarify those parts without even being asked, simply because he has anticipated the hearer's confusion.

In communication, people need to share meanings of words and messages. It is important for them to know that communication is transactional—that is, it takes place between people under some kinds of rules which we agree to follow. One of the rules is that if someone looks angrily at us after we have made a remark, we need to figure out what it was we said to make them angry. Another rule is that if the listener smiles and nods, we are thereby permitted to continue with that kind of message. So our transactions are affected by the kinds of feedback we receive—whether negative, which pulls us up short, or positive, which encourages us to go ahead. In Chapter 5 we discussed meanings of words. If the meanings we can have for words may vary from person to person, so do our emotions vary. It is important in our communication transactions to be aware of both content and emotion.

There is a tendency in all of us to sometimes pretend we understand when we really do not. It is not considered intelligent to ask, "What do you mean by. . . ?" and we may try to avoid looking stupid. As a result, we may miss some important message by pretending and give the other person feedback which is false. Two factors are important here: first, that we try to give more honest feedback about our depth of understanding, and second, that we make it easy for the other person to say he did not understand. If you can reduce the other person's anxiety about asking questions by suggesting in advance that you may not be making it clear, you may receive more honest feedback. On the other hand, we may have to swallow our pride and admit we do not understand, and thus provide more honest feedback to the other person's message.

Preparing the way for a message has been called "feedforward" for an obvious reason—it sets up the possibility of getting feedback. Making use of appropriate feedforward, as in the example above, should assist the feedback process. You may also precede a statement you make with a feedforward phrase such as, "If you have no plans for tonight. . ." or "Let's talk about next week's assignment. . ." which gives the cues to your listener that you expect a response and what directions the discussion is going to take.

The concept of feedforward should not be described as apart from feedback, but rather as a specialized activity within a total feedback system. Feedforward will help anticipate actions. It may be an intrapersonal plan for "What will I do if. . ." or "If the chair is empty, I will sit by Sally because there is something I want to tell her," or "If dad says no when I ask for the car, my following argument will be. . . ." When communication actually begins is difficult to pin down. Two people riding together on a bus as strangers will make a number of moves to test whether or not the other is ready to talk, and what they will talk about. Feeding forward in our communication will usually result in more appropriate responses in one another as we begin to operate the give-and-take of communication.

We mentioned above that not only content but also emotion is involved in the feedback process. Our attention to feedback will help us verify *who we are* in relation to others, as well as *what is said.* In Chapter 9 you will read about "needs" we have in communicating in relation to others. Keep in mind that we discover who we are by watching the reactions of others. By developing an ability to give and receive feedback, we also may better meet our interpersonal needs. Some of these needs are implied in the following suggestions based on workshop experiences.

In workshops where training has been conducted on giving and receiving feedback, it has been shown that our "guesses" about how others see us have been significantly improved when we are given feedback.[2] Just having feedback available, however, is not enough. We need to know how to handle it—that is, how to give it appropriately and how to receive

[2]Gail E. Myers, Michele T. Myers, Alvin Goldberg, and Charles E. Welch, "Effects of Feedback on Interpersonal Sensitivity in Laboratory Training Groups," Journal of Applied Behavioral Science, *vol. 5, no. 2, 1969, pp. 175–185.*

THE DYNAMICS OF INTRAPERSONAL COMMUNICATION

it intelligently. Some suggestions for giving and receiving feedback follow.

We generally can look more objectively on what we do than what somebody says we are. Our behaviors, or actions, are only a momentary part of us and therefore we feel more comfortable about being challenged to change them. If someone calls us "dishonest," it sounds quite different from their saying we acted "dishonestly" in a given situation. We cannot tolerate very well an attack on "us" which is what much criticism sounds like. If someone is critical of our *behavior,* we can more easily accept responsibility for that action, rather than tell ourselves we are a product of our genetic inheritance and for that reason cannot possibly be blamed nor think of changing.

To describe behaviors we use adverbs—e.g., loudly, kindly, happily, grumpily, or sincerely.

Avoid the use of adjectives relating to the qualities of the person, to his personality—e.g., bigmouth, kind, happy, sorehead, or sincere.

Behaviors include those things a person does well as much as the things he does badly. In describing behaviors we tend to concentrate on those which need improvement, but a person can often learn much from feedback about those actions which facilitate, support, or improve communication. Descriptions of behaviors should not be evaluative or selective, but should comment on what went on.

Focus Feedback on Behaviors rather than on the Person

Observations are those things which could be seen or heard by anyone, but inferences are your own interpretations or conclusions about what went on. If we spice our observations with inferences, we tend to obscure feedback, so we must be careful to differentiate when we are making inferences, or extensions of our observations.

Observations involve what is going on, not what happened at some previous time or some persistent characteristic you have noticed over a long period. In training groups, the term "here and now" is used to keep participants involved in what is happening and hence more concentrated on observations public to everyone. Research has shown that feedback given as soon as appropriate after observation will be more specific, more concrete, and generally more accurately reported.

Observations should be reported in terms of degrees of more or less, not as black-and-white, either-or, dichotomies. This helps us keep in mind the "quantity" of the behavior rather than a category which is too frequently judgmental and subjective. Behaviors are very active, alive, and related to other behaviors in a more-or-less continuum rather than in a static good-or-bad polarization.

Focus Feedback on Observations rather than Inferences

Focus Feedback on Description rather than Judgment

As in the case of focusing on behaviors, to use description is to avoid evaluation of the other person or his actions. Description attempts to remain neutral, but judgment takes sides.

Concentrate on the "what" rather than the "why." Again the "what" of the behavior is observable by others and therefore can be checked for accuracy. The "why" of a person's behavior is inferred and leads us into the dangerous area of "intentions" and "motives" and the emotionalism which goes with it. It may be useful at times to explore the "why" of behaviors, but this should be done with the help and consent of the person being discussed. Most of us enjoy playing "shrink" to all our friends, but we should realize that our analysis of the other person's behaviors may be more subject to our own aberrations than to theirs. If we concentrate on the "why," we may miss much of the very useful "what" of feedback.

Focus Feedback on Sharing of Ideas and Information rather than on Giving Advice

(1) We need to feel a joint responsibility for the outcome of the feedback encounter and be ready to assist the other rather than direct his responses.

(2) Telling another what to do with the information we give does not leave him free to determine what the appropriate course of action *for him* will be. Advice giving is a poor attempt at problem solving which does not give the other person leeway to make his own choices.

(3) Explore alternatives rather than provide solutions. If we concentrate on a variety of available responses, we can help move toward a more satisfactory answer. Too often we have ready at hand a list of solutions waiting for the problems to come along which might fit. When we offer someone a solution, ready-made from our own experience, it may not be useful to the other based on his experience or because the problem may not be exactly as we saw it.

Focus Feedback on What It May Do to Who Receives It

(1) If giving feedback is only making *you* feel good, you may not be helping as much as you are imposing.

(2) Be aware of how much feedback another person can handle at one time. Avoid the long recitation "and then you did . . . " after the recipient has given you some feedback that he is full to the brim. After that time you are only satisfying your own need, and not his.

(3) Emotional reactions may result when feedback is given at the wrong time or place. This is particularly true in the more sensitive and personal areas of human behavior. Even if you have some worthwhile points to make, they should be presented with the recipient in mind.

Bronowski, J.: *Science and Human Values,* Harper & Row, Publishers, Incorporated, New York, 1965.

Hayakawa, S. I.: *Language in Thought and Action,* rev. ed., Harcourt, Brace and Company, Inc., New York, 1964.

Johnson, W.: *People in Quandaries,* Harper & Row, Publishers, Incorporated, New York, 1946.

Lee, I.: *Language Habits in Human Affairs,* Harper & Brothers, New York, 1941.

THE DYNAMICS OF INTERPERSONAL COMMUNICATION

PART TWO

SELF-CONCEPT, ROLES, AND BEHAVIOR—WHO AM I?   Chapter 8

If one human lived alone, without contact with other people, the chief concerns of this person would be internal. That is, he would need to know how many hours sleep were needed, what kinds of foods to eat or avoid, when and if to wash, how much activity to engage in, and generally how to spend his time. He would be mainly concerned with the sensory world, or empirical world, as we have described it earlier.

As human beings, however, we live in a world of other people. While our bodily functions and our immediate sensory surroundings are of importance to us, we have an added dimension—human association—to concern us. Research on sensory deprivation, where a person has been suspended in water, in a soundless, dark environment, has indicated that a subject will begin to hallucinate and become "abnormal" in the sense that he is horribly aware of the absence of sensory stimuli. Isolation from human contact has been reported by prisoners in solitary confinement and other enforced situations of being cut off from others, and appears to be equally devastating to the subject. It is more difficult to measure this result, but it is safe to say that a whole range of aberrant behaviors may be attributed to some degree of human isolation.

How often have you heard the expression, "Oh, he just wants some attention," whether applied to a misbehaving child or adult? It is not that simple to dismiss the need in most of us for attention. Being ignored is perhaps one of the most undesirable reactions most of us face. We may be argued with, bawled out, called names, or frowned on, but our need is to be recognized. As we were told in our beginning physics laboratories, "nature abhors a vacuum," this same characteristic is true of nature's child—man. He hates to be in a communicative vacuum. He would like to get approval from others and have a sense of belonging, but he will better tolerate being abused than being ignored.

In this chapter we will explore some considerations of our behaviors in relation to the roles we play in our communication. Our assumption is that we behave in relation to others and the situations we find ourselves in. We do not behave in a vacuum. If we affect others, and are affected by our communication in each role we play, it is important for us to know something about how we select our roles, and how we test them. We will also relate our behaviors to our self-concept. Who we think we are is of great and continuing interest to us, and we spend a good deal of time trying to find out about ourselves.

> *All the world is a stage,*
> *And all the men and women, merely players,*
> *They have their exits and their entrances;*
> *And one man in his time plays many parts.*
>
> *William Shakespeare,* As You Like It,
> *Act* II

ANOTHER OPENING, ANOTHER SHOW

In our discussion of the roles we play, let's consider an analogy to the theater. A most obvious kind of role taking occurs on stage when an actor assumes the name, the personality, the verbalizations, and the moves of a character in a play. It is clear to us in the audience and usually clear to the actor, that the role is being played and that that part in the play is not the man playing it, except for a few hours a day.

On opening night the actor is uncertain how his role will be received. He has been coached by a director, he recites the lines provided by a playwright, and he is made up with the help of assistants. Other technical people aid his performance with lights, sound, and props. When the curtain comes down, the actors are rewarded by applause. After the opening night performance, there are reviews in the press which give some feedback on the performance, and are eagerly awaited.

That point is important in the analogy, because in our own communication, every contact can be an opening night. We don't have to wait as long for the reviews, because there is usually instant feedback available to us from our "audience."

Taking the theater analogy to our own communicative roles, point by point, let us first emphasize that we all take many roles in our daily lives. We are not entirely the same person "on stage" as off, and we not only play many roles in our lifetimes (as Shakespeare said), but we play many different roles in any day of our lives as we move from one set of associations to another. While it may be obvious to us as we watch a stage performance that the *actors* are playing roles, it is far less obvious to us in our own actions.

As we mentioned, we have an "opening night" with all our contacts in the sense that we are trying out a new communication and have a chance to get reactions. Even our talking with close friends may find new ideas, new relationships, to give us a chance to test our role. Each time we join a new group or encounter a different person, we take on a role. No matter how hard we may concentrate on being "the same" in every situation, we are not permitted to. Like a flowing river, the currents of conversation and actions make it necessary for us to adapt because we are being viewed by changing audiences.

THE DYNAMICS OF INTERPERSONAL COMMUNICATION

In our roles we are subject to many forces from our past experience. Our parents and friends have helped write the script we will read. Our associations in the past will supplement our role by giving us some direction on how we might act, just as there is a crew assisting the actor in the theater. We may have rehearsed some of our behaviors, but we may also be called on to ad lib, or improvise, much of our new role. How well we perform will be reported back to us by the others in our group, and we will pay more attention to some than to others—we will want and respect the judgment of some "reviewers" more than others. We are constantly seeking an answer to the question "how did I perform?"

This is the story of Jackson, as told in workshops and seminars to illustrate the complexities of role taking. It is only partial, because it focuses on Jackson himself and does not complicate itself by placing all other participants in a similar central spot. (If you want the challenge of additional discovery, you may want to imagine what happens when each of the "others" in Jackson's world takes the role in the center focal point.)

THE MAN IN THE MIDDLE

At stage one, Jackson is a real live human being, who breathes, eats, goes to work, helps raise the family, and plays golf at the club. He is a physical entity almost six feet tall, with a weight, hair color, and characteristic walk which his friends can recognize. When the people in his life meet him on the street, they know this is their acquaintance named Jackson. He occupies space, and has a perceivable identity which changes only gradually, except when he buys new clothes, cuts his hair differently, or grows a moustache. He is, therefore, a collection of sufficiently identifiable features, so that many people would notice his picture in the paper, or pick him out of a crowd.

At stage two, with the addition of some boxes over his head and the heads of others, we begin to develop Jackson beyond the physical attributes we can all agree on. Jackson has a picture of himself in relation to what he believes, who he likes, what he knows about his job, how he manages his children, and how he can cure his golf slice. In his day he will talk to many people, and only a few of them are represented in this illustration. Each of those he talks with has a picture of Jackson: how honest, how smart, how important, etc. It is at this stage that Jackson's pictures are talking to the pictures others have of him. When Jackson talks to the men working for him, he has his own picture of himself, and the men have theirs of Jackson (plus, of course, their own pictures of themselves, but we said we were not going to complicate this illustration that way).

Jackson

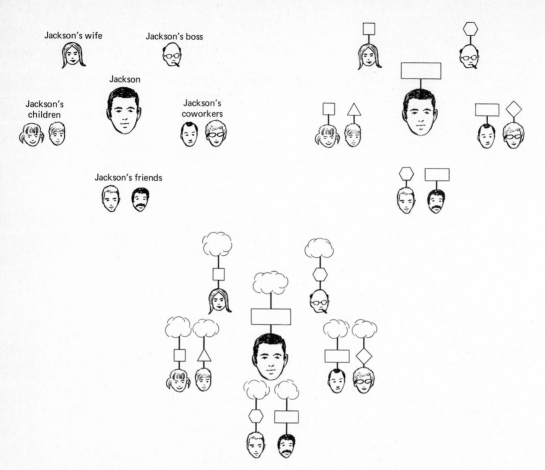

Figure 8–1 Stage one—Jackson and a few of the people in his world. Stage two—Jackson has a mental picture of himself, and the others have their mental pictures of Jackson (the boxes). Stage three—Jackson has an ideal version of what he would like to be like, and those around him also have their idealized Jackson (the little clouds).

What these men hear from Jackson will depend on how they see him. How effective Jackson is in communicating with them depends on how well he understands the kinds of pictures these men have of him. If the boss calls him in, it would be important for Jackson to know the kind of picture the boss has of him so he can understand what is being said. Does the boss trust him to carry out a job? Does he overexplain an assignment because he thinks Jackson is less smart than Jackson thinks he is? Going around the circle, we have many pictures of Jackson in the heads of the people he knows, and it is not likely that the pictures are identical. His wife and his children may see him differently, and the men at the club probably have another picture of him. Jackson very likely ad-

THE DYNAMICS OF INTERPERSONAL COMMUNICATION

justs his role from boss to employee to husband to father to golfer as the demands of his associates come into play.

Who is Jackson? Is he the pictures in his own head—those in the heads of his friends? More likely he is none of these for very long, but partly all the pictures, and he changes as his role changes. There may be no "real" Jackson except as he is seen by others. Jackson's communication will be affected not only by the pictures he has of himself in relation to others but also by the pictures they have of him. He finds out about these pictures by getting feedback from others and trying out his new guesses about the pictures.

(The first thing to know is that these pictures exist, and second that how others see us will affect our communication. When we seek and receive feedback, we may accept, reject, puzzle over, or misunderstand the feedback, depending on (a) how well it is given in terms of honesty, clarity, and consistency and (b) how we are prepared to receive it.)

If Jackson enjoys playing golf with his friends, he seeks some assurances that it is all right to do so. His friends will give him feedback by inviting him to join a foursome, by being pleasant when they are together, by making frequent dates for golf, by telling him they enjoyed it and telling others who in turn may report it to him. If they don't want him to play in their group, they will send signals to him, such as filling up the group without him, playing at times not convenient to Jackson, exhibiting rude behaviors during the play or afterwards, or suggesting to him (very unusual) or to others (more usual) that he is a bore on the golf course and they wish he would leave them alone.

Jackson has a choice: he may accept what he sees and hears as disapproval of his presence and seek another group, or he may ignore the messages of disapproval and continue to play with the group. If the information that he is not wanted is too hard to take, he may rationalize that they are not good enough to play with, too good, or they want to make too heavy bets, or that they always play at some time which doesn't fit his schedule. If he ignores the feedback he receives, the others will ask, "Why doesn't he understand that we don't want him?"

This brings us to stage three, a further complication of the process of roles and behaviors. Above the picture Jackson has of himself is a cloudy, ethereal, kind of ideal self—what Jackson would really like to be. This is a part of his self-perception—a kind of wish he makes about himself.

In the same way, above the pictures of his associates is a cloud of their idealization of what they would like Jackson to be. If he is pictured by his assistants as grouchy and mean, their clouds would be probably a wish that he were friendly and kind. If the boss expects Jackson to be punctual and alert, that will be part of his cloud and his expectations of Jackson. If the boss also pictures him as punctual and alert, the picture and the cloud will have a lot in common, and the boss will react in a predictable way toward Jackson. If, on the other hand, Jackson shows up late for work, the boss has a picture of him as being tardy, while his ideal for Jackson is punctuality. This conflict will be reflected in the messages the boss sends Jackson, and unless Jackson has some idea of what is wrong, he may be confused and disappointed by some of the boss's reactions. (We should remind you again that we are only focusing on Jackson, and that each other actor in this drama also has an "idealized self" to consider besides the "idealized Jackson.")

Jackson's wife married an ideal man, a kind knight in shining armor, and she has her idealizations about what he should be like—often she wished he were more attentive in opening doors and spending time with the children, and wishes he would pick up his dirty socks. When Jackson tells his wife that he is going to play golf, the response he gets may have nothing to do with his golf playing and he may have a hard time figuring out why she said she had to do the laundry.

Some of the idealizations may be more predictable than others. If Jackson is conscious of the value systems of his associates, he may come closer to understanding their ideals for him. In many of his activities there are rules to be followed: a boss should praise your good work as well as criticize your errors; husbands should help around the house; golfers do not talk while a player is putting; fathers give their children allowances; you don't lose your temper in the office, etc. In many of these instances, Jackson can guess pretty well how his "others" would like him to behave. He may choose then, whether or not to live up to those expectations. At least he is aware of how his behaviors may be viewed if he knows some of the values these people expect him to live up to.

Principles

Before we leave the Jackson story, let's suggest some principles we may draw from this example:

1. The greater the discrepancy between the pictures we have of ourselves and the pictures others have of us, the greater the chance for misunderstanding and ambiguous feedback.
2. The greater the discrepancy between our picture of ourselves and our ideal selves, the greater will be our dissatisfaction with our communicative behaviors.
3. The greater the discrepancy between the pictures others have of us and their idealizations of what we should be like, the less chance there is for satisfactory relationships to develop.
4. Our pictures of ourselves and those others have of us are the result of behaviors toward each other.
   a. We find out what we are like by having people respond to us; that is, from the feedback we get from them.

    THE DYNAMICS OF INTERPERSONAL COMMUNICATION

b. Others find out what we are like by collecting their reactions to our behaviors toward them.
5. Our idealizations for ourselves are related to our value system, and the expectations of others toward us are likewise related to theirs.
a. The role we play has much to do with our idealization of how a person in that role should act.
b. We depend on feedback from others to tell us not only how they perceive us (their pictures) but also how they would like us to behave (idealization).

In the rest of this chapter we will explore in more detail some of the ways we develop roles and act them out, and how this process is related to giving and receiving feedback. We will discuss self-concept and how we get our ideas about ourselves, and finally, how behaviors are the medium of exchange we use not only to get things done but also to adjust who we are.

ROLES AND ROLE TAKING

The story of Jackson may have bothered you because he sounded a little phony in his potential for changing his role to meet new situations or adjusting to people. You may also resist the idea that you play many different roles. One of the values we encounter in our society is that we "are somebody" and that implies a constant, dependable, person rather than the wishy-washy, changeable, fickle one. We accuse people of "play acting" or of "performing" when we feel they have stepped out of the role we have cast them in. Our culture tends to prize the image of the strong-willed individual who remains steadfast when tempted to act out a different role, or step out of character.

We do not argue with the idea that an individual "is somebody." The thesis of this chapter is that the "somebody" which you are is a complex of interpersonal behaviors which we call roles, and these occur in relationship to one another.

Furthermore, our role behavior is prescribed. Our relationships follow more or less loosely defined rules which we begin learning at a very early age. This does not say that we always follow the rules as they are prescribed. But when we don't, we are taking a special role which takes effort, may lead to unpredictable results, and may cause anxiety to those involved.

Role definitions are usually the product of the value system of a society, a group, or an individual. They are acting out what is normally expected (the norms) and the expectations of acceptable behavior for a whole array of special circumstances.

Another characteristic of roles is that some we may choose and some are chosen for us. If you are born with black skin, your role may be prescribed in many ways. You do not choose to be born a boy or a girl, but once started in life there are certain things which you are expected to do because of your sex. Boys don't cry; girls play with dolls. Boys become engineers, and girls, housewives. Breaking out of these chosen roles can be difficult partly because those around you are more comfortable if they can keep you predictable and stereotyped.

The strength of role identification is detectable in even young children as they begin to choose which parent or older children to act like. A child of our acquaintance in the seventh grade believed he had "flunked" his Kuder preference test. The test, which is given to find out what the child enjoys and prefers doing, was administered by a teacher who after scoring reinforced the norms that boys like to go camping and play ball, and girls like to listen to music and read. This boy felt his role as a boy was under serious question because his test results showed he liked music and reading. Some studies of other tests over the past few years have indicated that girls will outperform boys in mathematics up to about twelve years of age, after which the boys show superior abilities. One explanation offered to account for these data is that by that age the girls have been convinced that their role is not inclined toward mathematics and hence have lost interest and motivation. If you choose to step out of the role, you do so with difficulty, but it is possible to make subsequent choices which will alter your role.

Age is also a factor in choosing a role. You cannot choose the same behaviors as adults and children—a tantrum by a five-year-old may not be tolerated in adults. What you can wear and where you can appear are also determined for you in relation to age, sex, and other definable physical features.

You may choose to become a doctor. Once you have determined the general rules for being a doctor, you may adapt the role to fit your own needs. In other words, the choice is again there to be a model of the expected behaviors or to make the effort to modify the role in relation to others' expectations. The general practitioner in the small town may make house calls, while the specialist in the city may not.

In communication we are concerned with the aspect of roles which tell us who we can communicate with, what to communicate about, and how we will carry on the communication. In other words, the system of roles can help direct us to (1) the persons, (2) the content, and (3) the style of our communicating.

The Person

Who to communicate with is also determined (a) *for us,* as in the case of being assigned to a particular section of a class where you have a group of fellow students and a professor, or (b) *by us,* as in the case of meeting friends for coffee where you can studiously ignore the next table while you carry on your own conversations. In the same way, our parents are an "assigned" part of our communication environment, and we must communicate with them even if it is by not talking. When we walk into a store we select a clerk to help us, and the clerk is obligated to take that role just as we have the role of customer. In most colleges and universities, a student may talk to fellow students most of the time, to a professor fairly often, to a dean seldom, rarely if ever to a president or chancellor, and probably never to a trustee. If that same student were to become a professor in that institution, the role relationships would probably change his communication patterns.

What we communicate about is both cause and effect in our roles. As a student we may need to talk about the course with the professor, so as a result of the student professor role relationship we discuss that subject. If we were to sit beside the same professor on a bus, it is likely we would talk about the course again because of the student professor role relationship. Our roles have caused us to limit our conversational topic in both a formal (classroom) and informal (riding a bus) situation. In neither case is the professor obligated to talk about anything else, although through more personal contact with him you may find other topics which are appropriate to talk about. If you do, your role with fellow students may undergo a change.

The Content

We may talk about different things with our parents than with our peers. We talk about different things with boys than we do with girls. In a role of a liberal we talk about certain things, and as a conservative, others. We talk about different things in class and in the coffee shop, with strangers or with friends, and with those older or younger.

A third factor in our communicative role is the style we use when talking with others. If we have attempted a role of serious student, we will tend to use big words, ask "penetrating" questions, and affect an air of studiousness. Maybe our role is "one of the boys," so we will use the current slang, appropriate profanity, and adopt the postures and gestures, the inflections and speech rhythms of the group we have "joined." We will likely not use the same words or tone when we talk to a young child as when we talk to a peer. In the same fashion we will not put our feet on the coffee table and swear loudly in the home of friends we hope to impress.

The Style

Roles do not exist in isolation. We take on roles in relation to others. If we are a husband there is a wife, without which the defined role of husband would not exist. Parents do not exist as roles without children, nor professors without students, nor clerks without customers.

Because these complementary relationships will exist, we can say again: Any person may be called on to play many roles in the course of his normal communicating. The clerk in a shoe store must buy his groceries and move from his role as clerk to someone else's customer, into the new role of customer to the grocery clerk. The teacher who becomes a student in the summer to work on advanced degrees has taken an opposite role. Jackson is characterized as a boss when he talks with his assistants, but when he goes in to see *his* boss, he is an employee.

Not only do we switch roles in this fashion, but we also play the many roles which may not be complementary to each other. The shoe clerk may also be a husband, a father, a member of a church, president of the PTA, or Little League coach, as well as turning from clerk into a customer when he walks into a grocery store.

Roles you select for yourself will vary according to some predictable factors. They include:

1. Persons involved—what you think they expect of you
   a. present in this situation.
   b. absent but influencing the role.
2. Situation development
   a. current and immediate demands.
   b. past history of related situations and events.
   c. future implications of this situational outcome.
3. Your image of yourself in relation to persons and situation
   a. Role consistency—trying to remember how you acted before and to predict how you will be called on to act in the future.
   b. Active participant—Can you choose what role you will play or are you already typecast, and what are the consequences of changing?

We always communicate from a point of view, from our way of looking at the world. In previous chapters we developed material on what factors account for the way we see our world such as our language, our habits of observing, our perceptions, our logical habits of making assumptions and inferences, etc. These become a part of our communicating with others and help establish the position from which we play our communicating role. This point of view will include how we think a person in that role should behave. How do clerks in a store act, or fathers? If we understand our role, and the roles of others, we can expect to better understand communication with others.

SELF-CONCEPT

This internal point of view is called by various names: self-image, self-concept, self-perception, etc. All the terms have a common thread of *selfness* and of *seeing.* How do we see ourselves, not as an absolute being

THE DYNAMICS OF INTERPERSONAL COMMUNICATION

with static ideas and unchangeable behaviors, but in relation to the roles we will be forced to play or choose to play? How do I see myself as a student? How do I see myself as a speaker, a listener, a thinker, or in relation to my parents or my peers?

One interesting way of looking at ourselves is in terms of the groups we are trying to impress. Although we may often deny that we are out to impress anyone, the fact is that we are generally conscious of what others will say or do in reaction to what we say and do. Even by attempting to "go against" an established norm or value of society, we are conscious of who is watching us. When we wrote earlier that communication is not random, we included the consideration of the effect our communication has on others and our predictions of its outcome. Because we have had experience in our lives with people who are still "looking over our shoulders," we are never quite free from considering them. Because we are in contact with people whose reactions interest us, we are not free from them. We may speak and act in relation to these groups who look over our shoulders. We feel responsible for doing and saying those things which will receive approval (or disapproval) from a combination of people looking at us, not only those present, but also those out of the past, and possibly those we anticipate in our future.

We choose our models for our behaviors from those we admire, and avoid acting like those whom we do not. The "reference groups" then help us develop our self-concept and thus our ways of behaving. It makes little difference if the reference group is one from which we are seeking approval or a reference group we are trying to embarrass. Our behaviors are always in terms of someone else, and in that respect we are never quite free. It is possible to look at the "generation gap" in terms of those reference groups each side of the gap is trying to impress, and how it affects not only the self-image but the conflicting images perceived by either group.

The field of personality and self-concept is becoming more and more the subject of research. Some of the earlier developments in theories of self-concept are very descriptive and might be useful to review here.

Most writings center around the idea that we, first, find out who we are by contact with others, and second, get confirmation or denial of this concept in additional contacts.

Laing[1] is very specific about our discovery of ourselves in relation to others. We find out who we are from others and then make modifications in ourselves in relation to what additional information we get.

The relationship between ourselves and others in the development of our self-concept may be viewed from two directions. One hypothesis states that we relate our symbolic behaviors (speaking and acting) to our

[1]R. D. Laing, The Divided Self, *Quadrangle Books, Inc., Chicago, 1960.*

own internal situation and then try out these behaviors on others.[2] When we get responses from others, we make inferences on how well that behavior was accepted and then may want to make adjustments. This view argues that our firsthand knowledge of ourselves comes from analysis of our behaviors, and the behaviors of others (being secondhand) cannot be as deeply understood. So we necessarily understand ourselves better from our own behaviors.

Another hypothesis[3] argues that self-concept develops when the child begins to view himself as an object of other people's reactions. In this view, the concept of self is developed through communication but does not precede communication. The child acts toward himself as he sees others acting toward him, and in the first stages of this "role taking" merely imitates without any interpretation the roles of others. As the child becomes more accustomed to using symbols, he begins to understand the roles he takes and he differentiates among those acts which others make toward him. Growing to maturity, the person finds it impossible to play all the roles of others. He can, however, make some generalizations and develops the concept of the "generalized other" which is a synthesis of what this person has learned about those common or general roles of all the other people in a group he observes. Each of us could develop this "generalized other" as a set of expectations as to how we should behave, and in this way develop our self-concept and our ideal self.

It may be that we use a combination of these apparently divergent methods of developing our self-concept and maintaining it.

Berlo[4] argues we may begin our role taking as a useful exercise in learning, and then gradually apply the "generalized other" as we adjust our roles and our ideals about ourselves.

Most writers make use of the term "empathy" to describe that quality which makes us feel what we think the other person is feeling. Empathy in this sense is essential to discovery of self and maintenance of self-concept as well as to our appreciation of the behaviors and self-concepts of others. Without some link to the motives of others as well as to their behaviors we are making only incomplete inferences when we study their reactions to us. It may not be possible to know fully the grief of a mother whose son has been killed without experiencing it with her, but empathy explains how we may grieve with her and to some degree share her experience. When we considered Jackson's being able to change his roles, there was a quality of empathy involved rather than a manipulative attempt to alter his own character.

[2]*S. Asch,* Social Psychology, *Prentice-Hall, Inc., Englewood Cliffs, N. J., 1952.*

[3]*G. H. Mead,* Mind, Self and Society, *The University of Chicago Press, Chicago, 1934.*

[4]*D. K. Berlo,* The Process of Communication, *Holt, Rinehart and Winston, Inc., New York, 1960.*

Without empathy we isolate ourselves from the experiences of others to the degree that we live only by our own feelings and limit our "knowing" to those things we have experienced. From our symbolic world we can greatly extend those opportunities to experience joy and sorrow, happiness and discontent. By hearing others tell their experiences and interpreting their reactions we broaden our range of empathic relations. By reading, by seeing movies, by watching TV, and by all the individual and mass media reporting of human activities, we tend to extend our own narrow lives into an appreciation of what kinds of experiences have their effects on making people (and ourselves) what we are.

Another aspect of self-image which has to be taken into account is

THE TWELVE YEAR PUT-DOWN

One of the greatest challenges faced by teachers of college freshmen and sophomores is the large number of these students who feel that they are inadequate human beings. It is not difficult to understand why so many of our students feel this way, when you stop to realize that they have been taught to feel exactly so for twelve long years.

The tragedy of American education is that even our best students usually receive an essentially remedial education. In most U.S. classrooms, at whatever level of schooling, the student is perceived to be in a state of ignorance which must be remedied. By exposing young people in our society to a mandatory twelve years of being thus perceived, we assure the creation of an inferior citizenry. For whatever else our young people learn in this system, they tend to learn to perceive themselves as inferior.

Put yourself in the college freshman's shoes: "For twelve years you have gone to school to be told what you do wrong! Your grades were determined by your errors. A low grade resulted whenever your errors were abundant. A high grade resulted from a notable lack of error. After twelve years in a system which has assumed your ignorance and emphasized your errors, you now probably feel quite inferior. By essentially assuming your incompetence for twelve years, the educational system has gone a long way toward assuring your incompetence, because you have formed your self-image from those images of your self which have been most persistently communicated to you by the systems in which you operate. Twelve years in a system of negative reinforcement has tended to make you a master of the art of feeling inferior." © 1970, Noel McInnis, The Center for Curriculum Design, Evanston, Illinois. Reprinted by permission of the author.

the effect our self-image has on our behaviors. Dr. Maxwell Maltz,[5] a plastic surgeon, places great emphasis on the effects of self-concept in how we can accomplish our aims. His book on the subject of what he calls "psycho-cybernetics" applies that term to the directions we make ourselves go (cybernetics) in relation to our inner selves. A person who feels he is ugly will respond to others in a defensive or overly aggressive manner because he is sure they must also think him ugly.

Even before Couet popularized the belief in self as a determining factor in success with his "every day in every way I get better and better," there has been an attempt to gain mastery over human overt behaviors and actions by thinking about improving. There are today many "schools" for training self-confidence which are based on a more or less scientific hypothesis that a "man who believes in himself can accomplish anything." Research has indicated that to a degree this may be true. A study of basketball players who (a) actually practiced shooting free throws and (b) only mentally practiced, discovered both groups exceeded the performance of a third group which did neither. A professional tennis star keeps records of his matches on paper and replays them in his head. He also regularly "plays" his next opponent mentally before a match, as he prepares himself to meet the opponent's strengths and capitalize on his weaknesses, spending hours in this kind of reverie to build up his actual performance.

This practice is not much different from the salesman practicing his sales pitch, or the student rehearsing a presentation for class, or the actor mentally "getting into the part" before going on stage. As one studies for the content of a "performance," there is a tendency to predict the outcome as well. We may feel mentally ready, and this confidence becomes part of the actions which follow. If we are doubtful about our ability to carry out the activity, our performance may reflect this mental prediction.

A study of the verbal patterns of persons with low self-concept and high self-concept shows some tendencies which can be identified. In our looking at tendencies, let's not classify people, or decide a person who acts one way will always act that same way. Self-concept may vary with the situation or topic, and the relations of the others with whom a person is communicating. A highly verbal student in the dormitory may be tongue-tied in the classroom because he feels he gets along fine with his friends in a social setting but is a lousy student. A girl who is deeply sensitive in serious talk with other girls may become a giggling wreck in the presence of boys. A youngster may take advice and instruction from a teacher and not be able to listen at all when a parent tries to advise or explain the same

[5]M. Maltz, Psycho-Cybernetics, *Prentice-Hall, Inc., Englewood Cliffs, N.J., 1960.*

items. The way this person sees himself in relation to the others has a great effect on the changing patterns of communication.

The following are some verbal patterns which may characterize low self-concept:

—frequent use of cliché phrases or a few words ("you know," "like," "young people are like that," etc.) which are used not so much to help identify something in common with others, but because the person with a low self-concept does not trust his ability to be original;

—need to talk about self in terms of criticism, weaknesses ("all thumbs"), and difficult experiences which help explain why he is not better than he is;

—an inability to accept praise gracefully, often with a superficially worded disclaimer which invites additional proof;

—a defensiveness about blame to the degree that the person may be more anxious about who gets credit or blame in a project than actually getting the project accomplished;

—a cynicism about his accomplishments or his possessions; a hyper-critical attitude about those of others;

—a persistently whining or sneering tone of voice or posture as assumed in relation to his own or others' successes, as if to dismiss as luck or special privilege any accomplishments by anyone;

—a pessimistic attitude expressed about competition. (In the game of Monopoly "I always get the cheap properties and end up in jail.")

On the other hand, here are some verbal patterns which may characterize a high self-concept:

—original expressions, a rich vocabulary used in appropriate settings, an ability to "find the right word," or to use the balanced correct forms of address with others (Mister, Miss, first names, or nicknames);

—talks about self less frequently and may talk about others easily in terms of their accomplishments; needs less constant reassurance of his own personal worth;

—is able to accept praise or blame gracefully. In working on projects is likely to take risks and verbalize positions other than the "correct" ones; does not spend so much time figuring out the safe way of approaching problems to avoid blame;

—looks at his own accomplishments with a balance of credit to his ability and to circumstances, is willing to give credit to others for their part in what is done;

—a confident tone of voice; avoids condescending tone or attitude and is capable of saying "I don't know" or "I was wrong;"

—admits to a wide range of feelings and empathy for others whether or not these are popular;

—an optimistic attitude about competition; willingness to try new games, enter discussion about new topics with questions (risk displaying his ignorance in an effort to learn more);

—is generally less dogmatic about beliefs; less tendency to be biased, to stereotype others, or classify events too broadly.

We want to emphasize that this list is partial and that it does not necessarily describe a person—it describes some verbal patterns which may, in some circumstances or if found persistently, indicate low or high self-esteem for that particular relationship. We would discourage your taking this list and analyzing your friends. We would, on the other hand, encourage your looking seriously at your own verbal outputs in light of these possibilities to find out how often you may act in these ways. Do not then conclude that you *are* one or the other. You may conclude that in some situations you *act* in a certain way, and these actions may be changed if you feel like it. Also you may, and again only if you feel like it, ask someone who knows you well to tell you if you operate in one way or another (*a*) never, (*b*) seldom, (*c*) sometimes, or (*d*) frequently. We have left off the (*e*) always, because no one (including yourself) knows you that well.

BEHAVIORS

In this text we have been careful to distinguish between the person (as a total entity) and his behaviors. This is an important distinction. If we are to treat people appropriately, we need to recognize that we never see *all* any person is, and that any person will change as his experiences accumulate. In other words, it is inaccurate to label a person as dishonest, selfish, bigoted, smart, kind, etc. We will be more accurate if we *describe behaviors* which the person has exhibited, and limit our judgment to those.

The question of whether or not to disclose information about ourselves may not be a real question. We disclose with our behaviors constantly—sometimes intentionally, sometimes not. However we may try to hide certain things about ourselves, there is a strong chance that our behaviors will give us away. There is also a strong chance that we will not know the effects of these behaviors unless we remain open to (*a*) an understanding of the nature of behavior as a part of self and (*b*) a willingness to adjust behaviors in relation to the feedback we receive. In this way, our behaviors help us train each other.

Our behaviors grow out of what we feel about ourselves (self-concept)

THE DYNAMICS OF INTERPERSONAL COMMUNICATION

and what role we elect to play in any circumstance. If we adopt an habitual orientation to our world, it is likely we will exhibit some typical behaviors. It is from this pattern of behaviors that others will judge our "personality." Without some interaction, there is little chance that anyone can develop a picture of us—right or wrong—in terms of behaviors. It is from the established pattern of typical behaviors that we begin to categorize one another and begin to make predictions on how the other will behave. It is then we boast that we "know" someone. In a game of chess it may be more useful to know the other person's style of play than all the strategies of the game. If you can predict what moves the other will likely make in response to your moves, you will play more effectively. The accomplished chess player will predict many moves in advance because he assumes certain logical progressions of play. If he is playing a person who does not follow a chess logic on moves, it may make a very confusing game of it.

In human interaction we are caught in a dilemma. On the one hand, the society places such high value on dependability, steadfastness, and reliability, that it would seem we should strive to be predictable in our communicative behaviors. On the other hand, novelty, imagination, creativity, and spontaneity are prized highly, so we might therefore want to establish ourselves as less predictable.

To resolve this apparent conflict we should remember that not only are our behaviors a source of judgment from others, but also a testing ground for ourselves. If we do not develop some patterns of behavior we have very little to test, and yet if we do not add some novelty to our behaviors we cannot learn new things about ourselves. The answer, then, seems to be to do both and try to select wisely those events and circumstances in which to make familiar and typical moves or in which to try some new behaviors. In all this discussion, it is imperative that we remember that our behaviors will not necessarily be "consistent" in all the roles we play, and are therefore not the total of us when taken by any one group we have interacted with.

Our behaviors are then only bits and pieces of us, given out a few at a time in selected circumstances to selected people. In summary for this chapter on roles and self-concept, it may be useful to add these characteristics of behavior:

1. Behaviors, although only a portion of us at any one time, are still ours. They are our responsibility. We invented them. We must take the consequences of them because they belonged to us.
2. Behaviors may not always be the same but may vary as our relationships vary.
3. Behaviors may, however, demonstrate tendencies (or habits of behaving) which may force others to, sometimes mistakenly, label or

categorize us as the predictability of our behaviors increases.

4. Our behaviors are a testing procedure we use on others.
5. Our behaviors are a source of judgment of us by others.
6. Our behaviors are, for better or worse, an overt expression of our intentions.
7. Our behaviors are subject to change as we may like, and others may give us opportunity to change.
8. Our behaviors are visible tokens of exchange with others from which we can learn more about ourselves if we attend to the feedback we get about them.

BIBLIOGRAPHY

Cooley, C. H.: *Human Nature and the Social Order,* Charles Scribner's Sons, New York, 1902.

Goffman, E.: *The Presentation of Self in Everyday Life,* Doubleday-Anchor, New York, 1959.

Goffman, E.: *Encounters,* The Bobbs-Merrill Company, Inc., Indianapolis, 1961.

Gross, N., W. S. Mason, and A. W. McEachern: *Explorations in Role Analysis,* John Wiley & Sons, Inc., New York, 1958.

Jourard, S.: *The Transparent Self,* D. Van Nostrand Company, Inc., Princeton, N.J., 1964.

Komarovsky, Mira: "Cultural Contradictions and Sex Roles," *The American Journal of Sociology,* 1946, vol. 52, no. 3, pp. 184–189.

Laing, R. D.: *The Divided Self,* Quadrangle Books, Inc., Chicago, 1960.

Laing, R. D.: *The Self and Others,* Tavistock Publications, London, 1961.

Reeder, L. G., G. Donahue, and A. Biblarz: "Conception of the Self and Others," *The American Journal of Sociology,* 1960, vol. 66, no. 2, pp. 153–159.

Satir, V.: *Conjoint Family Therapy,* rev. ed., Science & Behavior Books, Inc., Palo Alto, Calif., 1967.

Strauss, A.: *Mirrors and Masks,* The Free Press of Glencoe, Inc., New York, 1959.

Tagiuri, R., and L. Petrullo (eds.): *Personal Perception and Interpersonal Behavior,* Stanford University Press, Stanford, Calif., 1958.

Wapner, S., and H. Werner: *The Body Percept,* Random House, Inc., New York, 1965.

ATTITUDES, BELIEFS, Chapter 9
AND VALUES—WHO SHOULD I BE?

We often feel that our personal world is unique, peculiar to us, unshared by anyone. We have great difficulties explaining to someone else a feeling or an experience. Even when we manage to describe the feeling and the experience with words, we doubt that others know them as we do. The life of a black man in a ghetto is filled with experiences that no white man can ever understand in the same terms the black man does.

However, man is peculiar. At the same time he intuitively believes in his uniqueness, he also assumes that he lives in the same world others do. He assumes that what he sees is what others see. Despite our feeling of uniqueness, our daily lives are spent usually in a world we assume is more shared than unique.

This may be communication's vital function. Were it not for human communication or human contact we would live alone, exclusively in our world of uniqueness, without getting confirmation of our experiences.

Confirmation of our experiences involves not only the physical world— when we check our perceptions with others to test their reliability—but also the social world—when we compare our ideas about religion, politics, morals, etc., with others to test their validity.

Because human beings are symbol-using creatures, they can create for themselves rules of conduct which go beyond the mere survival needs of the species. When a female animal raises young, she does so because she is programmed to do so in order for the young to survive and for the species to continue to exist. When human parents raise their children, considerably more is involved in terms of feelings, societal expectations, laws, duty, etc. Human beings create value systems, form beliefs about the nature of their world, and as a result, learn to respond to their environment in some ways more than in others.

In an earlier chapter (4) we looked at the relationship between assumptive systems and *intrapersonal* communication—how the systems of assumptions we hold color our perceptions of things and people, and shape some of the meanings we develop from our experiences. In this chapter, we will examine how values, beliefs, and attitudes—the ingredients of a person's assumptive system—are formed, held, and changed through *interpersonal* communication.

A FEW DEFINITIONS
Values

Values are fairly enduring conceptions of the nature of good and bad, of the relative worth we attribute to the things, people, and events of our lives. Values are usually embodied in complex moral or religious systems that are found in all cultures and societies, from the most "primitive" to the most complex and industrialized. Values define for people the parameters of their actions. They indicate to those who share them what is desirable, to what degree it is desirable, and therefore what one should strive for. They also provide man with a guidance system which is supposed to enable him to choose the "right" alternative when several courses of action are possible.

The labels, "bad," "good," "moral," "immoral," and other words we use in making our value judgments do not stand for any desirable quality of the object or people we apply them to—value judgments are applied by human beings to objects—they are not "in" the objects. Something is good to a particular individual or group only because it is defined as good.

Were it not for our ability to communicate and to use language, evaluating, that is, making value judgments would not be possible; without symbols we could not be told by others that something is good or bad. Communication is what makes our system of morality possible. Judgments about beauty or ugliness are in the same category as those about goodness or badness. "Beauty lies in the eye of the beholder," wrote Shakespeare. We cannot discover beauty—we can only discover how people define it. It is a man-made dimension.

Values grow out of a complex interaction between human basic needs and the specificity of a given environment. For example, all humans need to eat in order to survive, but they do not all value the same foods. In America, beef is commonly eaten while in India, the sacred cow must not be touched. What is valued in a particular area, region, or country, is partly determined by the availability of certain foods. Values thus differ from place to place because of the variety of ways specific needs can be fulfilled. However, in order to understand values, we need to have some idea about basic human needs.

Maslow's Hierarchy of Human Needs   A widely accepted description of man's basic needs is that of the psychologist, Abraham Maslow.[1] According to Maslow, man is motivated by five basic needs. He describes the needs as follows:

1. *Physiological*—Man's need for food, water, and sleep.
2. *Safety*—Man's need for shelter, clothing, and protection from his environment.
3. *Social*—Man's need to belong, to be accepted, to be loved, and to have friends.

[1]*Abraham Maslow,* Motivation and Personality, *Harper & Brothers, New York, 1954.*

4. *Self-esteem*—Man's need to be respected.
5. *Self-actualization*—Man's need to be what one can be, to develop oneself to his highest potentials, his need to give love and respect.

In addition to a description of the basic needs, Maslow further contends that the needs are arranged in a hierarchy, that is, man's most basic needs must be fulfilled to a large degree before he can concentrate on the fulfillment of the higher or less basic needs. According to Maslow, man must first concentrate on his physiological needs—food, water, and sleep—as these are vital for his survival. This need is followed by the safety need which is only second to the physiological needs in man's hierarchy. Once the needs for shelter and protection are met, man's energy is free to be directed toward the fulfillment of the social needs —to belong, to have friends, and to be accepted. Once these needs are satisfied, at least to some degree, man can concentrate on the self-esteem need and later the self-actualization need. This description is overly simplified. The passage from one need to another is never clear-cut. Actually, man may operate at all need levels simultaneously. Maslow is talking, however, of the bulk of man's energy. Man may seek fulfillment of his physiological and self-esteem needs at the same time, but until he satisfies his hunger, he is going to spend more energy trying to find food than trying to be respected and admired.

What man values at a given time is based on the needs that he tries to fulfill at that particular time. The indictment of "materialism" directed to the generation who lived through the 1929 depression in America, by a generation who lived mostly in post-World War II affluence, may be a reflection on a change of need levels. Once people know a certain level of material affluence which satisfies physiological and safety needs, they can reject what they no longer need, since it fails to fulfill the next need level which has become more prominent.

Values are fairly enduring and resistant to change because they are tied to fundamental human needs and because they are learned very early in life in a somewhat absolutistic way. Thou shalt, and thou shalt not. However, many values that are held by a given group of people can be, and often are, conflicting. In order to act, people must decide which of the conflicting values is more important, more basic, take precedence over the other (for example: thou shalt not kill, yet it is OK to kill the "enemy" in war).

Beliefs

Beliefs represent the way people view their environment. Beliefs are characterized by a true-false continuum and a probability scale. The existence of ghosts, for example, may be closer to the false end of the continuum for some people than for others. That man evolved from the ape is still debated by many who place Darwin's theory of evolution closer to the false end of the continuum, while they place the story of Genesis closer to the true end of the continuum. Beliefs represent what we agree with and what we usually think is true. Some things we believe to be absolutely true; some others we believe to be probably true; and some we are not sure about; some we think are false, probably or absolutely. According to the social psychologist, Milton Rokeach, a belief system "may be defined as having represented within it some organized psychological but not necessarily logical form, each and every one of a person's countless beliefs about physical and social reality."[2]

We cannot observe a belief—we can only observe a person's behavior and assume it came about because of a particular belief. Beliefs are not necessarily logical. They are largely determined by what we want to believe, by what we are able to believe, what we have been conditioned to believe, and by our basic needs which may influence us to have a certain belief in order to satisfy the needs.

According to Rokeach, there are many types of beliefs, and they are not equally important. The beliefs which came from our direct, personal experiences and are confirmed by the people around us are the most significant to us, and the most stable. Some other beliefs may not be supported by others. These may be highly personal views of reality not confirmed by others. Still another kind of belief we acquire secondhand from those people whom we perceive as authorities.

Attitudes

Attitudes are tendencies to respond to things in particular ways. Actually, attitudes are never seen directly. We infer their existence from what people do. If they seem to act consistently in a similar fashion in a particular set of circumstances, we infer the existence of an attitude which predisposes them to act that way. Attitudes include positive or negative evaluations, emotional feeling, and certain for or against tendencies in relation to objects, people, and events.

Attitudes are human responses, and they can be examined along three dimensions: their direction, their intensity, and their salience.

Direction The direction of an attitude simply refers to how favorable, unfavorable, or neutral one tends to be in relation to an object, person, or situation. It refers to whether one is attracted to, repulsed by, or simply indifferent to a particular course of action; whether one evaluates a thing positively or negatively. We like someone, or we do not, or we do not much care. We approve of birth control, or we do not, or we are ambivalent about

[2]Milton Rokeach, Beliefs, Attitudes and Values, Jossey-Bass, San Francisco, Calif., 1968, p. 2.

it, oscillating between one direction or the other. We have attitudes on just about everything we know about. We will judge what people communicate to us about in relation to the background of our existing attitudes about that thing. When we do not know much about something, and thus have no particular attitude about it, what people communicate to us will most of the time help us form one.

Intensity   The intensity of an attitude refers to how strong it is. It refers to how much we like or dislike someone or something. You may not like science courses very much, but your dislike of mathematics may be stronger than that of biology.

Salience   The third dimension of an attitude refers to how important the attitude is to the person holding it. As we mentioned earlier, we have attitudes on just about anything we know about. However, we do not attach the same importance to everything we know about. There are things in our lives that are much more important than others. Salience and intensity should not be confused. There are some objects, people, or ideas we may have a very strong attitude about (high intensity), yet they may not be terribly significant (salient) to us. For example, we may be convinced of the merits of a certain toothpaste and only buy one brand—a strong attitude—yet toothpastes in general do not usually represent what is most important in our lives. There are probably other things that are more salient, such as our attitude toward freedom, individual rights, pollution, etc.

FORMATION OF VALUES, BELIEFS, AND ATTITUDES

The point we wish to strongly emphasize here is that values, beliefs, and attitudes are *learned*. One is not born an anti-Semit, a conservative, an atheist, or a football fan. One is not born fearing God, valuing freedom and human dignity, nor convinced that a steady use of mouthwash will make one a social success. All values, beliefs, and attitudes are learned from the people with whom we live and associate. Because they are learned, they can be unlearned, that is, changed, although change may often be resisted as we will see later in this chapter.

It is essentially through interpersonal communication that one develops his prejudices, assumptions, and outlooks on what life is like, or ought to be like. Our values, beliefs, and attitudes were formed because of the various human groups we were and are exposed to who "indoctrinated" us—and still do—in those values, beliefs, and attitudes they held dear.

To communicate with others is to influence them and to be influenced by them, because any time that we have human contact with others, their behavior and what they tell us affect us. Any time we learn something new, we change and become a little more like those who taught us. This is what makes society possible. Interpersonal communication thus fosters the minimum uniformity necessary for people to live and work together. Sometimes the indoctrination is successful. Sometimes it has a reverse effect; the son of an ultraconservative man becomes a radical. This common phenomenon may be explained in terms of what social psychologists call the reference group theory.[3] We identify ourselves with a lot of different groups of people—our family, our peers, organizations we join, etc. Some of these groups influence us more than others because we have a higher desire to belong, or we have a great admiration and respect for the group members whom we want to emulate. Oftentimes, the different groups we associate with have differing values, beliefs, and attitudes. Usually the group whom we identify with the most will be most successful in shaping our values, etc. The radical son may be radical simply to oppose his father, or because radicalism is a view held by the friends he associates with, or because he has derived some satisfaction from his communication with others when he has shown he was a radical. In any event, his belief is shaped by other people, including his father.

Once an attitude is formed several factors are influential in keeping it stabilized. Many of us resist change and expose ourselves only selectively to new information (for example, when we read a paper which reflects our political, social, and economic views or listen to a political candidate we like and plan to vote for).

Many research studies[4] have demonstrated that we actively seek reinforcement and get involved in those situations which we consciously or unconsciously believe will reinforce out attitudes, beliefs, and values. This has important implications for our interpersonal communication. We tend to seek people whom we think hold attitudes, beliefs, and values similar to ours. We choose to stay away from those people whom we think differ too much from us.

If we cannot avoid exposure to opposing views, we listen only selectively and thus hear only those things which confirm beliefs we already have; sometimes we may not even become aware that opposing views are being stated.

[3] T. H. Newcomb, "Attitude Development as a Function of Reference Groups: The Bennington Study," in Readings in Social Psychology, E. E. Maccoby, T. H. Newcomb, and E. L. Hartley (eds.), Holt, Rinehart and Winston, Inc., New York, 1958, pp. 265–275.

[4] J. Mills, E. Aronson, and H. Robinson, "Selectivity in Exposure to Information," Journal of Abnormal and Social Psychology, vol. 59, 1959, pp. 250–253.

As we pointed out earlier, man can hold many different attitudes, beliefs, and values, and it is quite common for some of them to be in conflict with each other. A group of psychological theories[5] called the consistency theories (or balance theory, dissonance theory, and congruity theory) deal with this phenomenon. These theories say (1) that man needs consistency among his values, beliefs, and attitudes, (2) that the awareness of inconsistencies will produce tensions, and (3) that man will usually do something to reduce the tensions.

THEORIES OF CONSISTENCY AND COGNITIVE DISSONANCE

In his theory of cognitive dissonance, Leon Festinger[6] refers to the same ideas when he states that (1) the existence of dissonance (inconsistency) will motivate people to attempt to reduce it to re-establish consonance (consistency) and that (2) when dissonance is present people will, in addition to reducing it, actively avoid situations or information likely to increase it. According to Festinger, two major factors account for the occurrence of dissonance: (1) new events or information may create dissonance between what a person does and what a person "knows" or believes, or between two opposite beliefs and (2) few things are black and white and clear-cut, so that most opinions or behaviors are likely to be to some extent a mixture of contradictions.

An example of a dissonance-producing situation is finding out that a close friend, whose opinion you respect a great deal, is politically engaged in a cause you despise. The two knowledges clash: that the person is a close friend whose opinion you respect and that he is supporting a despicable (in your eyes) cause. The clash will probably arouse some tension in you which you will try to reduce in some way. Dissonance might also occur in you when you get a low grade from a professor you admire and for whom you worked very hard or when you buy a stereo and find out later that it was considerably cheaper in another store.

Reduction of Dissonance

We seek to reduce the tension generated by dissonant situations by use of several "strategies." If you hold two conflicting values or beliefs, you will tend to reduce the dissonance created by conflicting information by changing one of the two beliefs, generally the least salient belief, or the one with the least intensity. Let us say, for example, you believe that

[5]F. Heider, The Psychology of Interpersonal Relations, *John Wiley and Sons, Inc., New York, 1958. T. M. Newcomb, "An Approach to the Study of Communicative Acts,"* Psychological Review, *vol. 60, 1953, pp. 393–404. P. Lecky,* Self-Consistency: A Theory of Personality, *The Shoe String Press, Inc., New York, 1961. C. Osgood and P. H. Tannenbaum, "The Principle of Congruity in the Prediction of Attitude Change,"* Psychological Review, *vol. 62, 1955, pp. 42–55.*

[6]Leon Festinger, A Theory of Cognitive Dissonance, *Row, Peterson & Company, Evanston, Ill., 1957.*

LSD is really not dangerous and you read a very convincing medical document giving ample evidence to the contrary. If your initial belief in the harmlessness of LSD is very strong, chances are you will reject the medical document. This rejection may take several forms. You may (1) belittle the source (they don't know what they are talking about; they don't really have enough evidence), (2) accuse the source of dishonesty or bias (that's just propaganda), (3) find new information which fits the belief you do not want to change (I read another report that said just the opposite), or (4) escape psychologically or physically (when you realize the report goes against what you believe in, you do not finish it, or you skim it in such a way that not much of it will create an impression).

Take the example of your highly respected friend whom you found supporting a political cause you despise. To reduce dissonance you can use one of several strategies. You can mentally change one or the other of the two conflicting elements, the friend or the political cause. If you choose to change the friend, you may decide that this person was really not respectable and admirable after all, and you were pretty dumb to have been fooled, and he no longer will be your friend. Consonance is then re-established. You now have a person you do not care for working for a cause you do not care for.

However, you can elect to change the other element of the dissonance, the political cause. Here again you have several options: (1) Pretend that the source through which you found out that your friend belonged to the organization was unreliable, lied, or did not know what he was talking about. In essence, you are saying that your friend could not possibly belong to that organization, so consonance is re-established. Sometimes, of course, such a strategy cannot be used—when you find out about your friend because he himself tells you. If he tells you, you vaguely make an attempt at reducing the dissonance by saying that he is joking, that he is not being serious, etc. But it usually appears soon enough that the friend is not joking and you are faced with the conflict. Another way to reduce the dissonance is (2) to find excuses for your friend. You tell yourself he really did not know what he was doing, he got brainwashed in some ways, or maybe early toilet training is the cause of his turning out that way. Essentially, however, the friend is not responsible. (3) Still another strategy is to tell yourself that if a person of the caliber of your friend belongs to such an organization, perhaps the organization is not so bad after all. Finally, another commonly used option is to *compartmentalize* your friendship and the political views of your friend. This process, often used in practice, consists of discounting your friend's political views and accepting him on the basis of certain other merits (his faithfulness as a friend or his sincerity in his relationship with you). Your awareness of his political views is filed somewhere in your brain but is consciously "forgotten" or ignored.

THE DYNAMICS OF INTERPERSONAL COMMUNICATION

All these strategies are based on *rationalizations.* Man has, unfortunately, a great capacity to fool himself, willingly or unwillingly. We very often believe what we tell ourselves simply because we want to believe it so badly—no harm is done when we tell ourselves accurate things. Rationalization, however, always involves an element of self-deception. When we depend on this strategy too often, we run the risk of not being very much in phase with reality.

Resistance to Change

Reduction of dissonance does not always involve rationalization strategies. There are times when instead of rationalizing away a new piece of information in conflict with one of our behaviors, we will do the "right" thing and simply change the behavior. For example, if you smoke and find out that smoking is dangerous and may lead to severe health problems, you may simply reduce the dissonance by quitting smoking.

However, it is never easy to change a behavior, an attitude, a belief, or a value. We tend to resist change because it is always difficult. We often regard change with mixed emotions. What we are used to, however unsatisfying it may be sometimes, still provides us with the ease that comes from habits, and a relative comfort from doing what comes easily and is well-known. We usually feel more confident toward something we know well because we know how to perform. We also know what rewards we can get and how to avoid unpleasantness. We know the ropes. When a new situation presents itself (it may be a new job, moving, going to a new school, joining a new organization, meeting new people, or being exposed to new ideas), we are faced with a dilemma. Change *does* have many positive aspects: doing new things is exciting. It is a relief from boredom, an adventure, the possibility to make new dreams. However, the risks are great because change always represents the unknown. We fear what we do not know well, and tend to hang on to the familiar.

As Thelen pointed out,[7] resistance to change can be self-generated and can also be encouraged by the group we identify with.

(1) We often resist change out of our need to maintain illusions of expertness—changing a behavior or a course of action might imply that what we did before was not good—something hard to admit. So we may rationalize our failures as successes (we did not accomplish anything today, but we sure had fun) in order to reduce the dissonance.

(2) We often feel that a change is too much of a task requiring far more energy than we have. We resist making the effort and rationalize that we just don't have the time for such major undertakings.

(3) Changes in one aspect of our behavior, we fear, may involve sub-

[7]*H. A. Thelen,* Dynamics of Groups at Work, *The University of Chicago Press, Chicago, 1954.*

sequent changes in our role or position in relation to others around us. Even where we might be inclined to try out new behaviors and learn new things, we are afraid to upset other people's expectations, to be given new responsibilities, or to lose our place in the system.

BIBLIOGRAPHY

Bennis, W. G., K. D. Benne, and R. Chin (eds.): *The Planning of Change,* Holt, Rinehart and Winston, Inc., New York, 1961.

Biderman, A. D., and H. Zimmer (eds.): *The Manipulation of Human Behavior,* John Wiley & Sons, Inc., New York, 1961.

Festinger, L.: *A Theory of Cognitive Dissonance,* Row, Peterson & Company, Evanston, Ill., 1957.

Festinger, L., H. W. Riecken, and S. Schachter: *When Prophecy Fails,* The University of Minnesota Press, Minneapolis, 1956.

Hovland, C. I., and M. Sherif: *Social Judgment,* Yale University Press, New Haven, Conn., 1961.

Lecky, P.: *Self-Consistency: A Theory of Personality,* The Shoe String Press, Inc., New York, 1961.

Lippitt, R., J. Watson, and B. Westley: *The Dynamics of Planned Change,* Harcourt, Brace & World, Inc., New York, 1958.

Packard, V.: *The Hidden Persuaders,* David McKay Company, Inc., New York, 1957.

Rokeach, M.: *Beliefs, Attitudes and Values,* Jossey-Bass, San Francisco, Calif., 1968.

Sherif, N., Carolyn Sherif, and R. Nebergall: *Attitude and Attitude Change,* W. B. Saunders Company, Philadelphia, 1965.

COMMUNICATION IN GROUPS— Chapter 10
THREE'S A CROWD

Groups are everywhere—small groups; large groups; formal organizations; informal gatherings; associations we join voluntarily; committees we are appointed to; groups we belong to for fun, for work, for prestige, or out of necessity. We do not—cannot—live in isolation. As the sociologist Glenn Vernon notes, "Most of our individual behavior involves interaction with others."[1]

We are involved with one another, and we exert influence on one another. The web of an individual's group affiliations is the link between the individual and his society. It is a complex web because each individual participates in countless groups. The day of the hermit is gone, and few people play, work, and live in a social vacuum. The average man in the street may be a PTA member, a supporter of his church, a black man, a father, a coach in the Little League, a student at a Community College, and many other things. A student in college may be part of his school choir, the college marching band, his high school alumni group, his family, the basketball team, the film club, the French club, the student council, his communication class, a jazz band, and the local political club. This list does not even include his informal associations with friends and teachers, on a one-to-one basis, or in larger groups.

WHAT IS A GROUP?

What do we mean by a "group"? If you think the answer is obvious, perhaps you need to take a closer look at the characteristics present in "groups."

First of all, let us make it clear that in this chapter we will deal with characteristics that are present in "groups" of *two or more people.* We want to emphasize that dyads, groups of two people, are a part, and an important one, of our discussion. Although dyads and different-size groups have characteristics of their own, there are many important processes occurring anytime people are together in an interpersonal situation.

What then are the characteristics present in "groups" of two or more people? What differentiates, for example, a committee working on a project or a couple on a date from a collection of people waiting for a

---

[1]*Glenn H. Vernon,* Human Interaction, *The Ronald Press Company, New York, 1965, p. 4.*

BOX 1

> *A small group is defined as any number of persons engaged in interaction with each other in a single face-to-face meeting or a series of such meetings, in which each member receives some impression or perception of each other member distinct enough so that he can, either at the time or in later questioning, give some reaction to each of the others as an individual person, even though it be only to recall that the other was present.*
>
> *Robert F. Bales,* Interaction Process Analysis, *Addison-Wesley Press, Inc., Cambridge, Mass., 1950, p. 33. Reprinted by permission of the author.*

BOX 2

> *A psychological group may be defined as two or more persons who meet the following conditions: (1) the relations among the members are* **interdependent**—*each member's behavior influences the behavior of each of the others; (2) the members* **share an ideology**— *a set of beliefs, values, and norms which regulates their mutual conduct. This ideology is developed as the members of the group work together on common tasks, and, in time, this ideology becomes, to some degree, peculiar to them as members of the group and sets their group apart from other groups.*
>
> *D. Krech, R. S. Crutchfield, and E. L. Balachey,* Individual in Society, *McGraw-Hill Book Company, New York, 1962, pp. 383–384. Reprinted by permission of the publisher.*

bus at a bus stop or from an audience at a movie theater? Is just being together enough to make a gathering of people, who happen to be in the same place at the same time, into a group? The answer given by most small group scholars is *no.* Just being together is not enough. There must be some other bond between the people involved. For Robert Bales,[2] the important ingredient is *psychological awareness.* People must be aware of each other so that they can later remember that each was present. (Complete definition in Box 1.) For Krech and Crutchfield,[3] the con-

[2]*R. F. Bales,* Interaction Process Analysis, *Addison-Wesley Press, Inc., Cambridge, Mass., 1950.*

[3]*D. Krech, R. Crutchfield, and E. Balachey* Individual in Society, *McGraw-Hill Book Company, New York, 1962, p. 383.*

THE DYNAMICS OF INTERPERSONAL COMMUNICATION

cept of *interaction* is essential, in addition to psychological awareness. It means that not only are people aware of each other's presence but they also exert a reciprocal influence on each other through speech or nonverbal communication. (Complete definition in Box 2.)

Paul Hare[4] is still more explicit in his definition of what constitutes a group. He maintains that there are five characteristics that differentiate between a "group" and a mere "collection of individuals." Let us stress here again that dyads are included in our discussion of group characteristics.

Interaction

The members of a group are in interaction with one another. Interaction does not mean solely verbal interaction, that is, people talking to one another. Interaction also refers to nonverbal communication. We can interact with one another through our facial expressions—smiles, raised eyebrows, and grim looks—through our gestures—shaking a hand, clenching a fist, nodding—or through our body movements and positions—walking stiffly or sitting in a slouched position on a chair. In its broadest sense, interaction or communication refers to people taking each other into account or existing in each other's world.

When a teacher lectures to his students, he is doing the talking, and presumably they are sitting in silence. Yet all are interacting. All are in one another's world. The students may stop listening, yet the teacher is still there and by his mere presence prevents the students from leaving the room. The teacher is in the students' world at that time, in that place, whether they like it or not. Some students possibly can tune the teacher out completely and get caught up in their own thoughts to the point of almost forgetting where they are and that the teacher is there. If and when this happens, interaction between the teacher and that one student has stopped.

Goal Sharing

Members of a group share one or more purposes or goals which determine the direction in which the group will move. Interaction does not occur randomly. It always has some purpose. People interact or communicate with one another for a variety of reasons. A common goal which can be achieved through interaction is necessary to make a collection of individuals into a group. A common goal without interaction is not enough.

Take the example of the people waiting at a bus stop. They share the same goal—catching the bus—yet they do not need to interact with one another to reach their goal; they are not a group. A class needs to interact with its teacher, if only by listening, to accomplish the common goal,

[4]*Paul Hare,* Handbook of Small Group Research, *The Free Press, New York, 1963.*

Figure 10-1 *From Larry Lewis, "Campus Clatter."* San Antonio News and Express, *Newspaper Enterprise Association, November 2, 1971. Reprinted by permission of the publisher.*

which is learning. If interaction stops—when students completely tune the teacher out—the goal cannot be reached.

In addition, the goal of the group has some influence on the kind of interaction that takes place in the group. If people get together for the purpose of socializing and relaxing, interaction will likely involve a considerable amount of small talk and idle chatting in a fairly free-for-all and casual atmosphere. If, on the other hand, the group got together to gain information on a certain subject, its interaction might be characterized by the silence of most group members listening to one or several other members providing the necessary information. If a couple is on a date, the purposes of that particular association will definitely influence how each person will interact or communicate with the other. Incidentally, if the purposes of each person are not compatible with those of the other, communication will be at best difficult, and the evening in all likelihood ruined.

System of Norms

Members of a group develop a system of norms which set the scene in which interpersonal relationships may be established and activities carried on. Norms are rules of behavior, the dos and don'ts of interpersonal communication. The "proper" ways of acting which have been accepted as legitimate by members of the group. Norms may be formalized in a set of written rules and regulations, particularly in large groups—no-smoking signs, campus regulations, traffic signs, laws—or they can be informally derived through group communication, generally in small groups. For example, a group of students conversing with each other may find it appropriate to use vulgar words or tell obscene jokes. The informal rule (informal because no one needed to state it specifically and overtly) is that such language is OK. However, the same students in a different group, let's say the classroom or with their parents, might not use such language for they might feel the other group had norms that implied this behavior would not be quite appropriate.

Norms specify the kind of behaviors which are expected of group members by other group members. Norms, thus, regulate people's behavior toward one another because they reflect what the group considers appropriate. For example, some groups develop a very competitive atmosphere where people talk very fast, interrupt each other, etc. In some other groups, such behavior might be considered rude and out of place. In some groups the atmosphere is very formal, stiff, serious, no-horsing-around-no-nonsense, and businesslike, with no closeness between members. Some other groups might develop quite a different set of norms whereby warmth, play, fun, and humor are praised and encouraged while stuffiness is ridiculed.

Norms are a very important aspect of group communication. Any group of people who interact over a period of time will develop norms of their own, and group members, in order to stay members, will be pressured into conforming to them to some degree.

The Internal and the External Systems   Norms developed within the group may or may not fit with the norms developed by the environment of which the group is a part. Groups, like individuals, do not exist in a social vacuum. Homans[5] calls these the internal system (norms developed within the group) and the external system (norms from the outside environment).

For example, a group of college students develop the norm of smoking in a classroom where obvious "no smoking" signs are displayed. The external system—the college campus—requires no-smoking behavior in certain areas. The internal system—what that group of students considers appropriate—condones smoking. The internal and external systems, of course, need not be at odds with each other. Most students would not wear a bathing suit nor a formal dress to class. In this case, both internal and external systems are in agreement with each other.

Social Control and Group Pressure   The existence of norms plays a fundamental role in the development of interpersonal communication. Groups not only create rules of behavior to be shared by their members but also develop a powerful pressure system which influences their members into conforming to these rules. This process whereby individuals are influenced or pressured into conforming to certain behaviors is called *social control,* or group pressure. It is particularly strong when individual members are very anxious to belong to the group. Most of us need to belong to certain groups, and the stronger the need for belongingness, the

[5]G. C. Homans, The Human Group, *Harcourt, Brace and Company, Inc., New York, 1950.*

more likely we are to conform to the group norms, for fear we will be rejected or ridiculed if we don't.

Modes of dress are no exception to group norms. The "hippie" garb is just as much a sign of conformity to the norms of a particular group as the coat, tie, and briefcase for the middle-class executive. The battle between parents and sons over the length of the son's hair reflects the fact that parents and son belong to groups which have different norms about hair length. Moreover, each group offers equally strong pressures toward conformity to those involved. For the parents, it may be, "What will the neighbors think?" or "You'll never get a job with hair like this." For the son it may be, "I can't show up in the band with short hair, all the guys have long hair." In both cases the pressures toward conformity stem from a fear of rejection from those who matter to us. Norms and social control play the same role if only two people are communicating with each other.

The Sherif and Asch Studies Two classic and pioneering studies are worth mentioning in the area of group pressure and conformity. Sherif's autokinetic study in 1935[6] and Asch's conformity study in 1951[7] demonstrated how groups can influence individuals into conforming to group norms.

In Sherif's study, the subjects were placed in a dark room and asked to press a key when they saw a light starting to move. They were then to estimate how far the light had moved from its original position. The light was actually not moving at all. The visual illusion was created by lighting a balloon which was alternately inflated and deflated. When the subjects were in the room alone their estimates ranged from below one inch to several feet. Almost every subject mentioned a different figure. The procedure was repeated, but this time the subjects came to the dark room *in groups.* Each group member was then to announce aloud his estimate of the distance the light had moved. This time, the variations in the subjects' estimates were considerably reduced. There was a sort of tacit agreement among group members that all the estimates should be more or less consistent with one another. A social norm was created by the first subjects to make their estimates known. They were, of course, quite unaware of their influence on the subsequent estimates of their fellow group members. None of the subjects was aware that when he was reporting his estimate he was in fact reporting the consensus of the group.

[6]M. Sherif, "A Study of Some Social Factors in Perception," Archives of Psychology, New York, 1935, vol. 187, no. 60.

[7]S. Asch, "Effects of Group Pressures Upon the Modification and Distortion of Judgments," in H. Guetzkow (ed.), Group, Leadership, and Men, *Carnegie Press.* Carnegie Institute of Technology, Pittsburgh. 1951.

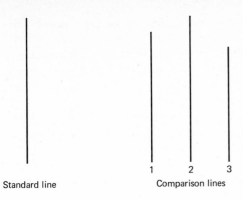

Standard line

1 2 3
Comparison lines

Figure 10-2 Example of the stimulus cards in the Asch experiment. Subjects were instructed to choose the line on the right (line 1, 2, or 3) which most closely matched the standard line on the left. In this case the correct choice is line 2, although lines 1 or 3 were selected by a majority of the subjects influenced by confederates of the experimenter.

The Asch study set out to determine what happens when people are asked to estimate something that is clearly not ambiguous and visually quite obvious and when the other group members—who are confederates of the experimenter—have been instructed to give the wrong answer.

One naïve subject and nine confederates of the experimenter (unknown to the naïve subjects, of course) were asked to compare the length of a line with the length of a set of three lines. The procedure was repeated twelve times with different sets of lines, and over one hundred naïve subjects were thus tested. On all comparisons, it was quite obvious what the right answer was. The naïve subjects, however, were always one of the last group members to make their answer known. All the confederates who answered before the naïve subjects were instructed to give an obviously wrong answer. The naïve subjects were thus faced with a conflict between what their senses were telling them and what they heard from a majority of those they thought were their fellow group members. What were they to believe: that their senses were more reliable and that all these other people must be all wrong, or that perhaps it was they who were in the wrong? Were they to rely on and conform to the judgment of several other people or stick to their own perceptions? The results showed 37 percent of the naïve subjects conformed to the judgments of the confederates and were thus in error.

If many of us rely on others for judging obvious physical stimuli, think of how the pressures to conform are greater for most of us when we deal with more ambiguous social judgments where a clear-cut answer is rarely given to any of us through our senses.

Stabilized Roles

If interaction continues over a period of time, a set of roles becomes stabilized. A role is the behavioral norm for an individual. It is what that individual tends to do habitually in certain specific circumstances.

Some people are likely to play leadership roles while others may feel more at ease in a more submissive role. Some people enjoy telling jokes and are often known to relieve tension by being funny. Some people may be looked to when information is needed because they have established themselves as knowledgeable in certain areas. Some people are very skillful at settling arguments or moderating conflict when it occurs. Roles in groups of two or more people are loosely defined at first, unless they are strongly prescribed by the environment in which the group is a part (as in student teacher relationship, for example). However, as the group continues to meet, roles will become more definite and better established. Most people in groups know who the talkers are and who the silent ones are, the smart alecks and the serious ones, the workers and the procrastinators. When two people of different sex are involved, patterns of dominance and submission, for example, can be noted quite rapidly. Part of this is culturally defined. Sex roles, as Margaret Mead[8] and other anthropologists have pointed out, are not inborn but culturally developed. Certain role behaviors become thus expected of men and women. One interesting thing about roles is that once they become established it becomes much harder to change them or to step out of them.

The longer a person has been silent in a group, the more difficult it becomes to break the silence and the more conspicuous breaking it will become. The reason for this is that once we have pigeonholed people into certain stereotyped roles, we become accustomed to their performing the role and this makes it easier for everyone else to anticipate, predict, and understand their behavior. This allows communication to run smoothly along expected paths. However, when someone steps out of his role, the pattern is broken. What is customary does not happen. The group is faced with a change of pace which may be startling or even threatening in some cases. A number of research studies[9] have shown, for example, that many women are pressured into intellectual underachievement because they fear that if they appear intellectually too strong they will not be popular with men and will have a hard time finding dates. Most women in our culture are quite aware that intellectual achievement is equated with masculinity and therefore is not a "feminine" role. They'd much rather play the traditional "feminine" role in order not to threaten masculine egos. However, a sizable number of women are today battling feminine-role stereotyping.

Sometimes a change of roles is welcome (for example, when an habitual joker finally decides to settle down and be serious so the work can get accomplished). Sometimes the change is resisted (for example, when

[8]Margaret Mead, Sex and Temperament in Three Primitive Societies, Mentor Books, New American Library, Inc., New York, 1935.
[9]Mira Komarovsky, "Cultural Contradictions and Sex Roles," The American Journal of Sociology, 1946, vol. 52, no. 3, pp. 184–189.

THE DYNAMICS OF INTERPERSONAL COMMUNICATION

a parent wants to be too "buddy-buddy" with his child, or a student tries to "play teacher" with his classmates).

Roles, however, are not static. People have ways to adjust to changing situations and environment by changing roles. Quiet little Susie in the classroom may well be chatterbox Susie back in the dorm among her friends. We often have to alter a familiar role, a familiar behavior pattern, to fit in with a group whose norms are different from ours.

Attraction and Rejection Networks

A network of interpersonal attraction or rejection develops on the basis of the likes and dislikes of people for one another. Actually, when people meet together for the first time, first impressions play an essential part in generating feelings about one another. People always have feelings about one another and often are not willing to admit this to themselves or to others. We put such a premium on rationality that we do not like to think of ourselves as emotional beings. Yet feelings and emotions are as much a part of human behavior as reason is. So we like some people, dislike others, feel relatively indifferent about still others, yet never completely so. Of course, as we interact more with other people, our first impressions of one another may change. We may come to like someone we did not care for at first, or vice versa. How often do we tell a real good friend after many months or years of solid friendship and affection that "When I first met you, I really couldn't stand you"?

WHAT TO OBSERVE IN A GROUP

All of us spend so much time around people in groups of various sorts that we rarely stop and observe what is going on between people and why group members behave the way they do. What is there in a group to observe? What should we look for if we want to understand interpersonal communication between two or more people?

Content and Process

Imagine a committee working together to plan a weekend dance at the local college or a couple deciding what to do for the evening. Communication between the people involved is happening at two distinct levels. If we observe *what* people are talking about, we are focusing on *content,* that is, the subject matter or the task upon which the group is working. When we focus on *how* the group is handling the content, we are focusing on *process,* that is, what is happening between and to the group members while the group is working. The distinction is an important one for the study of small group communication. Content and process communication are sometimes called "task and socioemotional" or "task and maintenance" communications. Both are going on at the same time in the group. What does the distinction between these two aspects of group communication refer to?

Task When a group of people get together, they do so with a purpose, a goal. The purpose may be purely social (a party, a group of friends having lunch or coffee at the student center together, or a date); people may get together to make decisions and plan activities (the typical committee) or to learn and gather information (classroom or work team) or to act (sport team).

BOX 3
CHARACTERISTICS OF
AN EFFECTIVE GROUP

Douglas McGregor, an industrial psychologist at M.I.T. drew on his observations of the management of large companies to characterize a well-functioning, effective, creative group.

1. *The atmosphere tends to be informal, comfortable, relaxed.*
2. *There is a lot of discussion in which virtually everyone participates, but it remains pertinent to the task of the group.*
3. *The task or objective of the group is well understood and accepted by the members. There will have been free discussion of the objective at some point until it was formulated in such a way that the members of the group could commit themselves to it.*
4. *The members listen to each other! Every idea is given a hearing. People do not appear to be afraid of being foolish by putting forth a creative thought even if it seems fairly extreme.*
5. *There is disagreement. Disagreements are not suppressed or overridden by premature group action. The reasons are carefully examined, and the group seeks to resolve them rather than to dominate the dissenter.*
6. *Most decisions are reached by a kind of consensus in which it is clear that everyone is in general agreement and willing to go along. Formal voting is at a minimum; the group does not accept a simple majority as a proper basis for action.*
7. *Criticism is frequent, frank, and relatively comfortable. There is little evidence of personal attack, either openly or in a hidden fashion.*
8. *People are free in expressing their feelings as well as their ideas both on the problem and on the group's operation.*
9. *When action is taken, clear assignments are made and accepted.*
10. *The chairman of the group does not dominate it, nor on the contrary does the group defer unduly to him. In fact, the leadership shifts from time to time depending upon the circumstances. There is little evidence of a struggle for power as the group operates. The issue is not who controls but how to get the job done.*
11. *The group is self-conscious of its own operation.*

D. McGregor, The Human Side of Enterprise, McGraw-Hill Book Company, *1960. Reprinted by permission of the publisher.*

This overt goal is directly related to the content communication in the group. For example, if the purpose for the group is to plan a weekend dance, much of the talking and interaction will focus on the actual planning of the event. The conversation may cover topics such as which band to get, what refreshments will be served, if any, what decorations to use, etc. This is content communication. It is communication directly related to the overt purpose of the group.

Process There is, however, another dimension of group communication which is not related directly to what the group talks about, but to how the group handles the talking about their task or purpose. Process involves how the members interact with one another, how they manage the feelings that develop as a result of their interaction with one another, and how they maintain the group as a group. While a couple on a date decides what to do for the evening, for example, feelings about each other are generated. Each will make attempts, more or less consciously, to make a certain impression on the other, or to maintain a certain image which is thought to be appropriate, and to favorably affect the other. All this is a part of process communication.

In most cases very little attention is paid to process even when it is a major cause of ineffective group action. Sensitivity to group process communication will better enable you to diagnose interpersonal problems and deal with them more effectively. Since process communication is present in all aspects of interpersonal communication, an understanding of its role is useful to anyone.

Specifically, what can we look for to recognize process communication?

Participation—who talks, how often, and how much. This is perhaps the easiest communication pattern to observe. Who are the most talkative members in the group? Who talks the least during the group discussion? If one pays attention to the mere quantity and frequency of the talking carried on by people in interpersonal situations, one can get a relatively accurate picture of the group structure and of the pattern of dominance and leadership in the group. In many groups most of the talking is done by only a few members. A careful observation of the group communication may reveal shifts in participation. The talkative members suddenly become quiet, and a silent member becomes talkative. There are usually reasons for such shifts since communication is never random. These reasons must be understood if one wants to be able to predict when such shifts might occur again.

The treatment of the quiet members is also important. Is their silence interpreted as consent with what is being discussed, disagreement, disinterest, hostility, fear, or shyness? Even when two people are involved, a pattern of participation is revealed.

BOX 4　A SYSTEM OF CATEGORIES USED IN OBSERVATION OF GROUP PROCESS*

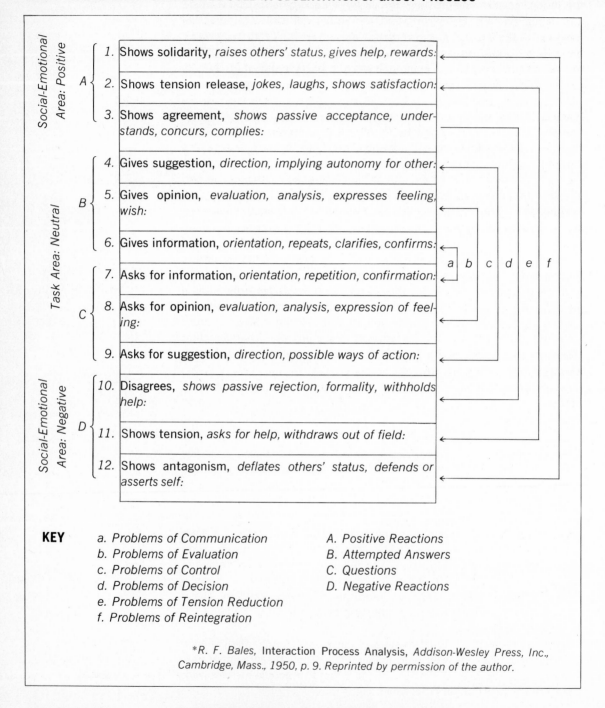

KEY

a. *Problems of Communication*
b. *Problems of Evaluation*
c. *Problems of Control*
d. *Problems of Decision*
e. *Problems of Tension Reduction*
f. *Problems of Reintegration*

A. *Positive Reactions*
B. *Attempted Answers*
C. *Questions*
D. *Negative Reactions*

R. F. Bales, Interaction Process Analysis, Addison-Wesley Press, Inc., Cambridge, Mass., 1950, p. 9. Reprinted by permission of the author.

If you are interested in doing a more systematic analysis of group participation, you can record members' communication behavior on a simple chart which shows the members' position in the group and the period of time the communication takes place. For purposes of recording, one communication is usually defined as an uninterrupted utterance.

The pattern shown as an example on Figure 10-3 indicates that most of the conversation was carried on between Peter and Harry with Sally supporting the two men, while John and Mary had little to contribute to the discussion. Obviously such an analysis is quite superficial and says nothing about the reasons for John and Mary's withdrawal.

An interesting feature of the interaction recording is that while usually the more quiet members are well aware of their lack of participation, the more talkative ones are quite surprised to find out how much they talked. The more talkative members usually know they are contributing quite often, but fail to realize the relative degree of their participation. Such an analysis can also be helpful in comparing groups with one another.

According to Figure 10-4, group A had a significantly livelier ten-minute discussion than group B. The total amount of interaction is 79 in group A and 18 in group B. There was either much apathy and silence in group B or a very dominating person who did most of the talking without interruption.

Participation—who talks to whom. The direction of the communication pattern is also quite important. Are group members talking to specific people in the group or to the group at large? Do group members tend to talk only to the same people?

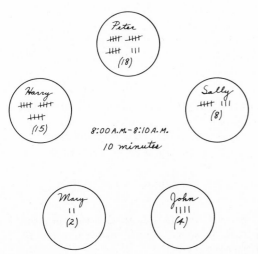

Figure 10-3 Sample of communication recording.

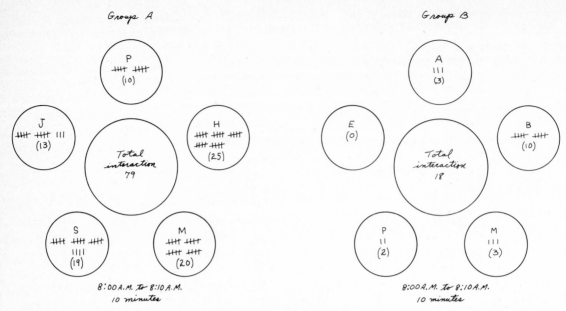

Figure 10-4 Communication recording: comparison of two groups.

On Figure 10-5 the notches on each arrow represent the number of times a particular member spoke and to whom he directed his comment. On this particular chart, it is evident that Harry did most of the talking, directed his comments mostly to Bill and Joyce, and finally was the one person in the group who received most comments from the other group members. Such a chart would reveal that probably Harry was assuming the leadership position, *for group leaders are often the people who talk the most and are talked to the most.*

The chart also identifies a subgroup within the group: Harry, Bill, and Joyce not only assume most of the talking, but do it among themselves, more or less ignoring the other group members.

Influence or leadership.[10]   Influence and participation, as pointed out earlier, are often found in the same group members. However, this is not always the case. Some people may speak very little yet capture the attention of the whole group. Others may talk a lot but may never be listened to.

Who is listened to may be the key for finding out who the influential

---

[10]*A detailed analysis of such a complex phenomenon as leadership goes beyond the scope of this chapter, or this book. If you are interested in learning more about leadership processes, we recommend the sources listed at the end of this chapter.*

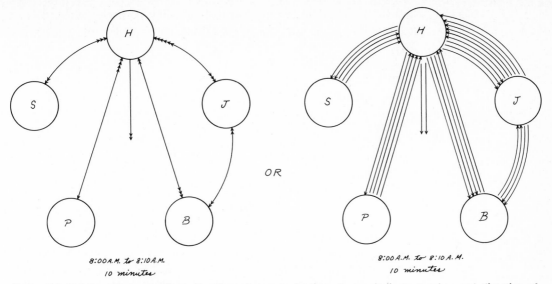

OR

8:00A.M. to 8:10A.M.
10 minutes

8:00 A.M. to 8:10 A.M.
10 minutes

Figure 10-5 Interaction recording: direction of communication. Arrows indicate number and direction of communication interactions. Either system of notation can be used.

members are in a group. Whose suggestions are generally accepted and followed may provide another clue.

Some members in a group may have no influence at all. It may be that they do not try to influence others, or they may try desperately yet unsuccessfully. Shifts in influence can also be observed as the problems under discussion change, as new people join the group, or as some members leave.

Sometimes several group members are rivals for influence, and a struggle for leadership ensues. It is interesting to note the effects of such struggles on the group as a whole. Group members may feel compelled to take sides; a risky business when it is not clear who will win the fight!

Decision-making procedures. Whether in a group of five, six, or more members, or simply with one other person, decisions have to be made in most interpersonal communication situations. Whether it be to decide which movie to see with your date or who should be elected president of the club, many decisions are made without always considering the effects of *how these decisions are made* on the group of people involved. Some people tend to impose their own views while others want everyone to participate and share in the decision-making process.

There are many ways decisions are made. Sometimes one person will make a decision and carry it out without checking with the other people involved. Your date picks you up and announces which movie you are going to see tonight, or someone in a meeting decides on the topic to be discussed and starts right in to talk about it. This is called the "self-authorized agenda."

Usually in any group when a suggestion is made it will draw support from some people. Looking at who supports whose decisions may reveal coalitions, cliques, friendship patterns, or who caters to whom. It is called the "handclasp" when it results in two members deciding things for the group.

Sometimes there is evidence of a majority pushing a decision through over other members' objections by calling for a vote, formally or informally. Informally when for example a wife tells her husband that "all the kids want to spend their vacation at Grandma's house" and the whole family ends up there, even though the husband would have liked to go fishing somewhere else.

At other times attempts are made to get all the people involved to participate in the decision-making in some way. This is called the "consensus method." Consensus, as you probably have already found with some of the exercises you have been through, is difficult to reach, for it involves compromises (somehow perceived by many people as "bad") and because it calls for a genuine discussion of the reasons why certain ideas are supported or disliked.

Finally, there are times in interpersonal communication situations when someone makes a suggestion that gets absolutely no response or recognition from other people (the son saying to his dad, "I would like to borrow the car tonight," and the dad answering, "Finish your homework"). This is called the "plop." The effects of a plop on the person who initiates it can be varied. He may try again ("OK, Dad, but can I have the car tonight?"), withdraw from the situation and sulk (to his room and slam the door), or become apathetic (go to his room and do nothing). Unless you observed the plop, you may not know how to interpret the sudden apathy or hostility of a group member.

Group atmosphere. Something about the way a group works creates an atmosphere which in turn is revealed in a general impression one can form by observing the group. People, of course, may differ in the kind of atmosphere they like in a group. Interpersonal communication can be characterized by a friendly, congenial, and warm atmosphere where conflict is reduced and unpleasant feelings are suppressed, or it may be characterized by an atmosphere of conflict, disagreement, and provocation. Group members may dislike each other and may not be willing to cooperate at all on the task at hand. Members who are unwillingly appointed to a committee or students who are forced to take certain required courses may be apathetic and withdraw from the communication. If enough people in the group feel that way, the whole group atmosphere will be permeated by this apathy. On the other hand, the group process may be geared toward easing the interaction and taking care of people's feelings when they get hurt. Small talk at times performs this very function. Cracking a joke at a particularly tense moment may relieve the tension and reestablish a friendly and working atmosphere.

Interpersonal communication can be looked at in terms of the functions it performs. These functions are related to the roles individuals play in a given interpersonal situation. Some of these functions center mostly

Interpersonal Functions

BOX 5

"Task functional behavior": *Behavior of members which is necessary for a group to get its job done.**

1. "Information seeking or giving": *Requesting or supplying factual material and objective data; seeking or giving relevant information about a group concern; asking and giving ideas, generalizations.*

2. "Opinion seeking or giving": *Requesting or supplying opinions and beliefs; evaluating; helping the group find out what members think or feel about what is being discussed, particularly concerning its value rather than its factual basis.*

3. "Initiating activity": *Starting the discussion; proposing tasks, goals, solutions; defining a problem or an aspect of a problem; suggesting new ideas, new definitions of the problem, or new organization of new material.*

4. "Clarifying or elaborating": *Giving examples, illustrations; paraphrasing; interpreting; developing meanings; trying to envision how a proposal might work out; clearing up confusions; indicating alternatives and issues.*

5. "Coordinating": *Showing relationships among ideas or suggestions; trying to draw together various trains of thought or effort of group members.*

6. "Summarizing": *Restating information, opinions, or suggestions in concise form after a group has discussed them.*

7. "Consensus testing": *Sending up a "trial balloon" to see if the group is nearing a conclusion or identifying points where agreement is not yet reached; direct checking with the group to see how much agreement has been reached.*

*"Adult Leadership," 1953, 1, 8, 17–18. Reprinted by permission of the publisher.

---

around the task area of interpersonal communication. Some center in the process area. Still some others, because of their detrimental effects on interpersonal communication, are called dysfunctional.

These task and process functions can be performed by one or more individuals. In most groups a sort of specialization gets established, and some people tend to perform task functions while others are more comfortable performing process functions. Traditionally, in the American family for example, the husband and father specializes in task (decision

BOX 6

"Maintenance functional behavior": *Behavior of members which builds and strengthens the group as a working unit.**

1. "Climate making and Encouraging": *Developing and maintaining a friendly, warm, relaxed, acceptive, and permissive atmosphere; seeking to reduce inhibitions; facilitating interaction; being responsive to others; praising others and their ideas; agreeing with and accepting contributions of others.*
2. "Gate keeping": *Attempting to keep communication channels open; helping others to contribute, participate, or "get into" the discussion by perceiving their nonverbal indications of a desire to participate.*
3. "Harmonizing": *Reducing and reconciling misunderstandings, disagreements, and conflicts when possible; reducing tension or relieving negative feelings by jesting; "pouring oil on troubled waters"; "putting a tense situation into a wider context"; encouraging others to objectively study differences; mediating as a third party to hostile, aggressively competing sides.*
4. "Compromising": *When his own idea or status is involved in a conflict, offering to compromise his own position; admitting error; disciplining himself to maintain group cohesion.*
5. "Expressing group feeling": *Sensing the group's feelings or mood about an issue and expressing it; sharing own feelings; describing reactions of the group to ideas or solutions; seeking the group reaction; empathizing.*
6. "Standard setting": *Expressing standards or criteria for group to use in choosing its content or procedures; applying standards in evaluating group functioning and production.*
7. "Evaluating": *Submitting group decisions or accomplishments against goals.*

"Adult Leadership," 1953, 1, 8, 17–18. Reprinted by permission of the publisher.

BOX 7

"Nonfunctional behavior": *Behavior of members which does not help and sometimes actually harms the group and the work it is trying to do.**

1. "Being aggressive": *Working for status by criticizing or blaming others; showing hostility against the group or some individual; deflating the ego or status of others.*
2. "Blocking": *Interfering with the progress of the group by going off on a tangent; citing personal experiences unrelated to the problem; arguing too much on a point; rejecting ideas without consideration.*
3. "Self-confessing": *Using the group as a sounding board; expressing personal nongroup oriented feelings or points of view.*
4. "Competing": *Vying with others to produce the most or the best ideas, talk the most, play the most roles, or gain favor with the leader.*
5. "Seeking sympathy": *Trying to induce other members to be sympathetic to one's problems or misfortunes; deploring one's own situation or disparaging one's own ideas to gain support.*
6. "Special pleading": *Introducing or supporting suggestions related to one's own pet concerns or philosophies; lobbying.*
7. "Horsing around": *Clowning, inappropriate or unnecessary joking; mimicking; disrupting the work of the group.*
8. "Seeking recognition": *Attempting to call attention to one's self by loud or excessive talking, extreme ideas, or unusual behavior.*
9. "Withdrawing": *Acting indifferent or passive; resorting to excessive formality; day-dreaming; doodling; whispering to others; wandering from the subject.*

In using classifications like those above, people need to guard against the tendency to blame any person (whether themselves or another) who falls into "nonfunctional behavior." It is more useful to regard such behavior as a symptom that all is not well with the group's ability to satisfy individual needs through group-centered activity. Further, people need to be alert that what appears as "blocking" to one person may appear to another as a needed effort to "clarify" or "mediate."

"Adult Leadership," 1953, 1,8, 17–18. Reprinted by permission of the publisher.

making, breadwinning, etc.) while the wife and mother is seen as the process element in the relationship (moderator of conflict, soft and gentle caretaker of feelings). A list of some specific task and process functions and of dysfunctional functions appear in Boxes 5, 6, and 7.

Needs and Hidden Agendas

People join groups with an overt reason or purpose—usually, the official reason they give closely parallels the official purpose of the group. A student will say he joined the campus service organization because he wants to work for the disadvantaged in the community. This reason for joining may be very real, yet it is usually not enough to explain why the student joined the organization, because human motivation is very complex. There may be a whole array of underlying motives, which he may or may not be conscious of.

For example, this campus service organization may be popular and may be considered the "in thing" to belong to by the people this particular student runs around with. Or perhaps the student is lonely, does not know anyone, and feels that by joining he will kill two birds with the same stone —he will do something useful and worthwhile and at the same time get to know other people and make friends. Perhaps the student wants to exert his leadership abilities and joins the organization with the intention of eventually running it or at least becoming influential in it. These motives which are added on to the initial overt purpose of joining are often called *hidden agendas.* When the group meets it has an agenda, the official reason for meeting and operating, and each member has his own little private hidden agenda which represents a need he will use the group to fulfill.

These needs or hidden agendas will manifest themselves through the group interaction and account in a large measure for *how* the group members handle one another or react to one another. What people do at the task level can often be explained by what is happening at the process level. If two group members cannot agree on a decision, for example, it may be that one of them, or both, want to win the argument to establish their leadership over the group. The content issue may be irrelevant; they would argue and disagree over any issue. These two members are not so much interested in solving the problem as they are in winning the argument for their own future role in influencing the group.

William Schutz[11] in his book *The Interpersonal Underworld* has identified three basic interpersonal needs which underlie most of our behavior around other people. These needs can be best represented as dimensions or continua along which we all fall. Schutz calls these interpersonal needs the need for inclusion, the need for control, and the need for affection.

Inclusion According to Schutz, the need for inclusion refers to the need to be recognized as an individual distinct from others. A person with a very high need for inclusion needs recognition and attention from others. Such a person likes to be in the spotlights, to be singled out, to be no-

[11]*W. Schutz,* The Interpersonal Underworld, *Science and Behavior Books, Palo Alto, Calif., 1966.*

ticed. At one of the extremes of the continuum, we find the prima donnas, or the obnoxious little kid who does anything simply to attract some attention, even if it results in punishment. To be punished is better than to be ignored. On the other hand, a person with a low inclusion need prefers not to stand out, would rather not receive too much attention, does not like to be prominent in the public eye.

According to Schutz, people at both extremes are motivated essentially by the same fear of not being recognized as an individual. The people high on the inclusion need will combat the fear by forcing others to pay attention to them. Those low on the inclusion need have convinced themselves that they will not get any attention, but that it is just the way they want it. Most of us are probably somewhere in the middle of that continuum. Our needs for inclusion may change as the people we associate with are different, and as the situations we find ourselves in change. We may wish very little recognition from a professor when we have not done an assignment and do not wish to be called upon, while at the same time have a strong need for attention from the girl sitting next to us whom we wish to ask for a date tonight.

The need for inclusion has some influence on the process of interpersonal communication. Imagine a situation in which two or more people equally high on the need for attention get together to plan something. Much of the energy they are going to spend in that interpersonal context will be spent establishing in the group a position from which they will get the recognition they need. However, if all members are recognition seekers, chances are they will have a difficult time securing attention from one another, since each will be so busy for himself. Much of the group's time, it can be predicted, will be spent vying for recognition from anyone in authority or from each other. Little else usually gets accomplished. A group composed of people high *and* low on inclusion will probably function in a smoother fashion.

Control The need for control refers to a striving for power, for being in charge, for running things, and for influencing one's environment. The need for control is not necessarily related to the need for inclusion. Some people enjoy being in charge of things even if no one is aware that they are running the show. These people are high on control while low in inclusion; the power-behind-the-throne type. Some people, on the other hand, may seek leadership or prestige positions not for the power they may bring, but for the attention they may produce. This is why it is not always easy to determine whether a person's behavior is influenced by one need or the other. We should be careful not to play "analyst" with our friends and summarily peg them into one or the other category.

Naturally, some people are quite low on the need for control and are not interested at all in taking initiative, responsibilities, in making decisions, or in leading a group. As for the inclusion need, a mixed group composed of highs and lows on the control dimension has a better chance of getting things done. Too many "leaders" and not enough "followers" may result in a constant struggle for leadership, and the ensuing climate of competition may not be conducive to accomplishing much. On the other hand, too many "followers" and no "leader" may result in apathy, and not much may get done either.

Affection   The need for affection refers to how close people want to be to one another. Some people like to be very intimate and enjoy warm relationships, even with relatively casual acquaintances. They enjoy telling about themselves on a personal level and expect a similar behavior on the part of others. They want and need to be liked. Sometimes people high on the need for affection are perceived by others as too friendly or coming on too strong.

Some people, on the other hand, prefer to keep others at a distance. They do not like to become too friendly, too rapidly. They do not wish to be too personal with others and share too much of themselves with people they do not know well. They may have a strong distaste for closeness and intimacy except with carefully selected people. These people are usually perceived as aloof, cold, or acting superior.

In the case of affection, a mixed group is not the best combination for productive interpersonal relationships. Aloof, cold people and warm people do not mix well. Each makes the other uncomfortable and hard to figure out. None is able to satisfy the other's needs.

Interpersonal communication is satisfying to us when we manage to satisfy our needs. In the case of interpersonal needs, we depend solely on others for their satisfaction. If others give us the recognition we seek, or give us a chance to exert influence when we wish to, or provide us with the close intimate atmosphere we like, we feel satisfied and we seek these people again in other interpersonal situations. We tend to avoid, when we can, that type of interpersonal communication situation where our needs are generally thwarted.

An understanding of interpersonal needs is essential, not only in facilitating our insights into group processes, but in helping us predict the situations that will be more or less satisfying and productive for us.

BIBLIOGRAPHY LEADERSHIP

Bass, B. M.: *Leadership, Psychology, and Organizational Behavior,* Harper & Row, Publishers, Incorporated, New York, 1960.

Gibb, C.: "Leadership," in G. Lindzey (ed.), *Handbook of Social Psychology,* Addison-Wesley Publishing Company, Inc., Reading, Mass., 1954.

Gouldner, A. (ed.): *Studies in Leadership,* Harper & Brothers, New York, 1950.

Petrullo, L., and B. M. Bass (eds.): *Leadership and Interpersonal Behavior,* Holt, Rinehart and Winston, Inc., New York, 1961.

Stogdill, R.: "Personal Factors Associated with Leadership: A Survey of the Literature," *Journal of Psychology,* vol. 25, 1948, pp.35–71.

Tannenbaum, R., I. R. Weschler, and F. Massarik: *Leadership and Organization: A Behavioral Science Approach,* McGraw-Hill Book Company, New York, 1961.

BIBLIOGRAPHY SMALL GROUPS

Bales, R. F.: "Task Roles and Social Roles in Problem Solving Groups," in Eleanor E. Maccoby, T. M. Newcomb, and E. L. Hartley (eds.), *Readings in Social Psychology,* 3d ed., Holt, Rinehart and Winston, Inc., 1958, pp. 396–413.

Bales, R. F.: *Interaction Process Analysis,* Addison-Wesley Press, Inc., Cambridge, Mass., 1951.

Barnlund, D., and F. Haiman: *The Dynamics of Discussion,* Houghton-Mifflin Company, Boston, 1960.

Bion, W. R.: "Experiences in Groups," *Human Relations,* 1948–1950, vol. 1, pp. 314–320, 487–496; vol. 2, pp. 13–22, 295–303; vol. 3, pp. 3–14, 395–402.

Cartwright, D., and A. Zander: *Group Dynamics: Research and Theory,* 3d ed., Harper & Row, Publishers, Incorporated, New York, 1968.

Collins, B. E., and H. Guetzkow: *A Social Psychology of Group Process for Decision-Making,* John Wiley & Sons, Inc., New York, 1964.

Deutsch, M.: "An Experimental Study of the Effects of Co-operation and Competition Upon Group Process," *Human Relations,* vol. 2, 1949, pp. 199–231.

Guetzkow, H. (ed.): *Groups, Leadership and Men: Research in Human Relations,* Russell & Russell, 1963. (Originally published by Carnegie Press, Carnegie Institute of Technology, Pittsburgh, 1951.)

Hare, P. A.: *Handbook of Small Group Research,* The Free Press, New York, 1962.

Hare, P. A., E. Borgatta, and R. F. Bales: *Small Groups: Studies in Social Interaction,* rev. ed., Alfred A. Knopf, Inc., New York, 1965.

Homans, G.: *The Human Group,* Harcourt, Brace and Company, Inc., New York, 1950.

Homans, G.: *Social Behavior: Its Elementary Forms,* Harcourt, Brace & World, Inc., New York, 1961.

Kelley, H. H., and J. W. Thibaut: *The Social Psychology of Groups,* McGraw-Hill Book Company, New York, 1959.

McGrath, J., and I. Altman: *Small Group Research,* Holt, Rinehart and Winston, Inc., New York, 1966.

Maslow, A. H.: *Motivation and Personality,* Harper & Row, Publishers, Incorporated, New York, 1954.

Mills, T.: *The Sociology of Small Groups,* Prentice-Hall, Inc., Englewood Cliffs, N.J., 1967.

Olmsted, M. S.: *The Small Group,* Random House, Inc., New York, 1959.

Schutz, W.: "What Makes Groups Productive?" *Human Relations,* vol. 8, 1955, pp. 429–465.

Schutz, W.: *The Inter-Personal Underworld,* Science & Behavior Books Inc., Palo Alto, Calif., 1966. (Originally published under the title *FIRO: A Three-Dimensional Theory of Interpersonal Behavior,* Holt, Rinehart and Winston, Inc., New York, 1960.)

Shephard, C. R.: *Small Groups,* Chandler Publishing Company, San Francisco, 1964.

Simmel, G.: *Conflict; The Web of Group Affiliations,* The Free Press of Glencoe, Ill., Chicago, 1955.

Slater, P. E.: "Role Differentiation in Small Groups," *American Sociological Review,* vol. 20, 1955, pp. 300–310.

Whyte, W. H., Jr: *The Organization Man,* Simon and Schuster, New York, 1956.

INTERPERSONAL TASK AND PROCESS—WE THINK AND WE FEEL

Chapter 11

Because humans *feel* as well as *think,* the merging relationship of task and process is almost automatic; it is continuous, it is linked to all behaviors. This ebb and flow of feelings and thought may have many different terms applied to it, depending on the writers or the discipline. Task in some speech texts has been called "instrumental," and process called "consummatory."[1]

Task may also be referred to as "content directed" with process taking the label of "emotion directed." In education we have begun to liberally use the paired relationship of "cognitive domain"[2] for task, and "affective domain"[3] for process. There is, in fact, a widening recognition of the effects we have on each other while we are getting the job done, and hence much study of the emotional, maintenance, affective, or process portion of our communication, by whatever name.

We have looked at the principle of task and process as it relates to groups (Chapter 10). Without attempting to make a distinction between what is a group communicative activity and what is interpersonal, we need to study a wider range of activities than touched on in the previous unit. This chapter deals with dyads (two-person groups), triads (three-person groups), as well as those numbers of participants we usually call groups, and as well as the "public" media.

Our discussion is a description of what is going on, whether or not it is recognized by the participants. The emphasis on task or on process in any given communicative act may not be easily defined, and each person involved may have a different feeling about how much "was accomplished" in either task or process. We will treat task as the primary relationship, in order to look at some activities, but we urge the reader to keep in mind the interrelationships of task with process.

Besides describing what is happening, this chapter does not attempt to advocate what should be, or establish a set of judgments on good or

[1]*T. Clevenger, Jr., and J. Matthews,* The Speech Communication Process, *Scott, Foresman and Company, Glenview, Ill., 1971, p. 161.*

[2]*B. S. Bloom, M. D. Englehart, E. J. Furst, W. H. Hill, and D. R. Krathwohl (eds.),* A Taxonomy of Educational Objectives: Handbook I, The Cognitive Domain, *Longmans, Green & Co., Ltd., London, 1956.*

[3]*D. R. Krathwohl, B. S. Bloom, and B. A. Massia (eds.),* A Taxonomy of Educational Objectives: Handbook II, The Affective Domain, *David McKay Company, Inc., New York, 1964.*

bad. When value judgments are made, they will be implied in terms of the "appropriateness" to the situation rather than to good behavior or bad behavior. In the long run, the more appropriate the behavior of individuals in contact with one another, the more likely they will have or develop healthy communicative habits.

In this chapter, we will also discuss *games* as a form of communication which occur with enough frequency to create a pattern we can identify. Once we see a *game* being played, we can recognize it again in another setting and at another time. Some patterns are more involved in task than others, but the usual form of a game occurs when we manage to *distort process* in the interest of winning the task.

It is unfortunate that we tend to split things in parts to study them, because we can mislead ourselves about their relationship. We should not think about task *or* process, but task *and* process. They are not competing opposites, but parts of the same activity, feeding on one another, inhibiting one another, generally inseparable in the ongoing activity of communication.

We have been late in emphasizing the effects of process in our communicating, partly due to the emotional nature of process itself. It has taken man a long time to become comfortable about having a psychological makeup, and he has resisted much probing into his "psyche." We have thought very highly of the person who could "keep his cool," who represented the unemotional, iron-nerved, gunfighter type, and we have made fun of the person who displays feelings too easily. We have believed in our culture that business should be conducted, relationships built, and most of our individual contacts should be ruled by intelligence and cold logic. If we can concentrate on the job to be done, we don't have to worry about having feelings. We know, however, that the feelings are there even in the most calculating and objective person's behaviors. Feelings are an inseparable part of human communication, in small degree or large, and are there whether we like to talk about them or not.

THAT UNEASY FEELING   How often have you come away from some communicative encounter having a vague, uneasy feeling that something went wrong. Our impressions of "something went wrong" are usually related to a distortion of the relationships between what we wanted done and what actually happened —both in terms of the task we hoped to finish and the feelings we had about ourself and others.

Distortions can occur when we get too serious or too casual, too personal or too distant, too simple or too complex, too fast or too slow, too short or too long, or any combination of excessive behaviors besides the obvious too-loud or too-soft communication. Some examples. You casually ask a friend, "How are you?" and he tells you, at length, about his problems with his girl, with his stomach, or with his studies. You wanted only a simple, passing relationship, but he draws you into his personal life to a depth you may even resent. In the motion picture *Bob and Carol and Ted and Alice,* the foursome was eating in a busy restaurant. The character Carol had been to a "sensitivity training" course and was full of "meaningful relationships" to the extent of trying to engage the head-waiter in deep discussion about his feelings. The headwaiter had a job to do, which did not include "meaningful" verbal relationships with cus-tomers, and the misunderstanding created left all participants confused.

You have been in an argument with a friend which ended in anger be-cause the topic—say it was where to have coffee or the correct answer to a test question—got lost in the discussion about the other person's per-sonality. This is called the "your watch is wrong" kind of argument, and the sequence is something like this:

"What time is it?"
"Four thirty."
"I've got four twenty."
"Why did you ask, if you knew?"
"Well, *your watch is wrong.*"
"I set it this morning."
"You couldn't have—unless it runs fast."
"It's a good watch, and I did set it."
"Are you sure it was this morning? You could forget."
"I'm sure. Don't you believe what I say?"
"Not always."
"So you think I lie?"
"I didn't say that. All I said was that your watch is wrong."

Another kind of argument develops this way:

"I think demonstrations are useless."
"You don't like demonstrations?"
"No."
"You're stuffy."
"You're irresponsible."
"You're afraid."
"Well, you're stupid." (Your watch is wrong.)

In this kind of meaningless argument, we tell each other a lot about how we feel as well as about the watch. In fact, the watch gets forgotten as we discuss each other.

Another annoying example of distorted communication is the situation where we find ourselves in a small seminar class conducted as a monologue by the instructor; or in a large auditorium-size lecture class where the instructor becomes very chatty and personal by disclosing much of his personal life to the hundreds in the hall.

In our everyday communication we encounter confusing situations. A friend wants to borrow a book for class and you find out he actually wants to get away from his studying and into a conversation with you. An employer asks the employee how he likes working there, and ends up giving him another menial job to work on at home without any extra pay. A telephone caller chats for a few minutes and then tells you she represents a photo studio with a special offer this week if you will just answer a simple question.

There are many situations we find ourselves in when we try to figure out what is happening. We may go away from such an encounter trying to guess what the other person wanted. Some relationships are very clear-cut, and all participants understand their respective roles. You step up to a Post Office window to buy stamps and you do not intend to share your inner feelings with the clerk, nor he with you. A psychological distance is provided to keep you from interfering with the sale of stamps, and to keep him from interfering with your mailing your letter.

In some situations you may have longer contact, such as filling out a complicated application for student aid at registration. In that situation you would like (a) information about what is right to put down on paper, (b) assurance that your informer knows his business, and (c) some emotional or process confirmation that you are worth talking to. It is to this part c that we turn when we get upset about our treatment by clerks, officials, parents, teachers, or other students. In a way we can tolerate another person's not knowing what to tell us better than we can tolerate their ignoring us or their condescension.

If, as we have said earlier, we cannot divide task and process into two distinct parts—like 10 pounds of task and 5 pounds of process—we still like to look for a balance in our encounters. The balance should be appropriate for the kind of situation we find ourselves in, and is recognized by us either consciously or by that vague feeling that things didn't go right.

We look for balance in our relationships along these three lines and may judge our encounters on this basis:

1. What you have "agreed" to do—what the situation calls for normally and your perceptions of what you expect, and what the other might expect from the encounter. (You might feel that an argument ought to follow a rule of using logic, using honest data, and not getting into personalities.)
2. What you felt you did—what you felt your part was in keeping to the

THE DYNAMICS OF INTERPERSONAL COMMUNICATION

ASSUMPTIONS ABOUT THE COMMUNICATION PROCESS

Assume that communication has failed between two people when:

B doesn't understand what A has to say—doesn't "get it"

B doesn't feel free (or is not concerned about) expressing himself further to A

Situation: A says to B: "This is the way to do this thing. . . ." B replies: "Oh yeah" (put your own paralanguage into this response). If you are A talking to B in this situation, what are your assumptions?

Assumptions by Jones:
That reply is a sign that B is not understanding and therefore you are not explaining well enough or completely enough or that B is too stupid to understand anyway.

Frustration by Jones; gets defensive; ego is threatened; attack on his ability to explain things clearly

Assumptions by Smith:
That reply is a sign that B has not exhausted his vocabulary about the subject; that the interaction between A and B is incomplete on this matter and some attempt must by made to find out why.

Curiosity by Smith as to what is going on inside B; not dismiss B's opinions; avoid pressuring B into understanding

(At this point it must be emphasized that we are not talking about "right" or "wrong" ways of dealing with B. These are two different methods of approaching communicative conflict—examples for generalization.)

Jones assumes that
1. what is going on is something logical
2. words mean something
3. the purpose of this interaction is to get B to understand and do it that way

Smith assumes that
1. what is going on is an interaction of sentiments, not logic
2. meanings are in B, not in words
3. purpose of this interaction is to give B an opportunity to express himself

Jones tends to watch primarily the "meanings" and logic of what he is saying, or, he listens to himself only. He tends to ignore the nonverbal system and seems to concerntrate on the verbal. He is concerned primarily with this one message and ignores what has led up to it or what goes beyond it.

Smith tends to pay attention to the emotional as well as the intellectual exchange—will listen to opposing points of view—watches the nonverbal as well as verbal system. He knows this interaction has a history and will have a future—it is a part of an ongoing relationship, not an isolated incident.

Smith's system often works better, not because it is morally right or because of any kind of magic, but because it more nearly represents what is going on.

structure and living up to the rules. ("I certainly didn't give any information in the argument except what I could prove or had heard from very reliable friends.")

3. What you actually did—what happened inside you and others which you would like not to admit, or which you have not been able to share with feedback. (When you told your friend that his information was not as reliable as yours, it made him secretly feel you had called him a liar. His watch was wrong.)

**TASK-EMPHASIS
CONTINUUM**

Figure 11-1 is a diagram of five general categories of communication with examples in each. These represent (from left to right) an increasing emphasis on task, with an appropriately decreasing emphasis on process. The activities described at the left end of the continuum are more likely to have less task involvement than the activities at the right end of the line.

It is difficult to locate any activity precisely on this line because we have to consider (a) what the participants will acknowledge openly is the purpose of the activity and (b) what may actually be happening in terms of the participants' desire to win, to obtain things or favors, to get action, to hurt, to lead, to control, to inform, to change, or to amuse. For that reason, the examples are located in relation to both factors: what we normally expect to happen and also what is usually going on. How the participants treat the situation will, of course, affect how much task and how much process is involved in that particular event. For that reason we would caution the reader to treat these examples, and these categories, as relative rather than discrete pigeonholes.

This grouping of activities is not a prescription of what should be done in each. It is a way of helping us see our communication in smaller pieces

Figure 11-1 Task-emphasis continuum diagram. Shaded area indicates the relative emphasis on task in each of the categories. Communication energies in each category not devoted to task may be assumed to involve process (the unshaded areas).

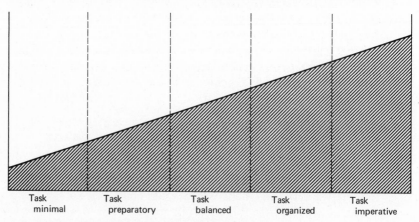

| Task minimal | Task preparatory | Task balanced | Task organized | Task imperative |

THE DYNAMICS OF INTERPERSONAL COMMUNICATION

to better understand the busy, day-by-day, flow of our interrelation-ships.[4]

The least emphasis on task probably occurs in our gossiping, our singing (alone or in groups for the fun of it), and our fighting, where no estab-lished rules govern our interactions. The distinction between fights and debates may be more clear if we say that the debate proceeds in an or-derly fashion to reach an end which may change an opinion or which may represent a winner for his superior performance. Fights are disorganized and are designed chiefly to blow off steam or express hurt or indignation. They may have the healthy effect of getting something off our chest, but they may also have the danger of hurting the participants emotionally and making additional interaction difficult if the fight is not well handled. The task, in this case, is so closely related to emotion (or process) that we put it toward the minimal end of the task continuum, along with gossip of all kinds. We tend to think of gossip as the kind of storytelling in which we spread stories (usually bad) about another. Gossip in this diagram includes the chatter about "who I saw at the store today," "what Sam was wearing at school," or other kinds of silence-substitutes we may employ to fill our surroundings with empathic noise.

Task Minimal

Malinowski calls it "phatic communion."[5] Berne calls it "stroking."[6] We may call it "circling." Sometimes we call it "cocktail chatter" or "small talk." These terms describe talking about getting ready to talk. They mean those exchanges we make with others to find out if we can get recognized, to find out if anyone else is "out there" to talk with, or to lead up to a continued relationship either at that moment or at some later time when we will have a task to perform together. Maybe this category should be called "task promissory" because the kinds of communication we will describe here are usually based on the promise of some future task rela-tionship rather than this communication itself being the task.

Task Preparatory

We tend to talk about "small talk" as if it were not a very important or even dignified thing to do. Yet it is significant to us, especially in terms of the process it provides. "Circling" will occur when we approach a car

[4]This continuum was suggested by D. Barnlund and F. Haiman's assembling of group speech activities into cathartic, social, learning, decision-making, and ac-tion, in **Dynamics of Discussion**, Houghton Mifflin Company, Boston, 1960. Those authors should not be held responsible for our categories or our examples.

[5]Bronislaw Malinowski, The Problem of Meaning in Primitive Language; Supple-ment I, in C. K. Ogden and I. A. Richards. The Meaning of Meaning, 8th ed., Harcourt, Brace & World, Inc., New York, 1946, pp. 315 et seq.

[6]Eric Berne, Games People Play, Grove Press, Inc., New York, 1964.

salesman. You comment on automobiles in general as if you are just kicking tires. He tries to find out what your real interests are, how much you can afford, what you are now driving, and may circle for some time with questions about your work, your family, etc. Rarely does anyone buy a car by simply walking into the showroom and saying "I'll take that one."

Phatic communion, as described by Malinowski, takes place between people who want to establish a speaking relationship for whatever reason. It may be a probing to find out if another is willing to talk and what kind of mood he is in and to get directions on how to proceed. It may simply be fulfilling a need to be recognized, to get personal confirmation that "I am worth talking to." It may give you a good feeling to be recognized by others and to say hello to them while walking across the campus or on the street. There are others in your world; you are part of their world, and therefore important. You matter to someone, if only to be greeted in passing.

Talking about the weather has become a symbol of small talk. This is frequently our best way to make contact with others. "Nice day" is not a meteorological analysis, but an invitation to talk, at least to respond. The information we gave when we said it was a nice day was probably information the other person already had. We really don't care that much what he thinks of the weather, anyway, but we care about what he thinks about talking with us.

You sit next to someone in a bus, a theater, in class. What do you do to establish contact? You likely do not begin a discussion of deep and important subjects. You test. You try him out: "Sure hot in here," "Hope this movie is good, the review was good," or "Wonder what prof will talk about today."

So much of what we learn about others and about ourselves comes from the "small talk" that we should not neglect it. Our relationship and our role may be established by this means. We also use this seemingly useless mode of communication to maintain our respective roles with others. There are rituals we perform in our greetings and our small talk which are carefully prescribed and which reinforce our relations with others.

Eric Berne describes these relationships in terms of "stroking."[7] When we meet people we have a well-developed system of acknowledging our relationships with verbalizations which may not mean anything—may not have any content. Stroking is highly systematized—we know who gets stroked—and also is reciprocal; we know how much we should get as well as how much to give.

For example, you meet a fellow student and say "Hi" (one stroke) and

[7]*Eric Berne, op. cit., pp. 35–40.*

he says "Hi" (one stroke), so you are even. If you say "Hi" and he does not reply, he owes you one, and you feel uncomfortable. That is known as a two-stroke exchange, and is used in casual relationships. In a more complex stroking exchange, you have to come out even, and the difficulty is in trying to break off a contact if it has "stroked" too long.

If a casual acquaintance has been away, say on vacation, the encounter with him on his return requires more than your usual stroke exchange. You have to ask him about his vacation, and he has to respond in some way.

Stroking, according to Berne, is highly organized. We fulfill the requirements, however, without thinking. There is an unstated balance to be created in our contacts we learn from somewhere, and the way we perform in this activity will affect others' opinions of us. If we habitually under- or over-stroke it will jiggle our relations with others and make contact difficult. Under-stroking may represent a preoccupation with other worries (if we feel kindly toward a person), or it may be interpreted as a generally sour attitude (if our feelings are not positive about the person). Over-stroking will usually result in our imbalanced feelings being directed toward the over-strokers being "pushy," or "aggressive," or "nosy," or our wondering what he is after.

Cocktail chatter has its own rules and is concerned with the same kind of balanced relationships as stroking. This kind of communication takes place not only at cocktail parties, but in any kind of casual gathering where people mingle as an assigned task. It could be a break between classes, the coffee break at work, or any kind of reception, grand opening, or spectator sporting event. It is often more difficult to find ways of breaking off an encounter than it is to establish one in this kind of setting. People are close physically, and they must either work at ignoring this fact or somehow acknowledge the presence of others. Once acknowledged, the right moment to break off contact may be sought, and when the stroking is balanced or when circling has been carried on without any advantages being established, the time to break must be faced. If you want to move along to another encounter, you must say something like, "Guess I'll go get a snack," and the person must excuse you with a releasing comment like, "Better get some soon, it is going fast" or "I recommend the anchovies." In cocktail chatter you may find out interesting things about interesting people and want to pursue them. You may find new kinds of encounters you enjoy. Without the "small talk" we would have difficulty establishing most relationships because none of us will take a risk of getting too serious, too soon, with strangers. Task may be minimal in some ways, but there is always the hope in this task-preparatory category that our encounters will lead to something, if only to proof that "I am a worthwhile person."

Task Balanced

This title does not mean to imply that equal amounts of task and process can be identified. It means that an interplay of task and process should, over time, be balanced to make the most effective use of the situation. In a discussion we cannot ride roughshod over another person's feelings and expect to have a satisfactory intellectual exchange. An argument should be balanced in terms of attention to cognitive data and emotions if we can achieve a solution or understanding. Even if you have overwhelming data, you can turn off your opponent by hurting his pride, making him angry, or otherwise attacking his emotional side when you would like to appeal to his intellect. The "balance" we suggest in the title, is a balance of *attention to* more than a balance of *time spent.*

If you sign up for a seminar class of five students, you expect to be able to talk. You also expect to be treated as if you had something to say, not just that you are occupying space in the room.

The affective domain[8] (process) has not yet been universally established as an integral part of all classrooms. In other words, we have not yet completely accepted the idea that the student in a classroom is something more than a brain waiting to be filled with data about history, speech, verbs, or vertebrate classifications. We deny sometimes the emotional portion of a class full of students in an attempt to add something to their knowledge. In spite of years of talking about motivation as a part of learning, it has taken us a long time to relate motivation to those process factors available in every class situation.

Student evaluations of instructors go far beyond how much the teacher knows about his subject. Invariably the teachers singled out for praise have a quality of attention to the needs of students beyond the information provided in lectures and textbook assignments. You might recall that the earliest public manifestations of unrest at Berkeley were against loss of identity by students and the early demonstrations featured students wearing giant IBM cards in protest against being treated as numbers and not as individuals. In this same regard, much of the criticism of higher education appears to be focused on the platitude of "loss of individuality" because of the massive enrollments in the large institutions.

Listen to the complaints of students who have been mistreated in a class. Sometimes you will hear documented charges of unfair grading against a teacher, but more often you will hear, "He treated me like I didn't know anything," or a similar remark indicating the student's worth as a person (not as an intellect) was really under attack. The recent student demand for "relevance" in education has more to say about *how* students are treated as human beings than it does about the *content* of the courses they enroll in. Relevance in most cases is a relevance to "me as a person" more than it is relevance of subject matter.

[8]D. S. Krathwohl, et al., op. cit.

A great deal happens to a student sitting in class. He interacts not only with the material of the lecture but also with the manner and attitudes of the teacher, the attitudes of his fellow students, and to his own expectations of the subject matter, the teacher, and himself. The classroom, then, is a highly charged and very busy communicative situation where real people react to one another, as well as to some "subject" as an intellectual abstraction. Balance in attention to task and process may produce more appropriate communicative outcomes.

If you go to be interviewed for a job you enter an organized situation in which the task is clearly spelled out for all parties. You will be asked questions, you know, and someone will want to know certain kinds of things about you. You will also be looked at, and possibly given some tests to complete. While the outcome is not clearly set by the rules of the game, you know that certain things may help you get the job and other things may not. For a personal interview you may dress up a little. You respond to questions honestly, but with some tendency to exaggerate your abilities toward the favorable end of the scale. At the same time, the interviewer may try to figure out what you look like when you are not being interviewed, and may also divide in half your claims of experience or abilities just by his own habit.

Task Organized

While the organization of the interview—or a debate, or buying, or selling—is marked by clear organization and prescribed roles of the participants, the outcome is not known. Therefore, some attention to process as well as task is necessary.

Buying and selling cover a wide range of possibilities. You might go to the drugstore and buy one toothbrush from a rack. In this kind of buying (and selling) the action of exchanging money for a commodity is very full of task, and little process is necessary. This does not say, however, that our lives could not be more pleasant if the clerk would offer help, and the person at the check-out cash register would greet the customer and finish the transaction with a "thank you."

Selling a car, buying a car, getting a job after the interview, hiring a person for a position from an interview, and predicting the outcome of a debate are all uncertain. In this task-organized category the task is spelled out, but the final outcome is in doubt. You followed all the rules of buying a toothbrush except that you didn't find one in the color you wanted. You showed up for the interview, filled out the forms, answered the questions, and did not get the job. You shopped for a car in five places and ended up keeping the one you had. On the other side, the clerk showed you five different brands and hardnesses of toothbrush bristles but could not find the color you wanted. The prospective employer had interviews with ten people for the job and selected one, although the procedure of the interview had to be conducted for all of them. Five car salesmen now have your name and address but so far have not sold you a car.

What goes wrong in these instances where the task is not completed? It is possible that the participants do not find the object they want. It is also possible that the participants damage each other emotionally ("I'll never buy a toothbrush—or a car—from that place") because something went wrong with the process.

Task Imperative

Here is a category of military orders or commands, demands from opponents to each other, invoices, and some kinds of lectures. The task is spelled out, and it will be accomplished or at least carried to a conclusion, however successful. A military commander could order his men to attack an enemy command post with reasonable assurance they would attack. If he ordered them to "capture" the enemy command post, they might do their best and fail, but the task had a conclusion.

Demands by a striking union do not mean that all will be met in the final settlement, but the demands mean that some kind of completion will come. It is not accurate to say that process has no place in union negotiations or any other kind of confrontation. Process may be very important. We tend, however, to view this kind of situation as one of clear argument, objective data, and a binding conclusion.

However we may feel about taking on the task (orders, demands, commands, etc.), it is imperative that we do so. We cannot worry about the involvement of process in a decision of whether or not to move. Some kinds of lectures and speeches are in this category, but it is difficult to categorize lectures because they offer a wide range of topics, speakers, situations, and audiences. An example of a task-imperative lecture would be the kind delivered to an auditorium of several hundred underclassmen by a master professor who sees his sole purpose as getting across his point of view or his scholarly data. If someone sleeps, that is not the professor's problem. If someone takes notes, or does not, that is not his concern. He is there to deliver the goods. If he hurts the feelings of someone in the audience by a reference to a religious group, that is not his concern either.

The military commander may try to keep his men motivated and reasonably content, but his main job is to get them to do the job as it becomes necessary. If he is leading a patrol and a dangerous situation develops, the squad cannot worry about hurting each other's feelings when one soldier yells "Get down, you _____." According to some reports, the military has undergone some modifications in its discipline. The actual combat situation will probably still continue to operate under an imperative condition, even though the U.S. Army has experienced situations in

THE DYNAMICS OF INTERPERSONAL COMMUNICATION

which orders were disobeyed, and those involved were not given traditional punishments.

Particularly this area of task imperative is one in which the primary emphasis is on content, the cognitive, the intellect, the knowing rather than the feeling.

On the basis of the discussion of task emphasis, we may be inclined to (a) identify our friends as a "task type" or "process type" or (b) identify the situations we find ourselves in as being primarily task or process. We would discourage such identification or labeling, except as it may help us understand the flow of our communication by stopping the flow to look at it.

BEHAVIORAL TENDENCIES

We have our own personal habits of responding to situations which then give others a pattern to judge us by. You may approach even the most serious matters with humor, or on the other hand you may tend to be serious about almost all situations. Your habits of responding to situations will begin to collect labels for you from those around you. How we see ourselves (self-concept) and what we think is expected of us (role) will in part determine these responses and in that way we confirm what others may already think about us.

We will be judged by the appropriateness of our response to many given situations. Do we spend a lot of time chatting with clerks who couldn't care less about what we think? Do we, on the other hand, treat even close friends very brusquely or in an off-hand manner? Do we immediately strike up a conversation with someone sitting next to us in a class or on a bus? Do we enter casual settings and never approach a stranger at a cocktail-party kind of gathering, but stay hidden inside ourselves by fiddling with the books on the shelf or the olive pits? Faced with solving a complex mathematics problem, do you immediately set out to solve it, do you try to find help from someone, do you decide the problem is funny and make up jokes about it, or do you respond to the problem in some other way?

We may react differently in dyads (two-person groups) than in triads (three-person groups) or than in larger groups. One of the factors involved in our behaviors is our attitude about "taking risks." When we approach a stranger, or when we enter a new situation, or when a group embarks on a new topic of discussion, there is "risk" involved to an individual who communicates. You may risk being "wrong" in something you do or say, or you may risk offending the values or beliefs of others, or you may risk having others change their image of you so you will have to adjust your behaviors. We tend to protect our self-concept and defend a role we are comfortable with. We will take risks in our communication only if our self-concept and our role stand a chance of coming out relatively undamaged, or if the issue is so important to us (saliency) that we overcome the threat.

If we are interested in preserving mainly a task image and role, we will take more risks in the process end of the task-emphasis continuum. That is, if we wish to be known as an efficient, coolheaded type, we will pay less attention to those items on the left end of the continuum such as gossip, singing, phatic communion, stroking, and circling. We are more careful with our behaviors in ordering, commanding, lecturing, or debating with logic.

If we are interested, however, in keeping an image of ourselves as process oriented, our role as the facilitator and icebreaker and not the problem solver or commander, then we will take more risks with the buying and selling, the demands, the ordering, and lecturing. We hesitate to risk our image for appropriate stroking, circling, gossip, or small talk, and we are very careful when we engage in those activities.

As a corollary to these preferences for taking risks, we must note that the person who sees himself as *both* the task leader and the process leader will have a very busy time of it trying to balance out the commands he gives to people with the smoothing of feelings to get the job done. Such versatility is difficult to achieve because of (*a*) the energy it takes to pay attention to a person's perceptions and evaluations of himself and others, and (*b*) the roles others cast him in, which will usually restrict a person to one end of the continuum or the other, and those roles are difficult to change once established.

GAMES

One way we have of dealing with the complexities of communication is to develop for ourselves or borrow from others some behaviors we will describe as "games." Although the main purpose of a game may be getting the task done, we manage with certain kinds of games to also win at process. Games then are a distortion of process for the purpose of winning, either a process goal, or a task goal, or both.

Stephen Potter, in a series of books, reported on the art of game playing with such titles as *Gamesmanship, One-Up-Manship,* and *Womanship.*[9] He suggests, for example, ways to win at tennis or golf even if your opponent is a superior player. "If you can't volley, wear loud socks" is typical advice designed to take away your opponent's physical advantage by psychological distraction. A golfer of our acquaintance, in true

[9]*Stephen Potter,* The Complete Upmanship, *Holt, Rinehart and Winston, Inc., New York, 1970.*

THE DYNAMICS OF INTERPERSONAL COMMUNICATION

Stephen Potter style, has been heard to say to an opponent "If you will turn your hands over slightly during your downswing, you can correct that problem in your drive" whether the opponent had any "problem" or not. This remark, made early in the game, was usually worth several strokes to the "gamesman."

Being "one up" is putting the other person "one down." Although Potter suggests many ways in which we do this, he has not by any means exhausted the possibilities, and you can find them all around you. The classroom is a complex of relationships between professor and students and among the students themselves. Professors are usually one up at the beginning of a course because students are defined as one down. From that time on, students may try to become "even" or to get "one up" on the professor by finding inconsistencies in assignments, errors in lecture notes, weaknesses in lecture arguments, or any way a student hopes to remove himself from a one-down position. Becoming friends with the professor is one way of getting "even" but if the whole class becomes friends with the professor, you have no advantage over other students, which may be another aim.

Games are, as we said at the beginning of this chapter, those distortions of interactions which occur frequently enough in enough situations to create an identifiable pattern. The wife who says to the husband, "It's eight o'clock" is not overtly nagging him to get ready but merely telling him the time in case he accuses her of nagging. She gets the job done but also remains safely in command of the process. The student who turns in a term paper and announces to the teacher that he was up all night for three nights getting it done is hoping to get more than the content of the paper evaluated and to place a sympathetic teacher one down when it comes to the grade.

Several factors are necessary in order for games to develop among people: (a) there must be clearly defined roles so those who are one up know it and those who are one down know it, (b) participants must be aware of their own self-image in relation to those roles, (c) there must be some kind of adversary situation or competition involved, either for resolving a task goal or maintaining an emotional edge on the other, and (d) the more prescribed the rules of interaction and the roles of the participants, the greater the opportunity for games. In other words, the more things we expect to happen and the more clearly we see ourselves in relation to others, the more opportunity there is for abusing the rules or the other person.

Games will be successful insofar as the winner is known, and the loser is somehow made uncomfortable. This discomfort may take the form of physical loss (money, prizes, labors, etc.) or psychological loss (embarrassment, confusion, anger, remorse, etc.). Very often the goals of a game are not the same for task as for process—we would like to win at the task and remain one up while we are doing it, but even if we were to lose the task (as a game of tennis or golf) and still manage to take away the winner's pleasure of winning, we have won the process.

"It's eight o'clock," says the wife. If the husband gets ready on time she can say, "You would not have been ready if I hadn't told you. . . ." and he gets angry. If he does not get ready on time, she can say "I told you, but you didn't listen. . . ." and he gets angry. Whichever way the task comes out (getting ready) she can win the process (being one up when he gets angry).

The "double bind" was described by Gregory Bateson[10] and his associates. This game is one of damned if you do and damned if you don't. It is a no-win situation for the victim. The mother says to the small child, "Come sit on my lap," and he feels wanted. Then when he is sitting on her lap she says, "My, you're heavy," and he doesn't know which message is the real one. If he refuses to sit on her lap and be too heavy, she can accuse him of not loving her.

Included in games is the process of button-pushing. The vicious form of this game is played by finding out what beliefs, objects, words, noises, etc., will make another person upset, and then making use of this information. A friend tells you she can't stand the sound of a fingernail on a blackboard, so at the first opportunity you scra-a-a-a-pe your nail down the blackboard when she can hear it; you pushed her button. The professor has an announced dislike for sleeping in class, so you pretend to sleep just to push his button. In each case, you have a defense that (a) either "I didn't know you were so sensitive about it," or superior self or (b) "I didn't realize that bothered you," or injured innocence. Either response is designed to leave you one up.

Button-pushing is a benign form of the game called "Hurt" which was developed publicly in the improvisations of comedians like Mike Nichols and Elaine May some years ago. In Hurt the design is to find a sensitive spot in the other person and work at it until the other gives signs of being hurt by keeping quiet, getting angry, crying, or quitting the game.

All of us have things which push our buttons. In questionnaires to student groups we have found that actions and physical objects (gum chewing, careless smoking, not placing the cap on toothpaste, too much makeup, etc.) are less offensive than verbal patterns which threaten our self-image (being accused unfairly of not doing my best, being dishonest, being stubborn, being embarrassed in public, being ridiculed, being sarcastic, etc.) or expressions of closed-minded attitudes ("That's the way we do it here," not listening to an argument, knowing it all, being a religious bigot, making racial slurs, not being open to suggestions, etc.). We can

[10]*Gregory Bateson, D. D. Jackson, J. Haley, and J. H. Weakland, "Toward a Theory of Schizophrenia,"* Behavioral Science, *1956, vol. 1, pp. 251–264.*

THE DYNAMICS OF INTERPERSONAL COMMUNICATION

push others' buttons very easily by what we say, not only by what we do. As consumers of services and purchasers of goods, we are slowly becoming aware of some of the games being played by those who would sell us things. The Better Business Bureaus in many cities have for years attempted to protect consumers against fraudulent activities, and more recently national attention has been focused on consumer activities which involve, if not fraud, at least not full disclosure of what is being bought, for how much, and on what terms.

Not all sellers of goods will engage in games. Not all games are fraudulent in terms of what a buyer receives. A great deal of buying and selling, however, is based more than a little on what the seller knows about "buyer psychology," that is, how we are somehow manipulated by process into the task of buying.

Advertising a shampoo does not directly tell us what it does for our hair; it represents the shampoo as making the user lovelier. A toothpaste will be represented as making you "kissable" rather than taking care of your dental machinery. An automobile will be made a youthful symbol, a symbol of power, of luxury, or of some kind of happiness—not transportation. A cola drink is sold as fun, fun, fun, and not refreshment. When cigarettes were advertised on television they were sold as a kind of romantic togetherness, freshness of spring, manliness for some brands, womanliness for some others. In brief, through "romantic fallacy" the commodity advertised became a fulfillment of our emotional and psychological needs rather than our needs to eat, drink, clean our hair or teeth, or drive to work.

One form of advertising game can be called "loose logic." A beer is advertised as being brewed by the oldest company in America, as if the age of the company was a determinant in the quality of their beer or your taste for it. A "mountain-grown" coffee advertises itself as being special because of that feature which is common to growing any coffee, just as a few years ago we were sold "shade-grown" coffee, little realizing that coffee plants grow in the shade as a rule not as an exception.

These are often coupled with another consumer game, "word magic," where we manipulate a product to give it an additional appeal.

We have already touched on the "romantic fallacy" kind of advertising in which immediate romance awaits the user. We buy a dentifrice (it is not called toothpaste any more), or hair preparation (instead of shampoo), or a breath freshener (it used to be mouthwash). A Chevrolet is no longer just a plain Chevvie, but may be a Sting Ray, Impala, or Bel Air, while Ford has a Mustang, Pinto, Thunderbird, and LTD.

There is also the "public service pitch" advertising where a product is tied to some national cause. Gasoline companies are capitalizing on "antipollution" beliefs by bringing out their low-lead gasolines in their advertising campaigns, regardless of how many automobiles may be using it. Another gasoline producer shows how careful they are in off-shore drilling

> ### MAN HOOKED OUT OF $66 IN SALU PARK "PIGEON DROP"
>
> *A 79-year old Alton man was robbed out of $66 Friday afternoon when two men worked the "pigeon drop" confidence game on him as he walked through Salu Park, according to Alton police.*
>
> *Jack Williams, 1933 Oakwood, said he was walking through the park when a man he did not know approached him and asked if Williams knew his uncle.*
>
> *Williams told the man he had not heard the missing uncle's name, and the man then explained that he had recently inherited $8,000 and wanted to contact the uncle. The man showed Williams a wad of cash as he told the story.*
>
> *Another man then joined the two and the first man repeated the story of his recent inheritance and said he had to go downtown for a briefcase with even more money that had been left him.*
>
> *The second man offered to drive the first downtown but the first said he didn't feel safe carrying the $8,000 and asked Williams if he would hold it in the park until the two returned.*
>
> *Williams said he would and the first man produced the wad with a blue handkerchief tied around it.*
>
> *He instructed Williams to place any money he might have in with the larger sum so that both parties would lose out if Williams was not careful and lost the money or had it stolen while the others were gone.*
>
> *Williams gave the man $66 and the man placed it in the handkerchief—or so it appeared to Williams—and tucked the blue bundle into Williams' shirt.*
>
> *Later, Williams walked to his son's house and told the story, and the son, suspecting something wrong, opened the handkerchief and found only newspaper the size of currency.* (Alton Evening Telegraph, June 5, 1971. Reprinted by permission of the publisher.)

operations to avoid those damaging oil spills which may be implied to be the fault of other companies. Life insurance companies show us how they invest in our cities to make life better for the disadvantaged. Chemical companies try to sell us an image of better living for everyone, better foods, an end to disease, etc. It is not too much of a leap for an advertiser from pollution to "fill it up" at a gasoline station, or aspirin from a company which is doing so much research on making life better.

These games we have cited: romantic fallacy, loose logic, word magic, and the public service pitch may be relatively harmless since the consumer will actually receive something in exchange for his dollar spent. Whether or not the product is as reliable as it is advertised to be, or whether or not it is really good for us, are personal decisions. But a transaction is made, and we get something for our purchase which at least represents the actual money spent, even if we do not achieve immediate romantic success or fame by that purchase.

Under considerable attack in recent years is the form of advertising called "bait and switch" which at its best is only a clever selling device, but at its worst is outright fraud and has been so labeled by watchdog agencies. It works like this: the advertiser announces a product—vacuum cleaners and sewing machines are the favorites—as "reconditioned like new for only $14.59." The buyer goes to the store and sees the item advertised. At this point the salesman will either (a) say their only reconditioned models have been already sold, or (b) demonstrate the reconditioned model so the buyer sees how poorly it operates. When the buyer finds out for himself that the $14.59 model vacuum cleaner would not pull dirt from the floor he has been baited and is ready for the switch. The salesman shows the buyer a new model priced at only $79.95 which is powerful, beautiful, and (lo and behold) available for only $14.59 down and easy monthly payments. The prospective buyer will fall for this switch often enough to have made "bait and switch" a classic in questionable selling practices.

Read the Label

Labeling of all kinds has come under scrutiny by agencies of the government. Efforts are being made to save consumers from their misperceptions of the symbolic world to help us avoid believing that the label or the picture is the thing it stands for. So widespread is this faith in words, that the following conversation was overheard at a carnival where a boy and his girl were standing in front of a sideshow tent arguing about the exhibit inside:

Girl: "Is that giant squid really alive?"
Boy: "It can't be. Not that big a one."
Girl: "Why not?"
Boy: "It just can't be. The tent isn't big enough. The tent is lots smaller than the sign."
Girl: "But it's alive. I know it is. The sign says so."

The enterprising advertiser probably knows more about how you react to the verbal world than you do. He makes use of that knowledge to sell his goods legitimately or to bilk an unsuspecting buyer who ends up not getting what he thought he was getting. None of us can become expert buyers of every kind of commodity; we can't know enough about buying fresh vegetables, household appliances, cars, books, toys, insurance, investments, pencils, or lawn seed. Even if we cannot know the quality comparisons of all items we are tempted to buy, we can all learn the principles of consumer games. We can be aware of the symbolic techniques used by advertisers and sales people to sell us things. We can analyze the arguments used on us in terms of the verbal mythology that words actually mean something. We can avoid being trapped by our own belief in the symbolic world.

One final example: Would you send the $2.50 asked for in this advertisement, with a guarantee that if the bugs were not killed according to directions you would get double your money back?

KILLS ON CONTACT all flying, crawling insects. Rid your home of these pests for only $2.50, postage 25 cents extra. Not harmful to children or pets when used as directed. No refills to buy; lasts for years with proper care. No moving parts to wear out. Leaves no unpleasant odor. Safe and easy to use. Operates on proven percussion principle; complete directions included free.

If you send your money you will receive just what was advertised: a fly swatter usually costing about fifty cents.

BIBLIOGRAPHY

Bennis, W. G., et al.: *Intrapersonal Dynamics,* The Dorsey Press, Homewood, Ill., 1964.

Berne, E.: *The Structure and Dynamics of Organizations and Groups,* J. B. Lippincott Company, Philadelphia, 1963.

Berne, E.: *Games People Play,* Grove Press, Inc., New York, 1964.

Festinger, L. and J. Thibaut: "Interpersonal Communication in Small Groups," *Journal of Abnormal and Social Psychology,* 1951, vol. 46, pp. 92–100.

Haley, J.: "The Art of Psychoanalysis," in S. I. Hayakawa (ed.), *The Use and Misuse of Language,* Fawcett Publications, Inc., Greenwich, Conn., 1962.

Heider, F.: *The Psychology of Interpersonal Relations,* John Wiley & Sons, Inc., New York, 1958.

Maurer, D. W.: *The Big Con,* The Bobbs-Merrill Company, Inc., Indianapolis, 1940.

Mead, G. H.: *Mind, Self, and Society,* The University of Chicago Press, Chicago, 1934.

Potter, S.: *The Complete Upmanship,* Holt, Rinehart and Winston, Inc., New York, 1970.

Szasz, T.: *The Myth of Mental Illness,* Harper & Brothers, New York, 1961.

Zalesnik, A., and D. Moment: *The Dynamics of Interpersonal Behavior,* John Wiley and Sons, Inc., New York, 1964.

NONVERBAL COMMUNICATION— Chapter 12
THE SOUNDS OF SILENCE

In an earlier chapter (Chapter 3) we contended that to be communicated at all an experience has to be translated into some symbolic code. As far as we know now, what goes on in a person's brain does not get transmitted to another person's brain directly without the mediation of a symbolic system. So far in this book, we have concentrated mostly on verbal systems, that is, communication through the use of words, and have neglected a fundamental aspect of everyday communication: nonverbal communication, or communication without words.

The study of nonverbal communication is relatively recent. For a long time people felt that, unless words were involved, communication did not take place. This attitude was, and still is, reinforced by the fact that in our culture we place a strong emphasis on the virtues of speech. In spite of a few wise sayings ("silence is golden," or "one picture is worth a thousand words") we value glibness, praise a "gift of gab," and consider silence in many social situations a weakness. In groups, silent members are more often than not perceived as the least influential members of the group.

This common attitude about silence, or the absence of verbalized noise, is rooted in a misconception about the nature of communication; that communication can be turned on and off; on when we talk, off when we do not. Nothing could be more misleading. There is no opposite to communication. As we will see in this chapter, one cannot *not* communicate. Our silences and other nonverbal aspects of communication are no more random than our words. They, too, are systematic expressions of meanings which we use, often quite unconsciously, in our interpersonal contacts.

The range of nonverbal communication is impressive. In this chapter, we will deal with four aspects of nonverbal communication: (1) silences, (2) how we send and receive nonverbal messages, (3) some cultural patterns of nonverbal communication and, (4) some characteristics of nonverbal communication.

SILENCES
Silences Occur in Interpersonal Communication

You and your new date are driving on your way to a movie. After some time of idle chatting about the weather, where you go to school, where she goes to school, what courses you are taking, and the kind of movies you like, you run out of things to say, and silence sets in—long, heavy, embarrassing silence. She just sits there, and you can't think of another thing to say. In desperation you turn on the radio.

You were just introduced to a person sitting next to you at a dinner and after the usual small talk neither of you finds a thing to say, and the best you can do is to stare at your napkin or appear very busy fiddling with the silverware.

These two examples are not unusual. They illustrate two principles about silence: (1) Silences are an integral part of interpersonal communication. They occur more often than we think. (2) Silences in many cases are perceived as embarrassing. We somehow feel they should not happen, and when they occur we try desperately to fill the gaps they create. Silences, however, are not to be equated with the absence of communication. Silences are a natural and fundamental aspect of communication, often ignored because misunderstood.

Effective communication between people depends heavily on silences because people take turns at talking and at being silent when listening. Unless one is silent, one cannot fully listen. Unless we know that silences are a part of the gamut of communication, we will continue to be afraid of them and avoid them instead of making full use of them.

Silences Are Not Random

Perhaps you have noted that we use the word "silences" in its plural form. This is deliberate. We want to stress over again that there are many different types of silences, each with a meaning of its own and different communication implications and consequences. When we say we like silence or are afraid of it, we really fail to acknowledge the many differences between types of silences. If one is to understand communication, he must differentiate between the many types of silences and meet them with an appropriate behavior.

For example, (1) silence when we are terribly angry, frustrated, gritting our teeth, ready to blow up and yet tensing up to not let the steam out, is different from the (2) silence which occurs when we are attentively listening to an important broadcast or a fascinating lecture or story. In both cases no word may be spoken, but what goes on inside you in terms of feelings, reactions, emotions, and thoughts is quite different. Not only does your silence stem from a different reason, but your actions, expressions, and movements will reflect that difference. (3) Silence when you listen but are bored is different from the preceding two silences. The silence of boredom expresses a withdrawal from the situation, a negative evaluation of what is going on, and implies an attitude of superiority which often offends those toward whom it is directed, if they perceive it. The bored student listlessly looking outside the window indicates through his facial expressions that the teacher is not worth listening to, a reaction the teacher will likely resent if he "reads" the student's silence. Earlier in this chapter we mentioned (4) the silence which occurs when we cannot think of a thing to say (on a date, at a dinner, or in any situation involving people we do not know well). During these social encounters, talk is expected. Silence represents what is feared the most, and when it occurs, makes us feel terribly inadequate and self-conscious. (5) Silence, when you think about a point made by a speaker, is different from (6) the silence which occurs when you do not understand what the speaker said. In the latter you may be so confused you do not even know what to ask in order to get some clarification.

(7) Silence can be reverent, meditative, or contemplative. Perhaps you silently pray; or perhaps you take a walk and encounter something so beautiful that you are speechless and the sight stirs deep emotions in you. (8) The silence of allness, the dogmatic "there is no more to be said on the matter, that's all there is to it" is quite different from the (9) silence of lovers or friends who may simply hold each other's hand, and do not need to say anything at all to communicate their feelings. The latter is a comfortable silence. A silence you do not need to break. A silence you treasure because it reflects the depth of a relationship. People who know each other well often do not need to talk to communicate well. A glance, an understanding smile, or a look is all that is necessary. Words are not needed. (10) The silence of grief is another type of silence. "So they sat down with him upon the ground seven days and seven nights and no one spoke a word unto him. For they saw his grief was very great" (Book of Job). This is a difficult silence. We know intuitively that words don't begin to express the sympathy or the concern we want to share with a person who grieves. Sometimes, just being there is enough. (11) Silence can be a challenge. The pouting child or the stubborn and angry friend, or the classroom toward the very last minutes of a period when the teacher asks, "Do you have any questions," and students almost dare each other to say one word which might trigger the teacher to continue talking after the bell.

This list of silences is not exhaustive. There are many, many different types of silences which mean a lot of different things. What we are trying to establish here is an awareness that silences cannot be lumped all together. Each must be interpreted on its own. The reactions to each of these silences should be different because they each mean something different. You do not respond the same way to someone who is silent because he shares grief with a friend, and to someone who is silent because he is angry. Oftentimes, though, we misunderstand a person's silence. We frequently think that silence is a sign of anger, hostility, or withdrawal, not realizing it may mean other things. Typical communication breakdowns between roommates often start this way. Mary does not speak to Sally one morning because she is thinking about an important assignment due that day which she must finish. Sally, who does not recall the assignment, thinks Mary is angry at her. Without checking any further, Sally starts pouting because she is upset to think Mary is angry at her. Mary, noticing Sally's silence, may decide not to speak to her until she is in a better mood, thus confirming Sally's conviction that Mary is angry at her. A whole chain of negative reactions can be easily set off, each girl's silence reinforcing her belief that the other must be angry at her. They are both on their way to a classic case of communication breakdown.

A sensitivity to silences is imperative to two-way communication. This means sensitivity to your own silences and to the silences of others to whom you would speak. If you are silent because you are thinking about a point the speaker made, or if you are puzzled by what he said, you should let him know. If someone is silent when you speak you must be able to read the cues that will tell you the reasons for his particular silence. Does he misunderstand you? Does he clam up because he is resisting what you are saying? Is he bored? Did you lose him? Unless you know (1) that silences can be interpreted in many different ways and (2) that you can learn to read the cues which will tell you what they mean, your interpersonal communication may not be as effective as it could be.

There are many cues available which help understand a person's silence. The way a person moves, his gestures, and his facial expressions will tell you a great deal about the reasons for his silence. We will analyze these in detail in another section of this chapter.

Silences May Be Appropriate or Inappropriate

Just as we may say the wrong thing at the wrong time, we may respond silently to a situation requiring talk, and not be silent when we should. When a person is engaged in some serious thinking, he will probably not welcome the friend who comes barging in and talks a mile a minute about some trivial things. When people are worshiping in church, they usually resent the loud intrusion by tourists exclaiming on the beauty of the ceiling or the woodwork.

On the other hand, in some social situations, you may be called a snob or someone may clap you on the shoulder and say, "Whassamatter, you're being awful quiet," when others think you should be talking. The conversation need not be significant, but silence may be perceived as an indicator you do not approve of what's going on or that you would rather be some place else. Even if this is true, you know that it is not polite to give that impression. So, usually, we all chat away at the same level as the rest of the crowd. We talk about the weather, the decor of the room, what we do for a living, and these simple exchanges set up avenues for further communication as we described in Chapter 11 under "phatic communion" (see page 154). Being silent in such situations seems to have very little virtue, as your social acceptability depends on your saying something, however inane it may be. Silence when the situation requires some

THE DYNAMICS OF INTERPERSONAL COMMUNICATION

form of verbal exchange makes you appear antisocial and drives people away from you. Another man's silence is not a reassuring factor. It is often perceived as something threatening. So, when your neighbor hollers at you, "Nice day," you usually come back with an equally profound, "It sure is." Both of you have made contact and feel reassured you are not isolated.

HOW WE SEND AND RECEIVE NONVERBAL COMMUNICATION

We said earlier that in order to understand another person's silence one should be sensitive to the nonverbal cues that are being sent out constantly. We send and receive a complex system of nonverbal signals which consists of tone of voice, body movements, gestures, things we surround ourselves with, and a whole range of messages conveyed by touch. Actually we often interpret these nonverbal signals without quite realizing it when we form impressions of people, when we decide whether we like someone or not. In our interpersonal communication we make many decisions based on an intuitive interpretation of the nonverbal code, such as when to laugh, when to move, when to relax or tense up, and when to continue or to end a conversation.

In this section we will examine the various ways by which we send and receive these nonverbal signals.

Paralanguage

The spoken word is never neutral. It is always affected by the tone of voice, the emphasis or inflections given, the breaks in the sentence, the speed of delivery, the degree of loudness or softness, and the pitch of the voice. These nonverbal factors are called *paralanguage.* As you know, a simple "yes" can express a lot of different feelings such as anger, frustration, resignation, disinterest, agreement, or challenge. A short sentence such as "I'll do it" may "mean":

"I'll be really happy to do it."
"I'll do it, but it's the last time."
"You always make me do what you want."
"All right, you win."
"Don't worry, I'll take care of it."
"You're so dumb I better take care of it myself."

Which of the "meanings" is implied can usually be determined by the tone of voice, the inflection of the voice, or the stress placed on each separate word. The meaning of the sentence does not lie in the words alone, but also in the vocal expressions, or paralanguage, which are always associated with the words.

Some years ago a record came out in which two renowned actors carried on a ten-minute dialogue using only two words "John" and "Marsha." The two talented artists managed to express so many different feelings and emotions that the story they were telling came through loud and clear. Meaning was exclusively carried through the paralanguage.

In everyday life we naturally rely on the words themselves *plus* their paralanguage features to develop our meanings about what people are telling us. There are times, however, when we get distracted and miss the words themselves. If we have to respond and do not wish to admit we have not been paying close attention, we will rely on the paralanguage features alone to interpret what was said. This happens often at cocktail parties where people involved in small talk do not pay full attention to what is said and respond almost automatically. It may be pouring rain but if someone says in a convincing tone that "It is really nice out, isn't it?" chances are the response will be an equally convincing "It sure is."

We often get upset not so much at *what* people say, but at *how* they say it. "He sounds so sure of himself, I always feel like contradicting him." We tend to respond to people in relation to these paralanguage features without quite realizing what exactly we react to. If we can learn to pay attention to how we respond to people's tone of voice or intonations, we will understand better why we may be attracted to some people and turned off by others.

Gestures

Gestures were probably one of the first means of communicating human beings developed, long before oral language appeared. All cultures have a system of meaningful gestures which either accompany spoken language or stand alone in conveying a particular message. We nod our heads to say "yes" (in some cultures, nodding means "no") and shake our heads sideways to say "no." The hitchhiker's hand gesture is recognizable in most automobile-using cultures. We extend our hand to shake someone else's as a greeting and not as a hostile gesture. The language of the deaf is probably one of the most sophisticated systems of sign language.

We usually accompany our speech with a considerable number of hand gestures. If you've ever tried to give directions to someone over the telephone, you probably have caught yourself uselessly waving a hand in the air. Some cultures are known to be more expressive with the hands than others. The French, Spanish, and Italian, for instance, generally Mediterranean cultures, are quite effusive with their hand gestures. Sometimes certain gestures become automatic. Students are usually quick to recognize the familiar gestures of their professors. Impersonators of famous people rely on pose and gestures, in addition to their voice imitations, to create their characters. Gestures are often used to give emphasis to our words. Sometimes, if a person's timing is bad, when the emphasis occurs on the wrong word, we get the impression that he may not be sincere.

THE DYNAMICS OF INTERPERSONAL COMMUNICATION

We are seldom immobile or expressionless. Our face moves and our body moves, and these movements communicate a great deal about our feelings, emotions, reactions, etc. Some of the time these movements are conscious and intentional, as when we deliberately smile at a friend, frown to express dissatisfaction, or raise an eyebrow to show surprise. Much of the time, however, these movements are so much a part of us they appear unintentional and unconscious. When we attempt to hide a feeling, we often give ourselves away without realizing it; the way we move toward or away from a person, the way we sit—tense, relaxed, on the edge of the chair, slouched, etc. We tend to lean forward when we feel involved and interested, and to lean back when we are not. The way we walk often indicates to others if we feel good, happy, cheerful or sad, gloomy, tired, or dejected. We indicate our perception of status by our postures. We tend to relax around people of equal or lower status and tense up around people whom we perceive as having higher status. We sometimes feel that someone is disrespectful simply because he talks in a more relaxed manner than we think is appropriate.

How we look at a person communicates a great deal. A teacher sensitive to nonverbal movements and expressions can tell a resistive, belligerent, challenging student before that student ever opens his mouth. There is no magic, or as we often call it for lack of a better word, "intuition" involved. It is a simple interpretation of subtle yet visible cues which are sent or given away by the student by his posture and the way he looks at the teacher. Whether our looks stay on a person too long or too little will also communicate something.

In this regard we have unconsciously developed a whole system of rules that we apply to our interpersonal communication. One of the rules says that *when we talk to someone we must look at them, and they must look at us,* preferably in the eyes or in the face. We usually feel uncomfortable when our listeners look everywhere in the room but at us. Students who look out the window, at the ceiling, or concentrate on what is happening in the back of the room irritate teachers because they violate the rule. Teachers who lecture without ever looking beyond their notes usually annoy students because they, too, violate the rule. We do not like, nor trust, people who speak to us without looking at us. Shifty eyes appear to mean insincerity.

On the other hand, rule number two says *if we do not talk to someone, we should not look at them*—or *if we look, we must talk.* Its corollary says that if you don't look, you don't have to talk. It is considered impolite to stare at someone we are not actively communicating with. When we are not talking to someone we usually avoid looking at him. If we do look and get caught by the person we have been staring at, we usually feel embarrassed and quickly shift our look away, or start talking. Observe what happens in public hallways, in schools, or in offices. Two people are walking toward each other from different ends of the hall. Most of the time they have noticed each other from a distance and need not acknowledge each other yet. However, as they get closer, they must do one of two things if they want to follow the rules: (*a*) They can pretend they do not see each other and thus do not have to say anything to each other (corollary of rule two: if you don't look, you don't have to talk). In that case, they will concentrate on their feet or on what they carry, or will look straight ahead of them in order to avoid meeting the other person's eyes. (*b*) They can look at each other, but if they choose this course of action, they must acknowledge each other by a few words or at least a nod of the head (rule two: if you look, you must talk). Sometimes the two people will meet each other's eyes and say, "Hi" just a little too soon. Then, when they actually pass each other, they must acknowledge each other again, which is usually awkward, since they did that just a minute earlier. They will usually overcome the awkwardness by joking about it. In any case, we find it difficult to look and be looked at and not to talk. If we look at someone and for some reason cannot talk to them, we will look away if his eyes meet ours or we will wave or smile. If we do not look away we have to acknowledge him in some way.

Object Language

Object language refers to the meanings we attribute to objects with which we surround ourselves. The clothes and jewelry we wear, our hairstyles, and the decorative objects in a house are all part of object language. They say something about us because they represent to some extent deliberate choices we make. Clothing and jewelry are particularly revealing. We usually dress differently for different occasions, and if we don't we are still communicating something about us, about our attitudes toward others, our sense of appropriateness, our upbringing, our values. Clothing is symbolic. Some young people's attire is rich in colorful symbols of their choice. Some people are so concerned about what they communicate with their clothes that they will only buy them in certain stores which guarantee them the particular kind of status they seek, whether they be secondhand stores, army surplus stores, or fashionable boutiques. A wedding band or an engagement ring communicate something quite specific about a person.

We often react to others in terms of what they wear and what this means to us. A man wearing a police uniform has told us nonverbally a great deal, if not about himself personally, at least about the role he can be expected to play in certain situations.

All material objects help us in making inferences about the person who displays them. We cannot ignore these objects and decide they do not count, just as we cannot decide that a person's words do not count. It occurs too often, unfortunately, that the inferences we make may be wrong or the objects' meaning misinterpreted. So do verbal breakdowns

THE DYNAMICS OF INTERPERSONAL COMMUNICATION

in communication. We must be cautious in interpreting the nonverbal messages communicated through dress and other material objects, just as we must be careful in interpreting a person's words, but we must remember that the choice of what to wear and what to say is still ours, and we have to take the responsibility for, and sometimes the consequences of, the misunderstandings they might generate. If we truly wish to communicate effectively with others, we cannot operate on the assumption that it's their responsibility to understand us. We have the responsibility of helping them understand us. Just as we do not speak Chinese to a Frenchman and expect him to understand, we perhaps should not be surprised that certain clothes or hairstyles may be misunderstood in some situations. If you think that you should not be judged for what you wear, remember that, whether you like it or not, this is a part of communication, and therefore says something about you.

Tactile Communication

Communication by touch is one of the first modes of communication of the human being. Infants learn much about their environment by touching, feeling, cuddling, and tasting. Linus' security blanket in Charles Schultz' cartoons is a symbol of all the objects children become attached to, which they particularly like to touch, feel, or keep. We communicate a great deal by touching. A pat on the back, shaking a hand, or holding a hand can express more than a lengthy speech. Lovers know this. Mothers do too. In their book, *Speech and Man,* Brown and Van Riper recall an incident told by one of their students which dramatically illustrates the power of a touch.[1]

A student was presenting to a class the view that verbal language, in the main, disguises the speaker, and that the real burden of a communication is sent in the nonverbal broadcast. This he illustrated with a story not to be forgotten. He said he was driving on a superhighway one morning at dawn, and an automobile approaching at a high speed began to sway crazily from one side of the road to the other. It eventually plunged off the road, crashed into a concrete pole which broke off and fell over the automobile, bringing it to a halt. The student stopped and ran to the man's aid. The victim was hanging out of his automobile, apparently dead, his faced covered with broken windshield glass. The student began to lift the glass from the man's face and the man shook his head slowly. Without opening his eyes, he mumbled, "Give me your hand." The student took the man's hand and in a

[1]*Charles T. Brown and Charles Van Riper,* Speech and Man, *Prentice-Hall, Inc., Englewood Cliffs, N.J., 1966, pp. 54–55. Reprinted by permission of the authors and the publisher.*

few minutes the man died. The student said, "In those moments I was told about death as no words will ever tell me."

In the American culture, except in a few well-defined situations, touching is linked with intimate interpersonal relationships, and is thus taboo for most other types of relationships. Many people thus refrain from touching others in more casual encounters for fear their behavior might be misconstrued or simply because they are afraid of or do not like physical contacts. When they must stand in line, Americans will usually form an orderly single line in which everyone waits patiently for his turn. In Arab countries, on the other hand, lines are almost unheard of, and considerable pushing, shoving, and touching are involved in most gatherings, and such behavior is not considered distasteful. American children learn relatively young to kiss sparingly their relatives hello and good bye. Spanish children not only frequently kiss their relatives, but adult friends and acquaintances, as well, when they encounter them and depart from them.

Touching is a powerful communicative tool and serves to express a tremendous range of feelings, such as fear, love, anxiety, warmth, coldness, etc.

CULTURAL PATTERNS FOR NONVERBAL MESSAGES

The anthropologist Edward T. Hall in his fascinating book *The Silent Language*[2] was one of the first scholars to probe into the cultural dimensions of interpersonal communication. Interpersonal communication does not occur in a vacuum. It takes place in a cultural context that is a system of norms and rules which determine to a large degree the variables of the communication process. We are usually unaware of the cultural factors which influence our communicative behavior because they are so familiar and "normal" to us. We sometimes see them when we contrast them to those of a foreign culture. The two most powerful factors which affect our interpersonal communication are time and space.

Time

Time is a form of interpersonal communication. In our culture, time is almost treated as a thing; we gain time, waste it, give it, and take it. Time is precious, a rare commodity in our rushed lives. Time speaks.

In the American urban white culture, punctuality is valued, and tardiness is considered insulting. Being late for an appointment or in turning in an assignment may lead to unpleasant consequences. However, what

[2]*Edward T. Hall,* The Silent Language, *Fawcett Publications, Inc., Greenwich, Conn., 1959.*

is considered "late" varies not only with each individual and his personal sense of time but also with the situation, the other people involved, and with geographic areas. For example, you may have a very important appointment with a person of higher status than yours—perhaps a job interview. Usually, you will try to be "on time," and this may mean about five minutes before the appointed time to five minutes after. If you arrive fifteen minutes after the appointed time, you would probably apologize and offer some explanation for your delay. The kind and extent of your apologies and explanations will vary according to how late you are. If you are only five minutes late you may not have to say anything; ten minutes late, you may feel you have to briefly apologize but not give any reason for the delay. Half an hour late, you would probably apologize profusely and need to explain thoroughly what kept you. An hour late, you might not expect the other person to be still waiting for you. If the other person is still there (as when you pick up your date at her house, and show up an hour late) you expect her to be very upset.

With a close friend the extent of tardiness may be increased without drastic consequences, but, here too, a scale will be established in terms of whether you owe an apology or not, and, if so, the extent of that apology. Apologies are needed at some point, however, because extreme tardiness may be taken as an insult or a sign or irresponsibility.

In some cultures, tardiness may not be perceived as insulting, and one can go to a meeting hours after the appointed time without upsetting anyone. In Mexico for example, it is not uncommon to arrive one hour and a half after the appointed time and still be considered on time. In America this would, of course, be considered very late and very rude. An American meeting a Mexican would feel insulted to have to wait so long and would probably expect a good story to account for such a delay. The American would be quite upset hearing no story, for the Mexican would, in his eyes, be on time and thus would not feel any need to explain anything. Unless we know and understand another culture's sense of time, we may get very frustrated, and this naturally affects the way we communicate with members of that culture.

Arriving early at an appointment also communicates as much as arriving late. In some circles where it is fashionable to be late to parties, the early arrival of a guest may throw the hostess in a panic, and she may be quite upset that her guest was not polite enough to arrive later.

Time communicates in other ways. A phone call at three A.M. somehow communicates a feeling of urgency and importance. People don't usually call you at that time of the night just to ask you how you are and to say, "Gee, it's been a while we have not seen each other."

If you are two hours late coming home during the day, your parents may be quite worried and upset, but their fears will be less intense than what they would be if you were two hours late after midnight.

Space

The space in which our interpersonal communication takes place affects us in many subtle ways that we are not always aware of. Each of us has a "personal space," a sort of invisible bubble around us, which we feel is ours and which we do not like to see intruded upon without express permission. While each of us sets his own personal boundaries, there are recognizable cultural patterns which regulate the handling of personal space and interpersonal distance.

The anthropologist, Edward T. Hall,[3] has identified three major interpersonal distances he calls "intimate," "social," and "public," which govern most of our interpersonal relationships. The "intimate" distance ranges from very close (3 to 6 inches)—soft whispers, secret or intimate communication—to close (8 to 12 inches)—confidential information—to near (12 to 20 inches)—soft voice. The "social" distance ranges from 20 inches to 5 feet, and the "public" distance from 6 feet to about 100 feet.

When people violate the unspoken rules of interpersonal distance (get too close when they should be at a social distance or stand too far when they are expected to be more intimate) we generally feel uncomfortable. When someone we did not invite comes too close to us, we tend to move away. Our territory is marked, and we may let others approach, but not too closely unless we specifically decide to let them. The uncomfortable feeling one gets in a crowded room often comes from the fact that too many people are too close to one another. If someone crowds you at the library or at the cafeteria by sitting too close to you, you unconsciously move away by moving your books, or your tray, or your chair away from the intruder. If for some reason the intruder moves closer, you try other avoidance behaviors. However, we rarely ask people in words to move away from us. If they do not respond appropriately by understanding our nonverbal avoidance moves, we usually change places in the library, or leave the cafeteria as soon as we can, feeling our lunch was spoiled.

Appropriate interpersonal distances vary from culture to culture. As Hall points out, the comfortable distance for most Americans to stand for social conversation is about 2 to 3 feet. In France, Mexico, Brazil, or in Arab countries, however, the comfortable distance is somewhat shorter than 2 feet. Should an American engage in conversation with an Arab, a subtle ballet is likely to follow: the Arab moves close to the American and looks intently in his eyes. The American, uncomfortable because the other one is too close, tries to re-establish a distance he finds less disturbing by moving back. The Arab, feeling the American is too far from him for social conversation, moves in closer, and the American moves back. Each feels somewhat upset about what they perceive as

___

[3]Edward T. Hall, op. cit., pp. 163–164.

"pushy" (the Arab moving in too close) or "unfriendly" (the American moving away).

Interpersonal distance is one of the ways we have to express feelings. We tend to move closer to people we like and away from people we do not, if we have a choice. We sometimes take great precautions to avoid walking near someone we do not like.

Special elements other than interpersonal distances also affect us. The arrangement of a room, the shape of a meeting table, or the size of a classroom in relation to the number of students occupying it all influence the development of interpersonal communication. Researchers have found, for example, that communication is distributed more evenly among people sitting at a *round* table than among people discussing at a *rectangular* table. At a rectangular table, people sitting at the ends are more likely to be talked to and to talk than the other group members.

CHARACTERISTICS OF NONVERBAL COMMUNICATION
The Impossibility of Not Communicating

We cannot not communicate. The nature of human communication is such that it is unavoidable. As we pointed out earlier, we can refrain from communication with words but we cannot escape nonverbal communication. To say nothing and remain silent is in itself a form of communication. We cannot stop from moving and expressing ourselves with our gestures and facial expressions. Whatever we do or do not do communicates something about ourselves. Interpersonal communication is inevitable when two people are together because all behavior has some message value.

Interpersonal communication may not be conscious or intentional, nor successful, but it takes place. Unless we know this principle and try to understand the communicative value of other people's behavior and our own, the potential for interpersonal breakdown looms large.

The Expression of Feelings and Emotions

Nonverbal communication is our primary mode to communicate feelings and emotions. We usually communicate about content and task through verbal communication. Verbal language is our primary mode to communicate cognitive information and deal with the business at hand. Nonverbal communication, however, is our mode to share feelings with one another and deal with the process of human relationships. Words usually carry *content information*, nonverbal communication expresses *affective information*. From the way we look at someone we may communicate love, hate, dislike, interest, trust, sexual desire, admiration, acceptance, scorn, etc.—a full range of human emotions which we do not usually express verbally. Gestures such as tapping our fingers or our foot can communicate impatience, boredom, or nervousness. Our face has innumerable ways of expressing likes and dislikes, approval and disapproval.

Information about Content

Nonverbal communication usually includes information about the content of a verbal message. Nonverbal communication gives us the clues that we need to interpret the verbal messages we hear. The same words (same content) said in different tones of voice should probably be interpreted differently. The tone of voice, among other nonverbal messages, is a clue as to which interpretation to make. Information about the content of a message is called *metacommunication*. Metacommunication refers to the nonverbal cues which tell us how we should understand what is said. Unless we are sensitive to that dimension of interpersonal communication, we may not interpret the words we hear adequately and increase the likelihood of having communication difficulties with those around us.

Reliability of Nonverbal Messages

Nonverbal messages are usually more reliable than verbal messages. In some interpersonal situations, the context of a message does not fit the affective information about that message. The man says "I love you," but somehow his tone of voice and other nonverbal signals he sends deny the very words he just spoke. He says one thing at the content level, but the opposite thing gets communicated nonverbally. What *is* the woman to believe? The words or the nonverbal signals?

A person assures you he trusts you, but his behavior toward you consistently denies his words. What are you to believe? The words or the behavior?

We know intuitively that words alone are not enough to establish the authenticity of a message. We know this because all of us know how easy it is to lie with words. We do it in many social situations when we assure a hostess we had a wonderful time and she replies she was delighted we could come, and neither really means the words spoken out of social courtesy. It is, however, much more difficult to "lie" nonverbally and express feelings we do not have. Talented professional actors are few. Most of us have difficulty faking over a long period of time the feelings we do not experience. A student will fake interest in the classroom for ten minutes maybe, but to sustain the fake interest for the whole class period without giving himself away is extremely difficult. Nonverbal expressions are thus considered more believable than words. If a verbal message conflicts with what is expressed nonverbally, we thus tend to believe the nonverbal message. We rely essentially on nonverbal cues to get our impressions of how honest other people are in their interpersonal relationships, rather than on what they tell us about themselves.

The people we trust are usually those people whose nonverbal behavior consistently confirms and reinforces the content of their verbal communication. We know they speak their true feelings, and they do as well as they say.

Benedict, R.: *Chrysanthemum and the Sword,* Houghton Mifflin Company, Boston, 1946.

Birdwhistell, R. L.: *Introduction to Kinesics,* University of Louisville Press, Louisville, Ky., 1952.

Birdwhistell, R. L.: *Kinesics and Contexts,* University of Pennsylvania Press, Philadelphia, 1970.

Bosmajian, H. A. (ed.): *The Rhetoric of Non Verbal Communication,* Scott, Foresman and Company, Glenview, Ill., 1971.

Calhoon, S. W.: "Population Density and Social Pathology," *Scientific American,* no. 206, 1962, pp. 139–146.

Fast, J.: *Body Language,* M. Evans and Company, Philadelphia, 1970.

Goffman, E.: *Behavior in Public Places,* The Free Press, New York, 1963.

Hall, E. T.: *The Silent Language,* Fawcett Publications, Inc., Greenwich, Conn., 1959.

Hall, E. T.: *The Hidden Dimension,* Doubleday & Company, Inc., Garden City, N.Y., 1966.

McLuhan, M.: *Understanding the Media: The Extensions of Man,* McGraw Hill Book Company, New York, 1965.

Ruesch, J., and W. Kees, *Non Verbal Communication,* University of California Press, Berkeley, 1956.

Satir, V.: *Conjoint Family Therapy,* rev. ed., Science & Behavior Books, Inc., Palo Alto, Calif., 1967.

Sommer, R.: *Personal Space,* Prentice-Hall, Inc., Englewood Cliffs, N.J., 1969.

Watzlawick, P., J. H. Beavin, and D. D. Jackson: *Pragmatics of Human Communication,* W. W. Norton & Company, Inc., New York, 1967.

BIBLIOGRAPHY

Chapter 13   LISTENING—IS ANYONE THERE ?

How do you feel when you are not listened to? Have you ever been in a situation where it became apparent that the person you were talking to was, in fact, mentally miles away from you and had not paid the least attention to your fascinating story? Pretty unpleasant, isn't it?

We can say quite safely without qualifications that people in general do not know how to listen. Yet we all have ears, and most of us have no fundamental physical deficiency in our hearing mechanism. Yet we do not listen well. Many of our interpersonal communication problems can be traced to just this: we do not know how to listen effectively.

Daniel Katz,[1] a communication scholar, wrote some years ago that the physical barriers to communication had all but disappeared, but that the psychological barriers remained. Mission Control can send the astronauts to the moon and back. We can watch live on television the first men landing on the moon and hear the President talk to the two astronauts standing at attention hundreds of thousands of miles away. Soon, telephone companies tell us, we will be able to talk to people on the telephone and *see* them on a private television screen hooked up with the receiver. The technological "miracles" surprise hardly anyone. Actually, they have become such a part of our American life that most people were quite bored with the third moon mission up until the time a crisis developed and it looked as though the astronauts were in danger and might not come back.

However, if the physical barriers of communication have disappeared, the psychological barriers still remain. We still do not understand our children, our students, our teachers, or our friends. We still have difficulty making sense to one another, and about one marriage in three ends up in divorce or separation.

Listening is a major ingredient of the communication process, and the tremendous lack of skill in that area is primarily responsible for many of the problems we experience with other people.

Norbert Wiener,[2] the mathematician, wrote that "Speech is a joint game between the talker and the listener against the forces of confusion." Unless both make the effort, interpersonal communication is quite hopeless.

[1]*Daniel Katz, "Psychological Barriers to Communication," in* Mass Communication, *Wilbur Schramm (ed.), The University of Illinois Press, Urbana, 1960, p. 316. (Originally published in* Annals of the American Academy of Political and Social Sciences, *March 1947.)*

[2]*Norbert Wiener,* The Human Use of Human Beings, *rev. ed., Doubleday & Company, Inc., Garden City, N.Y. 1954.*

THE DYNAMICS OF INTERPERSONAL COMMUNICATION

A few statistics will give you an idea of the extent of our problem. For years Ralph Nichols and his associates[3] conducted many intensive studies at the University of Minnesota to test the ability of people to understand and remember what they hear. The listening ability of thousands of students and hundreds of business and professional people was examined. In each case the people listened to a short talk and were later tested on their grasp of the content. These studies led to the following conclusions:

THE PROBLEM

1. Immediately after the average person has listened to someone talk, he remembers only about half of what he has heard—no matter how hard he thought he was listening.
2. The University of Minnesota studies, confirmed by studies at Florida State and Michigan State,[4] showed that two months later people will only remember 25 percent of what was said. In fact, people tend to forget one third to one half of what they hear *within eight hours.*

To summarize these statistics simply, we can say that whenever we listen to someone talk *we miss about half of what he tells us,* and two months later will remember only one fourth of what was said. When you think of all the time we spend being talked to, and all the energy we expend trying to remember the things we are told, it seems as though the whole thing was a pathetic waste of time. Think of all the hours you sit in a lecture hall listening to your professors, or all the time spent in an office listening to someone telling you what to do and how to do it. Think of all the hours spent telling things to your friends, colleagues, and parents. Perhaps not even one fourth of what you tell them will register and stick. What is the use of hearing lectures if you neither understand nor remember what is being said?

There are many complex reasons for poor listening. Oftentimes, we deliberately tune someone out because we don't like him, or we are bored or simply tired. However, many times our poor performance in listening is involuntary. To gain insight into the reasons for poor listening, we must dispel three myths which are quite pervasive and have obscured our understanding of the process.

SOME CAUSES OF POOR LISTENING

[3]*Ralph Nichols and Leonard Stevens, "Listening to People,"* Harvard Business Review, *vol. 35, 1957, no. 5.*

[4]*J. J. Kramar and T. R. Lewis, "Comparison of Visual and Non-Visual Listening,"* Journal of Communication, *1951, p. 16.*

Myth One: Listening Is a Natural Process

If we believe that listening is natural, then it follows we never need to learn it. Breathing is a natural process. No one had to teach you how to breathe. This was the very first thing you did, all on your own, the minute you were born. The myth that listening is something natural we do normally, unconsciously, and automatically is most detrimental to our improvement in that area. You will never learn what you believe you already know. If something is natural, inborn, automatic, then there is not much *you* can do about it. You have it, or you don't. You are good at it, or you are not.

An Ohio University study[5] showed that the average adult spends 70 percent of his waking time communicating in some form or another. It also showed the average adult spends his communicative time in the following way:

 9% writing
16% reading
30% speaking
45% listening

45 percent listening. Just about half of our time is spent listening. Think of a normal day and how you spend your communicative time. You spend many hours listening to people talk to you. If you logged your communication in its four forms, you might not be far off the 45 percent for the listening part. Yet, when you look at what we are taught from the time we are small children, you can see that learning to write and read takes up many of our school years. Actually, twelve years of English is not unusual, and when you go to college you still have to take English composition. All the years are spent to master the difficult skill of writing, a skill you will probably use only 9 percent of the time. Think how difficult it was to learn to read and how slowly many of us still read. Perhaps now you may be taking a speed-reading course to improve your skill. A skill you only use 16 percent of the time. Speaking was also a skill you had to learn. Your parents or teachers spent years trying to get you to say, "I am not" instead of "I ain't."

But, who taught you how to listen? Did you ever have a course in grade school, high school, or college to teach you how to listen more effectively? The answer is probably no. There are unfortunately too few of these courses available in the formal educational system. Why? Because for too long people have assumed that listening was natural and need not be learned. This is sheer nonsense. Listening is a skill just as writing, reading, and speaking. It needs to be learned. It certainly can be im-

[5]*Paul T. Rankin, "Measurement Of the Ability to Understand the Spoken Language," unpublished doctoral dissertation, The University of Michigan, 1926.*

THE DYNAMICS OF INTERPERSONAL COMMUNICATION

proved. Most of us learn how to listen on our own, picking up the habits of those around us. Unfortunately, those around us are not much better off than we are, for they picked it up on their own, too. You do not know many people of whom you can say, "He really is a good listener." So most of the time we pick up bad habits that will hinder our interpersonal communication for years.

Myth Two: Hearing and Listening Are the Same

Although, as Clevenger[6] pointed out, the relationship between hearing and listening is a complex one, and despite the fact that in some cases it is difficult to distinguish between the two processes, generally, hearing and listening are two distinct processes. Most of us, unfortunately, treat them as one and the same. We do this when we assume that just because we have uttered some words in front of someone else he will know and remember what we said. The fact that the someone else was awake and not deaf is no guarantee that he listened to what we said. The fact that we "expose" students to some facts and ideas about a particular discipline in a lecture is absolutely no guarantee that they learned anything at all. They may have heard the noises made by the professor as he was talking, but that is no assurance that they listened and retained.

Hearing is a natural process. Provided your ear is not damaged and that your brain is functioning normally, you cannot help but hear sounds of a certain intensity. Hearing is essentially a process of energy transformation (the technical term is "transduction" and refers to a process whereby energy in one form is transformed into another form). What happens during the hearing process is the transformation of acoustic energy into electrochemical energy. It happens like this: A sound wave hits your eardrum, a thin but tough membrane stretched across the auditory canal. The eardrum, as a result of being hit, vibrates. The vibration is transmitted next to three little bones (ossicles), the anvil, hammer, and stirrup. The bone vibration is then transmitted to a fluid in the cochlea, the endolymph. These vibrations are still acoustic waves. As the waves move through the fluid they will disturb tiny little hair cells. Depending on the amplitude and frequency of the waves, some hair cells will be stimulated more than others. If a given hair cell is stimulated above its threshold, it emits electrochemical impulses which will activate the eighth cranial nerve. From then on we are dealing with the nervous system and no longer the ear itself, and the brain will then reconstruct a representation of the initial sound. At that point, you heard. Naturally, there is more to hearing than just the process of energy transformation through the ear mechanism. The nervous system is involved, too. We have little or no control

[6]Theodore Clevenger and Jack Matthews, The Speech Communication Process, Scott, Foresman and Company, Glenview, Ill., 1971, pp. 65–80.

of the process of hearing. If our hearing mechanisms and our brains are normal, we cannot help but hear.

But we can help listening whenever we want to. We can tune out any speaker, any time, at will. Listening is a higher cognitive process which is under our control. Why, then, do we decide to tune out? Basically, the problem is caused by the fact that we think much faster than we talk. The average rate of speech for an American is about 125 words per minute. This is slow going for the human brain, which can process, with its 13 billion cells, about 800 words per minute. In listening, the difference between the speaking rate and the thinking rate means that our brain works with hundreds of words *in addition* to those we hear. It means that our brain will continue to think at high speed while the spoken words arrive at low speed. We can listen and still have some spare time for our own thinking. The use or misuse of this spare time holds the key to how well a person can listen to the spoken word.

Most of us misuse the spare time by going on private sidetracks. We daydream while we are "listening" to a friend or to a lecture. At first, this presents no problem, for we are able to catch every word the friend or the professor is saying, and still think of what we are going to say next, or what we are going to do tonight, etc., and there is plenty of time to do all this extra thinking. Actually, we can hardly avoid doing this since it has become a strong habit over the years. So we go back and forth between what the speaker is saying and our private world. But sooner or later we stay a little too long on one of these mental sidetracks, and when we get back to the speaker, he is ahead of us. We lost something he said. If it is something important we may not understand the rest of his conversation, and therefore we find it easier and easier to slide off on our sidetracks for longer periods of time. When the speaker is finished, it is not surprising that we actually heard only half of what he told us.

Figure 13-1 Diagram of the human ear.

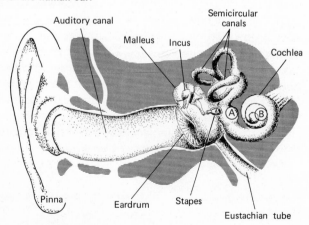

THE DYNAMICS OF INTERPERSONAL COMMUNICATION

The previous two myths were centered around the listener and explained what makes it difficult to listen well. The third myth is oriented toward the speaker and what makes it difficult for him to be listened to well.

Myth Three: We Speak to a Mass Audience

When we find ourselves talking to several people, we often assume that we are being heard in the same manner by every one of our listeners. This assumption is implicitly based on the premise that we are talking to a mass audience, that every individual member of that audience is identical and therefore will respond in like manner to what is heard. First of all, the individual members comprising any audience are not identical. They are quite different people with different interests, different needs, and different motives for being there and listening to us. Some are friends, some are enemies, some are smart, and some are dull. Some are happy to be there, some can't wait until they can get away. Some have pressing problems at the time, some are relatively free from strong anxieties. These individual differences account for the fact that these people may or may not go on private sidetracks, may or may not stay very long on their sidetracks if they do tune out once in a while. It also explains the fact that they may all tune out at a different time and literally hear different parts of the conversation. No wonder we often come out of a conversation asserting very dogmatically that "He said such and such" and find that another person who was also there affirms emphatically that he certainly did not. You almost feel as though you had been listening to two different speakers. Perhaps the half you missed was the half the other person heard.

MORE EFFECTIVE LISTENING

If listening is essentially up to us, how can we become better at it? How can we acquire better habits? No amount of reading and hearing about it will ever make you better. Listening is a skill, and as for any skill, practice is essential. What we can do in a brief section here is to draw your attention to some things to watch for, but you will have to do the watching. You will have to try it for yourself over and over again. As you incorporate some of these suggestions in your behavior, you might find that listening comes a little easier, but progress will be slow and hardly noticeable at first. Listening is hard work. Unless you are willing to stand the difficulty and make the effort, your habits will not change.

For convenience, we have grouped our suggestions into three main categories. The first category deals with the differential time between the speed of the spoken word and thinking.

Use Spare Time More Effectively

Instead of going on private sidetracks which have nothing to do with the topic being discussed, think about what the speaker is saying.

Think Ahead of the Speaker

Try to figure where he is getting at and what his next point will be. This may be easy with some speakers who are well organized and who present their points clearly. However, most of us are not that clear and organized, and it may make the work of the listener very hard. However if you are interested in getting what the speaker has to say you may have to do his organization for him if he did not do it for you.

Summarize What the Speaker Is Saying

Break what is being said into the main points and the supporting points. Most speakers tend to repeat themselves and often go on tangents that may or may not be related to the topic. As a listener, your task is to sift what is important from what is only supporting material. The speaker sometimes helps you make the distinction by emphasizing a point with his voice, or repeating it several times, or telling you that this is a key point to be remembered. Teachers will often use the blackboard to write what they consider their main points and key words.

Identify the Speaker's Evidence

Ask yourself questions about the speaker's sources and their validity. Do you find the evidence convincing, complete, valid? *Listen between the lines. Listen for the two broadcasts.* To listen effectively one has to listen to two broadcasts at the same time. The first broadcast is the content of the discussion, the words the speaker is saying, the topic itself. The other broadcast comes from all the nonverbal signals the speaker is sending while he is talking. His tone of voice, his gestures, and his facial expressions. The second broadcast tells you about the speaker's feelings and gives you a great deal of information on how to interpret what the speaker is saying.

You will remember that in our discussion of meaning we emphasized that one must understand both the nonverbal and verbal aspects of a message if one wishes to understand fully what another person is trying to communicate. Listen for the feelings the speaker is putting across. Don't be misled by the apparent triviality of some statements, or by what appears to be only "small talk." Oftentimes we do not know of any other way to make contact with others, and what we are truly saying to another person goes beyond the words we use. A little girl coming home from school in tears saying she hates school and does not want to go back may really be saying that someone made fun of her at recess and she was hurt. Unless the parents listen for the little girl's feelings, and try to make it easy for her to tell the story, they may brush her aside by saying that "This is ridiculous, and of course you want to go back to school." They would thus miss the point entirely.

Listening between the lines is very difficult. It takes a great deal of sensitivity and patience, for people have innumerable ways of erecting defenses and hiding behind them. Only patience and a willingness to

THE DYNAMICS OF INTERPERSONAL COMMUNICATION

spend the time deciphering the more subtle dimensions of a person's communication will make us successful in our attempts to understand others.

Human beings are not machines. They have feelings, emotions, which play a fundamental part in their interpersonal communication. There are things we like and things we do not like, things we are afraid of or ashamed of, things we like to hear and things that are so threatening we would rather not hear them at all. As a result, quite unconsciously, we have a tendency to tune out what we do not want to hear and to listen better to what we agree with. If something is said which might cause us to change our perception on something, a threat of dissonance has been introduced. Any potential change in our perceptions involves strong feelings, and the first of these feelings are usually confusion and frustration. To reduce the frustration, we often flee mentally from the situation by tuning out what the listener is saying, or by distorting it so that we won't have to alter our perceptions. This is not done deliberately by any of us. Actually if and when we are told that we are doing this, we very righteously deny it. Our emotions often blind us to what is actually happening in us.

When we do not agree with a speaker, we have a great tendency to prepare a rebuttal while he is still talking. We hear the first few words or sentences, get an idea of what the speaker is saying, decide we don't agree, and here we go preparing our answer and waiting impatiently for our turn to speak. Sometimes, we don't even wait, and we interrupt the speaker who never gets a chance to finish his thought. Unfortunately, when we do not hear a speaker out completely, we really do not know for sure what he is saying. We may think we do, but incomplete statements may not represent a fair sample of the speaker's thoughts. People we do not agree with are often the most difficult people to listen to. Usually we have little difficulty listening to someone telling us how great we are or how smart we are, but listening to a professor who tells you your paper certainly did not deserve any better than a ''D'' is a lot more difficult.

We again arrive at the concept of the open mind. We must be willing to listen to information which goes contrary to our belief system. And even though you think that your paper deserved better than a D, you should be willing to hear the other side. He may happen to have some good reasons that will make sense, even to you, *if you are able to let them come in,* rather than shutting them off, on the basis that the prof obviously dislikes you and that's why you got a D.

We know that children's spans of attention are very small. The younger the child, the smaller the span. In fact, most adults also have a short span

Freedom from Distractions

of attention and have difficulty concentrating over the same thing for too long a period of time. Naturally this varies with each individual, but think of the difficulty you have as a student listening to a fifty-minute lecture, even when the lecturer is an outstanding professor. Because it is hard to sustain attention for very long, we get distracted very easily. The sources of distractions come from (1) within us, when we daydream, (2) from the outside environment (outside noise, people passing by, someone waving, the temperature of the room, etc.), and (3) the speaker himself. This last category merits some discussion.

We often get distracted by a speaker's accent, his mannerisms, the way he is dressed, the language he uses, his delivery, etc. Some people simply won't listen to a person because he wears long hair, or is dressed too conservatively. Or if they are willing to listen, their listening will be affected by the preconceived ideas they have because of the speaker's dress or appearance. This of course is hardly conducive to effective listening. It is difficult to fight off these distractions. Yet as we become aware of all the little things that can get in the way of good listening, we might be in a better position to train ourselves to overcome them. In addition to the physical distractions created by the appearance of the speaker, his use of language may turn us off. Most of us react very strongly to certain emotionally loaded words, trigger words. Whenever these words are pronounced by someone it's as though a red flag had been waved in front of our nose, and we react, usually emotionally and strongly. These words, of course, are different to each of us. If we can try to identify these words, they somehow lose some of their impact on us when we hear them, and at least we may not block out what a speaker has to say simply because he used one of our pet peeves.

Ralph Nichols and Leonard Stevens in their book *Are You Listening?*[7] make these suggestions about listening habits which we have summarized below:

Ten Worst Listening Habits Are:
1. Calling subject "uninteresting."

2. Criticizing speaker's delivery, personal appearance, necktie, etc.
3. Getting overstimulated and preparing rebuttal.
4. Listening only for facts.

Ten Best Listening Habits Are:
1. Tuning "old professor" in to see if there is anything you can use.
2. Getting his message, which is ten times as important as his appearance, etc.
3. Hearing the man out before you judge him.
4. Listening for main ideas, principles, and concepts.

[7]*Ralph G. Nichols and Leonard A. Stevens,* Are You Listening?, *McGraw-Hill Book Company, New York, 1957.*

THE DYNAMICS OF INTERPERSONAL COMMUNICATION

5. Trying to make an outline of everything you hear.
6. Faking attention to speaker.

7. Tolerating distractions in meeting.

8. Evading difficult material.

9. Letting emotion-laden words affect listener.
10. Wasting differential between speech speed (100 to 300 words per minute) and thought speed (cruising 800 words per minute).

5. Listening two or three minutes before taking notes.
6. Good listening is not relaxed. There is collection of tensions inside.
7. Getting up and doing something about it—by shutting a window, closing a door, requesting the person talking to speak louder, etc.
8. Learning to listen to difficult material.
9. Identifying 100 greatest word barriers.
10. Making thought speed an asset instead of a liability by:
   a. Anticipating the next point to be made.
   b. Making contrast and comparison.
   c. Identifying the man's evidence.
   d. Practicing mental recapitulation.

ACTIVE LISTENING

There is another dimension to listening which the psychotherapist Carl Rogers and his associates have pointed out.[8] This other dimension goes beyond the psychiatrist's field to permeate all areas of interpersonal interaction. Listening is more than a skill to improve communication. Listening, or active listening, as Rogers calls it, reflects a whole orientation to life and to people. This orientation implies that *to listen is to have the creative power to imagine how it would make sense to say what the other person is saying.* It implies that the other person is fundamentally important and worth listening to, worth giving some of your attention, energy, and time. In a sense, you cannot fake active listening because it is not enough to pay attention to the suggestions we listed in the preceding paragraphs. You must *feel* deep inside of you that people are important in their own right, and you must feel that by listening to them you are sharing with them your feelings of respect. Active listening, Rogers points out, must be firmly based on the basic attitudes of the listener. You cannot use it as

[8]*Carl Rogers, "Communication: Its Blocking and Facilitating," Northwestern University Information, 1952, vol. 20, pp. 9–15.*

a technique if your fundamental attitudes about people are in conflict with its basic concepts. If you try, your behavior will be empty, and everyone will recognize it. Unless we have a spirit which genuinely respects the potential worth of an individual and trusts his capacity for self-direction, we cannot begin to be effective listeners.

What does active listening consist of? Very simply, to listen to a person *without passing judgment on what is being said, and to mirror back what has been said to indicate that you understood what feelings the speaker was putting across.* It seems simple enough. However the implications of this procedure are tremendous. By withholding judgment and by showing that we understand the feelings of another man, we tell him that he is free to say more, we tell him that he does not run the risk of being judged and found stupid or silly. We remove the threat that another person always presents to the defenses of another man. Effective communication is free to happen once that threat has been removed. By mirroring what another person says we help build a climate in which we can be accepting, noncritical, and nonmoralizing. People then feel safer.

Remember the example we gave earlier of the little girl coming home very disturbed over her day in school and crying that she did not want to go to school ever again. As a parent and as an active listener, what can you do to find out what is bothering the child? Her statement that she does not want to go back to school may be her only awkward way to indicate to you that she has a problem, and she may not even know herself exactly what the problem is. Asking her why she does not want to go back to school may not get you anywhere because chances are she will tell you that she hates it, and she won't know specifically why. If you tell her that this is a stupid thing to say and that of course she does not mean it and she likes school and wants to go back, you are passing judgment and telling the child she does not know what she is talking about (no one, not even a seven-year-old, likes to be told that), that you know better what's good, and that you know better than she does what she is really feeling. That's precisely the one thing no one knows better than this little girl. She knows better than anyone else what she is experiencing inside of her at that moment, even if she is not articulate enough to tell you. The result of your response will probably be more tears, and the child will clam up. You will still not know what really is bothering the girl.

As an active listener, you would simply mirror to the child what she just told you. "So you feel bad about school today." This simple sentence tells the girl you have been listening to her, that she communicated her feeling to you adequately, and that you are not passing any judgment. She is free to say more and probably will. "Yeah, I don't want to go back. I hate recess." If the mirroring process continues you will probably get the whole story from the child very easily. (She hates recess because today everyone teased her, and no one wanted to play with her. She felt awkward and left out—feelings no one really likes to experience. Her way out was to decide not to go back to school so she would not have to experience this again.) Once she has communicated her feelings and feels that she was understood, it will matter a lot less and chances are she can cope better with the problem.

All of us want to be listened to and understood. When we are not, we feel we are not worth much since people won't even think enough of us to take the time to listen to us. What do you hear most people complain about? Not being listened to. "I can't talk to my parents, they never listen." Or, "I can't talk to my son, he just won't listen." Or, "I am quitting this job. My boss never listens to anything I say. It's as if I did not exist."

To listen actively to another human being may be the greatest gift you can give a person. The power to listen is a remarkably sensitive skill, perhaps the greatest talent of the human race. It is certainly the skill that makes interpersonal communication truly effective and rewarding for all concerned.

BIBLIOGRAPHY

Barbara, D.: *The Healthy Mind in Communion and Communication,* Charles C Thomas, Publisher, Springfield, Ill., 1962.

Brown, J. I.: "The Objective Measurement of Listening Ability," *Journal of Communication,* 1951, no. 1.

Duker, S.: *Listening Bibliography,* Scarecrow Press, New York, 1964.

Duker, S. (ed.): *Listening: Readings* Scarecrow Press, New York, 1966.

Johnson, W.: *Your Most Enchanted Listener,* Harper & Brothers, New York, 1956. (New edition under the title of *Verbal Man: The Enchantment of Words,* P. F. Collier & Son Corporation, New York, 1963.)

Nichols, R. G., and L. A. Stevens: *Are You Listening?,* McGraw-Hill Book Company, New York, 1957.

Whyte, W. H., Jr: *Is Anybody Listening?,* Simon and Schuster, New York, 1952.

LABORATORY MANUAL

INTRODUCTION
General Comments

You will find this laboratory manual, as well as the accompanying text, somewhat different from others you may have been used to. Books tend to be full of information for you to acquire. The accompanying text material provides a *method* for you to practice, as well as some information for you to acquire. The method of the text and the course is based on a simple premise that *people tend to learn better by discovering for themselves than they do by just being told.*

In communication study, particularly, we feel it is important for the student to experience his communication and the communication of others. We need to watch communication going on around us. A laboratory situation is a relatively safe place to experience human communication, and it can be an interesting place to observe the limitations of human communication.

Another reason we believe experiences with communication can be valuable is because there is only one person who can do anything about your communicating—and that person is you. No one can change your communication habits for you. In the laboratory situation you can try out new communication behaviors if you want to, or you can refine the behaviors you feel are your successful ones. Only you can make the exciting discoveries of your own communication strengths and weaknesses, and only you can decide to change if you like.

Laboratory learning is, of course, not new. Any biology or chemistry student has put in hours of work in a lab. Although laboratories are somewhat newer in the social sciences, the applications are growing for laboratory learning in our educational settings. In communication laboratories there are no test tubes or microscopes. The apparatus is our language and paralanguage, and the experimenters are you the students and your instructor. In the process of laboratory learning you will be both the observer and the observed. You will learn about communication by practicing it with other people in a protected environment where you will be able to see and analyze the consequences of your behaviors. In the laboratory you will hear yourself and others talk. You will raise questions about identity, alienation, relating, and caring. You will discuss roles, norms, games, values, and strategies we hide behind and masks we wear to protect ourselves. You will have the opportunity to examine your communication value system and how it affects you.

Finally, we hope you will discover that our communication is so involved with our attitudes that communication is much more a state of mind than it is a garble of words.

Class Activities or Exercises

Recommended activities are grouped according to the subject matter of the chapters of the text. Some exercises, naturally, will demonstrate several different principles of communication, so it must be admitted that the arrangement of the exercises is somewhat arbitrary. In addition to the activities for which you have worksheets in this book, your instructor may add some other projects or class exercises from time to time.

Recurring in most of the following laboratory manual chapters is the laboratory theme of activity groups such as Picture Makers, Forum Discussion, Role Players, and Observers. How these groups will function is described in detail at the beginning of laboratory manual Chapter 2. Election of a steering committee may be accomplished during that same session if it is decided to follow that course.

Feedback blanks are provided in each of the following chapters. This is designed to give students another means of interacting with one another and with the course. Honestly given, the laboratory feedback can reflect a growing awareness of communication maturity for the class.

Cases for study are included in many chapters. It should be noted that the importance of the cases and the case method in communication study has resulted in our setting aside an extensive discussion of how groups solve problems by the case method as an introduction to laboratory manual Chapter 5. By the time you have reached the activities in Chapter 5, you will have begun to work with cases and the material will be relevant to your own group deliberations.

Assignments and Projects

Besides the activities you will have during class time, there are many other opportunities to explore human communication through a variety of assignments and outside class projects. Your instructor will assign those which are most appropriate to the time involved and the interests of the class. In addition to the assignments suggested in this manual, the instructor may add tests or other assignments which do not appear.

Personal Improvement Blank

Related to the laboratory experience, this brief response sheet may be assigned as a self-study help which you will tear out and turn in. The questions asked and the topics advanced will put a premium on your introspection and understanding of communication principles as they relate to your daily life.

Journal

The instructor may assign you the project of maintaining a journal of communication happenings. These will become a collection of your own observations of communication around you. Although the assignments for journal entries do not appear in every laboratory manual chapter, it might be useful to continually keep a "communication diary" of the things you notice about the communicative behaviors of yourself and others.

Scrapbook

A collection of newspaper clippings, notes, letters, printed ads, and other published or written materials will help you analyze the communication habits of the people who make news and who suffer from the same communicative difficulties as the rest of us. (While the journal makes a record of your own private life and observations, the scrapbook will tend to be more sweeping in its scope and more distant in its relation to affecting your personal life.)

Communication Case

Another kind of outside assignment is the case which you construct from your own experience or the experience of others. The purpose of this assignment is to have the student describe and analyze a communication breakdown. The case should present a relatively complex problem which is still largely unsolved. If the problem is too simple and uncomplicated all we have is an illustration which can be read with interest but which leaves little room for creative analysis. For that reason the case should contain a record of misevaluations and breakdowns amenable to analysis with the principles and concepts presented in this course.

It should consist of three distinct parts: (1) *The description of the problem.* This first part should be in sufficient detail so that it could be role-played. The case does not have to be of monumental importance to the future of the world, but can be representative of the tragedies which befall us in our relations with others as we observe our faulty communication over a period of time. The case can represent the everyday kind of mess we can make of our interpersonal communication. In this way you can deal with something you may know about firsthand. This first section is an objective report. Treat it as a third-person story even if it happened to you. Try to minimize personal judgments, slant, and inferences. This first section is only a description of events: what happened to whom, when, and where. It may be written as a narrative or a dialogue, or any form you wish. (2) *The analysis.* In this part you will analyze the communication difficulties from the point of view of the behaviors described in this course and text. Include if you like some recommendations about how the behaviors you report could have been improved by applying some of the principles discussed in class. If you want at this point to propose solutions and inject your personal feelings about the case, you may do so in this section. (3) *Your reactions.* A final part is to report the reactions you noted in yourself in carrying through this assignment from its inception (maybe when you first read this page) to the completion of your paper. You are asked for your reactions to the assignment at this point, not your reactions to the case itself or the people in it.

CHAPTER 1   YOU AND YOUR COMMUNICATION

As you can see, the titles of the chapters in this laboratory manual will coincide with the chapters in the text portion of your book. Exercises are chosen to fit the subject matter of each chapter, and assignments are built around the topics covered.

Because "You and Your Communication" is the opening chapter of your text, the main purpose of the exercises, activities, and assignments in this section will be to help you get acquainted with (1) other class members, (2) the kinds of participation this course proposes, and (3) the communication emphasis of the activities and the assignments.

You will be asked to respond spontaneously to most questions and exercises in the book. In the Acquaintance Questionnaire in this chapter, the quality of your responses will depend on your relaxing and giving your off-the-top-of-your-head answers. On the other hand, the Course Expectations Scale will require a little more introspection and thought on your part, and you are asked to hand it in unsigned.

This laboratory manual chapter will also be your introduction to the Feedback Blank which is filled out at the end of a session and not signed. There have been instances where a student has used the feedback as a punitive instrument—a sort of "here's my chance to get so-and-so"—and this is easily detected by the class and not very well accepted. Open, honest responses to the items asked will give students and the instructor an indication of general sentiment at the end of each session. If you are in doubt about the usefulness of giving and receiving feedback in communication, we would refer you to pp. 86 through 90 in your text.

Getting Acquainted Triads

1. Form groups of three students. The criterion for formation is that students should not know the other two members of the triad.

2. Participants in each group name themselves A, B, and C.

3. *Phase one:*
   a. Participant A takes three minutes to tell participants B and C as much about himself as he feels comfortable doing.
   b. Participant B repeats the process.
   c. Participant C repeats the process.

4. *Phase two:*
   a. Together, participants A and B take two minutes to tell participant C what they heard him say and what they inferred from what he has said or left unsaid.
   b. Participants B and C repeat this process for participant A.
   c. Participants A and C repeat the process for participant B.

Acquaintance Questionnaire*

Your instructor will read aloud each of the following incomplete statements. You will be allowed a minute between each statement to complete the statement. Write spontaneously. Don't think about the statements too much.

a. I am a _____

b. I am happy when I _____

_____

c. Ten years from now I want to _____

_____

d. This school is a _____

e. Next Saturday night I want to _____

_____

f. My three heroes are (1) _____

(2) _____

(3) _____

Giving Instructions

1. Break up into small groups of five or six students. For every group formed there is an assigned "order taker" who does not participate in the group planning but must be out of the room or segregated from the planning session.

2. You are to develop instructions for performing a very common task: you will instruct a person from outside your group, the "order taker," on *how to put on his coat.*
   In the preparation time (ten minutes) your group should develop a series of instructions to be given orally to your "order taker." You will assume that this "order taker" has never seen a coat, does not know anything about coats or what they are for, and will not understand any of

*Adapted from *Speech: Science-Art,* by Elwood Murray et al., The Bobbs-Merrill Company, Inc., Indianapolis, 1969, p. 74. By permission of the authors and the publishers.

the words used to name parts of the garment. He will just rely on what you will tell him to do—nothing more, nothing else.

3. After your group feels it knows just what to say to the "order taker" to make him complete his task successfully, you will call the "order taker" and begin the actual order giving. The "order taker" will stand beside a chair, a coat is hung over the back of the chair. Start telling him what to do. . . .

Course Expectations Scale*

Students usually expect to derive something of value from a course. In terms of your personal expectations, put a check mark on each line to show how you would rate the importance of the following outcomes:

By the end of this
course, I will . . .

Gain new knowledge of the subject

_____

| unimportant | mildly important | moderately important | extremely important |
| to me | to me | to me | to me |

Learn about the interrelationships
of facts and ideas

_____

| unimportant | mildly important | moderately important | extremely important |
| to me | to me | to me | to me |

Gain self-confidence

_____

| unimportant | mildly important | moderately important | extremely important |
| to me | to me | to me | to me |

Be pretty satisfied with the way
things went in the course

_____

| unimportant | mildly important | moderately important | extremely important |
| to me | to me | to me | to me |

Gain an understanding of other
people

_____

| unimportant | mildly important | moderately important | extremely important |
| to me | to me | to me | to me |

*From *Effective Speech Communication: Theory in Action,* by Huber Ellingsworth and Terry Welden, Scott, Foresman and Company, Glenview, Ill., 1970, pp. 37–39. Copyright © 1970 by Scott, Foresman and Company. Reprinted by permission.

Learn to think about questions and
analyze problems for myself

| unimportant to me | mildly important to me | moderately important to me | extremely important to me |

Improve my ability to take
part in discussions

| unimportant to me | mildly important to me | moderately important to me | extremely important to me |

Strive for excellence in my own
communication

| unimportant to me | mildly important to me | moderately important to me | extremely important to me |

Clarify my values

| unimportant to me | mildly important to me | moderately important to me | extremely important to me |

Derive social satisfaction

| unimportant to me | mildly important to me | moderately important to me | extremely important to me |

Gain a better understanding of myself
as a communicator

| unimportant to me | mildly important to me | moderately important to me | extremely important to me |

Obtain a good grade for the course

| unimportant to me | mildly important to me | moderately important to me | extremely important to me |

Feedback Blank One

1. Rate the productivity of this week's (session's) work for you. (Circle one number.)

                1   2   3   4   5   6   7   8   9   10

Not productive   Highly productive

2. Rate how you think the rest of the class felt about this week's (session's) productivity.

                1   2   3   4   5   6   7   8   9   10

Not productive   Highly productive

Comments:

3. Comment on your contribution in the small group or in the class exercises. Did you speak too much, too little?

4. Comment on the class activities this week (session). What did you like, dislike? What was helpful to you and why?

5. Other comments, criticisms, questions, suggestions, etc.

NAME _____

DATE _____ SECTION _____

Personal Improvement Blank One

Use this sheet to write your answers.
1. Briefly state what you hope this course may do for you.

2. After the first few meetings, what have you learned about yourself or about others in communication situations?

3. Do you think you will be able to be perfectly honest in your responses to the feedback, or do you think there is some inhibiting factor in spite of their anonymous nature?

Assignment One

An Estimate of Myself as a Communicator

Your own communication experiences have provided you with a wealth of information about yourself in your relationships with others. How you see yourself in your communication with others affects a great deal what you do. For this assignment you are asked to answer three questions:

1. How effective am I as a communicator in a one-to-many situation (having to talk to fifteen or more people)?

2. How effective am I as a communicator in small groups (committees, work groups, buzz sessions, etc.)?

3. How effective am I as a communicator in a one-to-one situation (talking to one other person)?

NOTE: It is essential that you write from your own point of view how you see yourself and not how you think other people see you. You do not need to ask anyone their estimates of your effectiveness. However, you should be prepared to have class members read your paper.

Allow yourself enough time to do some thinking about the three questions before you write anything down on paper.

Assignment Two*

Interview

Go to the health center on your campus to interview the doctor and/or nurses to discover their views on the communication problems they encounter in their work with students or other patients.

How does a doctor make sure his instructions are clearly understood by his patient? Are there any special problems in relating information to very sick patients? How does the use of technical terms affect the doctor-patient communication? Is it better to use technical terms, not to use them? Does the medical staff rely on information given by their patients or on observations and examinations? Why? How do they get information from their patients? Can most patients answer the doctor's questions adequately?

Ask the medical staff any or all these questions to get their reactions to them. Use this sheet to make your notes during the interview. Then, write a one to two page paper in which you will summarize your findings and conclusions after your interview.

*This assignment should be given to a group or to a few individuals to interview professional people on their use of communications. While medical people are suggested in the example, the same assignment could be made to involve anyone using technical language or terminology who must meet the public.

CHAPTER 2 PERCEPTION—THE EYE OF THE BEHOLDER

This laboratory manual chapter introduces the structured laboratory activities of Picture Makers, Forum Discussion, Role Players, and Observers. The remaining chapters will also have activities for these groups and this structure may be used as a consistent program in the laboratory. At the end of this introduction there are general suggestions for work in small groups which may prove useful when you are assigned to a picture-making group, a forum group, a role-playing group, or as an observer. Reference back to this set of suggestions may be helpful when you are working on activities in the forthcoming laboratory chapters.

Included in this chapter are instructions on conducting an election for steering committee. If a steering committee is used, it will be composed of from five to seven class members and the instructor. Its purpose is to help guide the class toward a more productive learning experience. Meetings are held outside of class time, so a requirement for membership on the steering committee would be availability to attend these sessions. Once the committee is elected, members may proceed to select their own officers and designate responsibilities. A steering committee *reporter* notes the discussion of the committee and reports on the session to the entire class. The steering committee *chairman* presides at the meetings. The *social chairman* arranges for name tags if they are used, introduces guests or visitors, and assists in arranging any breaks or social activities. The *librarian* helps the instructor collect materials (such as the fill-in pages from this manual or assignments) and return the assignments to students. The *group chairman* helps set up the small groups and guides their organizing. He also receives comments on the groupings. The *schedule chairman* helps keep the laboratory on schedule by reminding small groups when planning is over and when performance times are being exceeded. Any number of additional steering committee members may be elected without specific duties, but a *member-at-large* should be appointed to take over for any member who is absent. The meetings of the steering committee should be open to any members of the class who want to attend.

A continuation of the feedback system mentioned in laboratory manual Chapter 1 will be evident in this present and succeeding chapters. Other class activities are designed to demonstrate differences in perception. There is also a case to be studied, and it should be mentioned that in subsequent chapters more and more cases will be included. In laboratory manual Chapter 5 we will include a discussion of how groups work on cases.

Out-of-class assignments in this section are designed to make you think about your perceptions and the relationship perceptions have to our communication.

General Suggestions for Work in Small Groups

Picture Makers:

Think of these as visual aids (close to the empirical world). Drawing people or communication analyses or events may require speech "balloons" over heads, or "clouds" for thoughts. Sequences of panels may depict continuing action in a problem-to-solution presentation. You may divide the group to present consecutive or different interpretations of the problem. Some may draw, others interpret ad lib or foster group discussion. Be sure to include the audience in imaginative ways.

Forum Discussion:

May be "leaderless," leader-oriented, or some combination. Avoid having each member make a pleasant, pat little speech and then lapse into silence. Try for interaction of ideas—try involving the audience and other members of the forum. Do not discuss the topic so thoroughly in your planning session that you lose spontaneity in your performance. Planning time should concentrate on selecting the topic and getting some kind of agreement on the terms to be used in your discussion. One person may introduce the topic to the audience, explaining the limits your group has set on the key words used. You may want a moderator to open the speaking and review it at the end, making sure you stay within your time limit. The idea is to stimulate thought and discussion, not necessarily to reach conclusions or obtain group agreement—in fact, your discussion may have to end at the most heated moment or before all questions are answered. Good topics include personal experiences: "how we handled a communication difficulty in the office or classroom," "children should be taught honesty in the home"—something based on your own communication experience. The forum is not a UN Cabinet—family, campus, civic, church, classroom, etc., problems are much more real to most of us.

Role Players:

Warm-up (planning time) should concentrate on establishing a problem situation and assigning roles. Performance is more spontaneous if each actor understands his "character" and liberates his emotions through that character. A "stage manager" may set the scene and identify the characters for the audience. More than one act may show a problem, its developments, and possible solutions. Try using techniques such as:

Alter Ego (a person stands behind an actor and speaks his thoughts, interrupting by placing a hand on the actor's shoulder).

Soliloquy (an actor speaks his hidden thoughts himself, in asides to the audience by changing his voice or by some other sign to indicate he is communicating his silent thoughts).

Extensions (like alter ego, several players stand behind the actor to indicate his thoughts at different times of his life or from different points of view, i.e., a man this year, last year, etc. or a man as a father, a boss, a lodge member, etc.).

Observers:

Observers have an advantage in not being directly involved in the discussion preparation, so they have time to observe interactions and communication behaviors. It helps to compare functioning of groups to other meetings of the class. Improvements should be noted. The observer role is to provide the audience (all the class or the small group) with information and insights not available to everyone. Interaction during the planning session is very important, but also consider the effect of the group's efforts on the audience, the appropriateness of the problem chosen to demonstrate a principle, the development of the problem, the solutions offered, the clarity of the views expressed, and the communication behaviors of the group members (loudness, language, flexibility of delivery from preparation time and performance, tension in voices, nonverbal cues fitting the verbal ones, and other emotional responses to audience or situation). Observe not only the oral output, but the "feeling level" communication as well. Your report to the class should be brief (avoid the dull and pointless repetition of "then he said to her," and "she said to him," etc.).

Election of Steering Committee

Break up into small groups of six or seven students.

Step one: Caucus and prepare a tentative slate of candidates from members of the class. Nominate from the class at large any person you feel would be interested and productive as SC (steering committee) members. Candidates need not be chosen from your own group or from those who have had a communication class before. You may nominate as few as two and as many as seven of the class members. Make sure these nominees can be present at the SC meetings once a week for a half hour (the exact time and place of the meeting will be announced by the instructor).

Step two: Select one member from your group to meet with representatives of the other groups as an "electoral college" to make the final selection.

Step three: The "electors" (from step two) meet at the blackboard with their nomination sheets from their group and arrive at an agreement based on the number of times a person was nominated. If necessary, the electors may return to their groups for further instructions. If the group decides to have more than seven members or less than seven members on the SC, no difficulty will be presented.

Step four: While the "electors" are in session at the blackboard, the members of the groups will formulate questions about the course, schedule, communication, and activities. One or two good questions from each group would be appropriate for the time allotted. You may want to ask one member of the group to write down the questions you have decided to ask and have that person ask them during the question/answer session.

Step five: Members of the SC are announced, and they will start meeting at the time indicated by the instructor.

Nomination Sheet for Election of Steering Committee

I nominate:

_____   _____

_____   _____

_____   _____

_____   _____

Nominations are for membership on the SC. Officers of the steering committee will be elected by SC members during their first meeting.

First Impressions

Your instructor will distribute a description of an individual. Read it and then select from the following list those traits which are most in accordance with the picture of the individual you have formed in your mind. Underline one adjective in each pair.

1. Generous	Ungenerous
2. Shrewd	Gullible
3. Unhappy	Happy
4. Irritable	Good-natured
5. Humorous	Humorless
6. Sociable	Unsociable
7. Unreliable	Reliable
8. Popular	Unpopular
9. Important	Unimportant
10. Ruthless	Humane
11. Good-looking	Unattractive
12. Persistent	Unstable
13. Frivolous	Serious
14. Restrained	Talkative
15. Self-centered	Altruistic
16. Imaginative	Hard-headed
17. Strong	Weak
18. Dishonest	Honest

Agree/Disagree List on Perception

1. Indicate whether you agree or disagree with the following statements. Record (A) if you agree, (D) if you disagree on the left hand side of the sheet.
2. Form groups of six or seven students and reach a consensus for each of the statements. Record the group consensus on the right hand side of this sheet.

Individual			Group Consensus	
(A)	(D)		(A)	(D)
_____	_____	1. The perception of a physical object depends more upon the object than upon the mind of the observer.	_____	_____
_____	_____	2. Perception is primarily an interpersonal phenomenon.	_____	_____
_____	_____	3. The fact that hallucinations and dreams are as vivid as waking perception indicates that perception depends very little upon external reality.	_____	_____
_____	_____	4. The reaction we have to what we see generally depends on learning and culture.	_____	_____

216

_____ _____ 5. We tend to see what we wish to see or are expecting to see regardless of what reality is. _____ _____

_____ _____ 6. Given the undependable nature of perception, we can never tell the "true" nature of reality. _____ _____

_____ _____ 7. Though there may be reality "out there," we can never really know it. _____ _____

_____ _____ 8. We may eliminate the undependable in our perception by careful, scientific observation. _____ _____

_____ _____ 9. Scientific instruments, though they extend the limits of man's perceptions, do not make perception any more real. _____ _____

_____ _____ 10. What we perceive is no more than a metaphor of what is. _____ _____

_____ _____ 11. Perception is a physical response to a physical reality. It is only when we begin talking about our perceptions that we begin to distort them. _____ _____

_____ _____ 12. If we are careful, we can see the world as it really is. _____ _____

_____ _____ 13. We react to our environment on the basis of what we perceive that environment to be like and not on what the environment is really like. _____ _____

The Accident Case

John Howell had been waiting at the corner to catch the bus for work. As he was standing there, a light blue car driven by a young man of nineteen was involved in an accident with a white car driven by a twenty-six-year-old mother of two. John arrived at work and described the accident to Harry, a fellow worker.

"I was standing there at the corner waiting for the bus when I saw a blue car coming down the street at a fairly fast rate. At least it looked like the car was going fairly fast. The driver was a young fellow about nineteen or so who attends the university. He was on his way to class. Anyway he must not have been paying much attention to what he was doing because he hit a car in the intersection. He hit the car at the rear and the rear door was dented pretty badly. The college fellow was not injured, but the woman was shaken up and one of her children lost a tooth. It wasn't a bad accident, but it sure shows you can't be too careful."

Harry went home that night and told his wife that John had seen an accident.

"John saw a bad accident this morning. He was waiting for the bus when a crazy college kid came roaring down the street. John said he was doing ninety and nothing. He must have been late for class, and he was not paying attention to what he was doing. He was probably listening to the radio or something. A woman was waiting at the intersection, and this guy just plowed into her. He did not even hit his brakes. The woman was hysterical. One of her children was all bloody and lost one tooth. They should take the guy's license away from him. If anybody can't drive better than that, he doesn't deserve a license."

What will Harry's wife think when she reads about the accident in the paper saying that the woman was given a citation for making a dangerous turn and failing to yield the right of way?

Discuss the implications of the story.

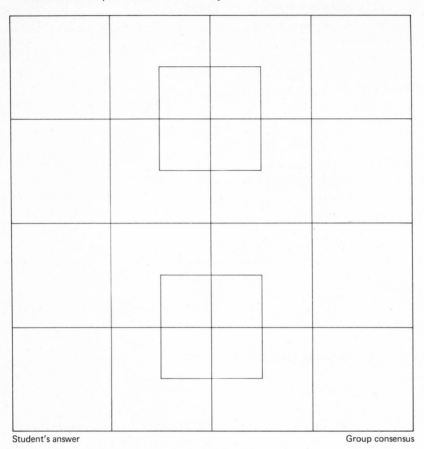

Student's answer   Group consensus

_____   _____

How many squares?

Laboratory Groups

Picture Makers:

Illustrate with pictures, diagrams, or any other nonverbal means a situation in which communication difficulties occur because the people involved have different perceptions of what happened.

Think of a situation which may have happened to you in real life. Toss several ideas among yourselves in the small group before you decide on the situation you will illustrate. Then concentrate on how to communicate to the class without the use of words. Do not choose something too obvious.

After you present the situation to the class, be prepared to discuss the consequences of the problem, why it occurred, and how it could have been prevented.

See the general instructions for work in small groups (laboratory manual p. 211) for specific suggestions on how picture-making groups can carry out their assignment.

You will have about thirty-five minutes to prepare for your presentation. You will have about five minutes to present it to the class as a whole. You may have another five to ten minutes to discuss the implications of the project *with* the rest of the class.

Forum Discussion:

Discuss the idea that we do not communicate about what's "out there" but about our perception of what's "out there." If this is true, how can we check whether or not our perceptions are "accurate"? In what situations are our perceptions more biased than usual? Is it at all possible to correct some of the biases that interfere with accurate perceptions? How? Are people willing to recognize their biases? Why?

In your planning time, ask yourselves these questions and try to prepare some answers. You may not all agree on the answers. In your presentation, ask the class to think about the questions and to arrive at some answers. Discuss the reactions. Try to formulate some final statement to conclude the discussion.

See the general instructions for work in small groups (laboratory manual p. 212) for specific suggestions in how forum discussion groups can carry out their assignments.

You have about thirty-five minutes to prepare your presentation. You will have about ten to fifteen minutes to talk with the rest of the class about your topic.

Role Players:

Role-play a situation in which people evaluated inadequately what was going on (distorted what they perceived, consciously or not) and how it affected communication. Show how it could have been prevented. Two acts might be indicated.

Choose a situation from your everyday experience. Make sure you understand what is meant by "evaluated inadequately." You might suggest examples to each other during your planning time. From these examples, one might stand out as the one to role-play.

See the general suggestions for work in small groups (laboratory manual p. 212) for specific suggestions on how a role-playing group can carry out its assignment.

You have about thirty-five minutes to prepare your presentation. You will have about ten minutes to present it to the class as a whole, and if time permits a discussion with the rest of the class will follow your presentation.

The acting out should be spontaneous. In the planning you should concentrate on the setting, the situation (what actually happens in your story), and the characters. Try to build the characters so that they have some substance and are not too pat. Specify to yourself in the group planning what kind of people the characters are—their age, their background, their beliefs, their personality. The more details you make up about them, the easier it will be to act out their role in the actual performance.

Observers:

There are many things one can observe when people communicate in a group situation. (See the general suggestions for work in small groups pp. 212–213). One of these things, perhaps the easiest one to observe, is the *amount* of communication taking place in a certain length of time—in other words, how much and how often, how little and how seldom people talk.

Another thing which can be observed is the *direction* of the communication flow, that is to whom people talk.

A convenient way to record what is going on in the group, as far as amount and direction of communication are concerned, is to use a *flow chart* or a *sociogram* as described in your text on pp 136–137.

In this example, *Jo* talked eight times—four times to Mary, three to Sue, and one to Jim. Jo received eight communications.

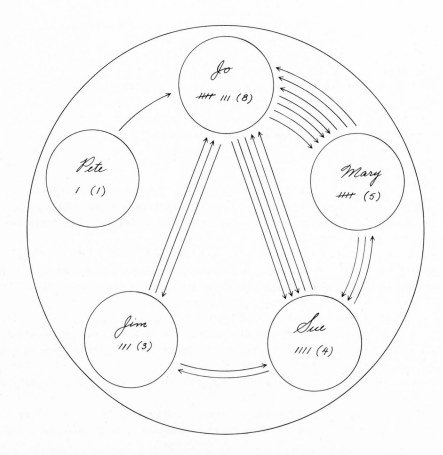

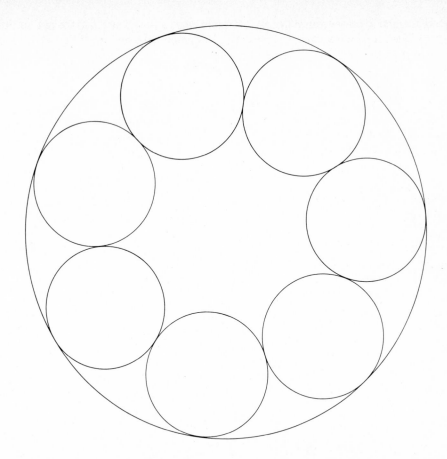

Mary talked five times—three times to Jo, two to Sue. She received five communications.

Jim talked three times—two times to Jo, one to Sue. He received only one communication.

Sue talked four times—two times to Jo, one to Mary, and one to Jim. She received six communications.

The number of bars in the small circles indicate how many times this particular person talked at the time of the recording. The arrows show to which person they addressed their comments. When a person talks to the whole group or when it is difficult to see to whom he is talking, the arrow should point toward the center of the circle.

If several observers are assigned to the same group, the observers can get together and decide to split their observations so each observer will be assigned to watch only two or three group members and record on his flow chart the amount and direction of communication of these group members only. At the end of the observation session, the observers can get together again and make up a composite picture of all the group members by putting all the flow charts together.

You will probably be asked to present your observations to the rest of the class. Use the blackboard to explain the flow charts to the rest of the class. Since this is probably the first time that this exercise is done in class, you will want to explain what a flow chart is to the rest of the class.

Be sure to identify by name on your chart the group members you are assigned to observe. In your report to the class, the use of names is optional.

Feedback Blank Two

1. Rate the productivity of this week's work for you.

                      1   2   3   4   5   6   7   8   9   10

Not productive   Highly productive

2. Rate how you think the rest of the class felt about this week's productivity.

                      1   2   3   4   5   6   7   8   9   10

Not productive   Highly productive

Comments:

3. At this point, how comfortable or at ease do you feel in this class? Why?

4. If you do not feel comfortable, can you isolate the reasons why?

5. Did you feel left out in any of the activities this week, in your groups or during any of the exercises? If you did, do you think anyone noticed?

6. What were your reactions to the comments on the feedback report this week?

7. Other comments, criticisms, suggestions, questions, etc.

Personal Improvement Blank Two

1. How would you relate the study of communication to your field of study or your profession (or your intended profession).

2. Give two examples of *adequate* perceptions you have observed recently.

3. Describe a situation in which your biases interfered with an adequate perception of the situation.

Assignment One

Perception Incident

Think about what happened to you this past week. Trivial as well as more important things, happy and sad things. Were any of the unsatisfactory events of the week due to inadequate communication? If so, were any of the communication difficulties traceable to differences in perception between the people involved or to distortions in what was perceived which caused subsequent difficulties?

Write a brief summary of such an instance and analyze its consequences on you and the people around you.

Assignment Two

Interview

Arrange an interview with a professional artist (painter, sculptor, musician, etc.) to discover his views on "Art as Communication." Report the results of your interview.

or

Talk to a public school teacher to find out how he views his communication role in the classroom. Report the result of your interview.

Assignment Three

Newspaper Clippings

Examine the newspaper accounts of a recent controversial event. Examine also the various reports of the investigation commissions if any was formed and if those reports are available. From your investigation of these sources, identify the communication barriers and breakdowns which were involved in the situation.

CHAPTER 3 LANGUAGE AND REALITY—THE TWO WORLDS WE LIVE IN

You will find again in this chapter the exercises and activities for the laboratory experiences of Role Players, Forum Discussion, Picture Makers, and Observing. In addition to these, there are other activities in making us aware of our attitudes about the maps we have of the territories in our experience.

A scrapbook is recommended in the assignments section of this chapter. It could be very interesting for you to maintain such a collection for the entire course. The reason for indicating the source of the clippings is to acknowledge that all sources for the same information may not approach the communication about it the same way. In other words, it is sometimes as interesting to know "who is saying it" as it is to know "what is said."

Descriptions of people are interesting to the student of communication because the biases we have about people tend to have such a strong influence on what we tell others about them. For this reason biographies of great and notorious people are subject to many interpretations and apparent inconsistencies depending on the point of view of the biographer—with the most biased biographies generally being those produced by the writer himself, or an autobiography.

Maps and Territories

1. Break up into small groups of six or seven students.

2. Compose a list of "maps" and their corresponding "territories" in the sense meant by the authors of your textbook in Chapter 3. Refer to Chapter 3 in the text for specific examples.
   You have about ten minutes to complete that part of the exercise. A representative of the group should write down the maps and their territories on a large sheet of paper provided by the instructor.

3. The class looks at all the examples generated by circulating to see each group's sheet.

4. The groups re-form and then select one particular map from their group's sheet or from any of the other groups' sheets. You will then discuss how the validity and reliability of this particular map can be checked. For example, how would you go about checking the claim of an advertiser that his toothpaste is better than "any other leading brand" in preventing cavities? If there are several ways to check a map's validity, state them.

5. Next, answer how you *personally* go about checking the validity of that particular map. If it so happens that you usually do not bother to check its validity, state some of the reasons why you do not.

Self-analysis Inventory*

1. Define communication in your own words.

2. How effective am I as an interpersonal (face to face) communicator?
   a. List communication strengths:

   b. List communication weaknesses:

   c. List specific measures that can be taken to overcome weaknesses:

*Joseph P. Zima, "Self-Analysis Inventory: An Interpersonal Communication Exercise," *The Speech Teacher,* 1971, vol. 2, no. 2, pp. 108–114. By permission of the author and the publisher.

3. Describe situations in which you have the most difficulty communicating with others. Why?

4. How satisfied am I with my progress in the following areas? Why or why not?
   a. Educational

   b. Occupational or career choice

   c. Social

d. Other

5. What are my most outstanding "hangups," both positive and negative (attitudes, prejudices, values, etc.)? Describe them below.
   a. Ones I am satisfied with:

   b. Ones with which I am not satisfied:

6. How do these "hangups" affect my interpersonal communication?

7. What kind of initial impression do I leave with others? (Why do you think so?)

8. Write a paragraph describing your personality as you see it, and comment on how *your* perception of "you" compares with *others'* perceptions of you.

Laboratory Groups

Picture Makers:

1. Illustrate with picture, diagrams, or any other nonverbal means, the kind of maps a teen-age son and his middle aged father have about drugs. Show how different or how similar the maps are. Try to show how the differences could affect their communication with each other.

or

2. Your performance will consist of selecting a class member not in your group and giving him specific orders, *without saying or writing a single word,* to carry through. In your planning, decide what the orders will be (don't choose something too easy and obvious) and what you will do to make yourself understood. Remember, you won't be able to talk or write. One member of your group should recruit a volunteer when you are ready for your presentation to the class. Then, explain to the class what your assignment is.

or

3. Illustrate with pictures, etc., the concept of allness or allness attitudes.

   The procedure to follow for the picture making exercise is to break up into small groups, choose one of the above topics, and spend thirty-five minutes planning together on how you will illustrate the topic for the benefit of the rest of the class. After the planning you will have about five minutes to present your illustration to the class and five to ten minutes to discuss it with the class.

   For more specific suggestions, see the general suggestions for work in small groups, laboratory manual Chapter 2, pp. 211–213.

Forum Discussion:

1. Break up into small groups of six or seven members.

2. The instructor will either assign you one of the following topics or tell you to choose one. You will have thirty-five minutes to plan with your group a discussion on the topic selected. You will then have ten to fifteen minutes to present the discussion to the rest of the class in any form you think is desirable and will get the whole class involved.

3. Topics. Your instructor may assign one of the following:
   a. Look at the following words: feedback, sender, decoding, message, noise, encoding, channel, transmission, stimulus, and receiver.

      Use whatever mental resources you have to determine the meaning of these words. Then, based on the meaning you give, place these words in the order which you feel illustrates best how communication between people takes place. Each word may be used more than once if you wish.

      When you are done, present your product to the rest of the class and explain it. Be prepared to answer questions and to justify what you did. Do not use your textbook. Use the blackboard for your presentation to the class.

   b. Can a map ever be completely accurate? Why or why not? What do you think are the characteristics of a "good" map? Of a "good" map maker?

c. Can people formulate different maps of the same event? Give examples from your own experience. What happens if these people who have different maps of the same event try to communicate with one another?

d. What are some of the assertions we can make about human beings that will apply always and to all?

e. How is feedback involved in the socialization process? How is it involved in the education process? How is it involved in the communication process? Are there any similarities or differences?

f. Through the recording function of language, man is able to live in the past, present, and future simultaneously. Explain.

g. We have said that most everyone has communication problems. Do you agree? What is a communication problem? In a class or group discussion you have had recently, did you have a communication problem or did you notice someone else having one? What, exactly, happened? Why was it a communication problem? What types of communication problems can you identify among the people you know?

h. Have you ever been in a crowded room and felt alone? Have you ever talked to someone for a while and felt that absolutely nothing that was said made sense? How would you describe these situations? What do you and your friends do to overcome the feeling of loneliness? What prescription would you give to an incoming freshman at your school to help him overcome loneliness? What skills would he have to have?

i. How might each of the following interfere with or facilitate one person's communication with another: cigarettes, pipe, beer, extreme anger, "pot," allness, dirty feet, a frown, a book?

j. It is not unusual to encounter people who have strongly held stereotypes (allness attitudes) about certain groups. The implicit attitude is that all the members of this group or that group are the same. "You've seen one, you've seen them all." When shown an exception to the stereotype—a real person belonging to the hated group yet different from the typical stereotype about the group—the person with the allness attitude will usually shrug it off as "the exception that confirms the rule" or "some of them are my best friends."

   Assuming you would like to make the person having the stereotyped attitude understand that he can't know all about any group and that people are not all alike, how would you go about it? If someone tells you that all long-haired kids are good for nothing and unpatriotic or that you can't trust anyone over thirty, what would you do to make him realize he has an allness attitude? What could you do to change his attitude? Discuss with the members of your group the problems involved in these questions and the possible strategies. There are no easy answers.

Role Players:

1. Break up into small groups of six or seven members.

2. Choose one of the following topics. You will have about thirty-five minutes to prepare as a group a way to illustrate the assignment by role-playing an example which will illustrate the problem. Refer to the general suggestions for work in small groups, p. 212, for specific suggestions about role playing.

3. Topics:
   a. Role-play a situation in which acting on the basis of inaccurate maps resulted in communication difficulties.
   b. Role-play a situation in which the people involved drew different maps of what was going on, and show how this affected their communication with each other.

                                        or

   c. Think of a situation in which communication broke down between the people involved. Describe the setting and define the people and what they are like. Then, act out what happened. Be sure to show in some way the feelings of the people involved during the communication breakdown. (Are they mad, irritated, impatient, confused, indifferent, stubborn, frustrated, etc.?) In what way does the communication breakdown inconvenience the people involved?

                                        or

   d. Role-play a situation in which allness or allness attitudes interfere with communication significantly.

Observers:

If you are an observer, read this carefully before you start observing your group. There are many things that can be observed in a group. One way of examining a group is to look at the content the group has dealt with—*what* the group has talked about, its topic, its task. Another way is to look at *how* the group dealt with the content—what happened to its members as the group dealt with its content. The latter method is called *process* as opposed to *content,* or task.

Most communication problems in groups are not content problems but process problems, or people problems. Problems are less created by what people talk about than by the way they talk about it and what they do to each other while they talk about it.

Here are some guidelines in the form of questions which should help you look at some of the things that pertain to the process of the group. We will concentrate for this session on (1) climate, (2) gatekeeping, (3) harmonizing, (4) aggressiveness, and (5) apathy.

1. Did anyone in the group attempt to develop and maintain a friendly and relaxed atmosphere? If so, what did the person(s) do?
   a. Told jokes
   b. Was responsive to others when they made a comment
   c. Praised others and their ideas
   d. Agreed with and accepted others' ideas
   e. Other—specify

2. Did anyone attempt to keep the communication channels open by helping others to contribute to and participate in the discussion? If so, what did the person(s) actually do?
   a. Directly asked someone who was silent what he thought about the issue being discussed
   b. Told the group that not everyone was participating and that perhaps the quieter members might want to
   c. Helped a group member to "get in" the discussion by telling the rest of the group to pay attention
   d. Other—specify

3. Did anyone attempt to reduce disagreements and conflicts when and if they occurred? What did the person(s) actually do?
   a. Acted as a mediator between the opposite sides
   b. Tried to reduce the tension by jesting or by the use of humor
   c. Tried to provide an "objective" side to the issue
   d. Other—specify

4. Did you notice any aggressiveness or hostility in the group? If so, in what way did it manifest itself?
   a. Criticisms about the topic, the task, the class setup were voiced frequently
   b. Criticisms about group members were expressed
   c. Criticisms about ideas presented or suggestions were often expressed
   d. Some group members were deliberately ignored, made fun of, etc.
   e. Other—specify

5. Did you notice any apathy in the group? How did it manifest itself?
   a. Few people talked
   b. Most group members looked bored
   c. Some group members engaged in talking about things unrelated to the group task
   d. Some group members removed themselves totally from the discussion by reading a book, doing homework, or writing letters
   e. Suggestions or ideas "plopped" a great deal of the time. No one responded to them and silence followed
   f. There were long periods of uneasy silence
   g. Other—specify

DO NOT SIGN

Feedback Blank Three

1. Rate this week's (session's) productivity for you.

                    1   2   3   4   5   6   7   8   9   10

  Not productive   Very productive

2. Rate how you think the rest of the class felt about the productivity of this unit's work.

                    1   2   3   4   5   6   7   8   9   10

  Not productive   Very productive

  Comments:

3. In your group, did you feel free to participate? Identify the group you were in.

4. Describe briefly how your group worked together.

5. Did that coincide with the observer's report?

6. Other comments, criticisms, suggestions, questions, etc.

239

© McGraw-Hill, Inc.

NAME _____

DATE _____ SECTION _____

Personal Improvement Blank Three

1. Give a few examples of "allness" behavior you have observed recently that interfered with interpersonal communication. Describe what happened and speculate on the reasons why the allness behavior was detrimental to the situation.

2. Speculate on the kind of communication patterns you tend to exhibit in:
   a. A group composed mostly of people you do not know well or at all. Do you talk much, little? Do you make the first move or overture to talk, or do you wait to be talked to before you respond? Do you feel at ease, ill at ease?

b. A group composed of people you know well, whom you feel relatively close to.

Assignment One

Scrapbook

Start a scrapbook of communication difficulties. For this chapter collect as many "allness statements" that you can find in magazines, newspapers, speeches, conversations, commercials, etc. Be sure to indicate the source of the clippings.

Assignment Two

Allness

Sometimes students respond to the nonallness principle by saying: "Well, if we can't know all, what's the sense of further studying? If we can't know all, then how do we know that we know anything?" How would you answer these questions? Why did you answer as you did?

Assignment Three

Biographies

Read three or four biographies of a given person by different authors. What kind of different pictures do you get? Why do you think that these different pictures emerge?

Assignment Four

Group Allness

Observe the next discussion group you participate in. What happens in the group when participants assume they say "all"? Analyze your observations and possibly give some "cures." Explain what you have found in a brief paper. Have you told all?

Assignment Five

Overcoming Allness

What are some of the popular recommendations for overcoming allness? Are they workable? Answer the question in a short paper.

CHAPTER 4 FACTS AND INFERENCES—LOOK BEFORE YOU LEAP

When you watch situation comedies on television or read stories about family troubles, you might watch to see how much of the difficulty is caused by confusion of inferences for facts (observations). This misevaluation of what is really going on when we watch others has furnished the plot for novels, short stories, movies, comic strips, and for dramas as far back as the written word has been recorded in history or folk tales have been sung.

Another form of inference-making occurs in riddles and in puzzles of many kinds. This chapter points up some of the situations in which we are tempted to judge by inferences when we need more data or need to rid ourselves of our habitual ways of looking at things.

In the assignments for this laboratory manual chapter you will have a chance to observe your own selective use of data (facts) in helping another person make a judgment (inference) from the data you choose to supply. In this way we tend to adjust the relationships of people around us by guiding their inferences.

The Uncritical Inference Test is by now a classic in the field of communication and William Haney's name has been associated with this kind of exercise especially in the management training field.

The Uncritical Inference Test*

Instructions

This test is designed to determine your ability to think *accurately* and *carefully*. Since it is very probable that you have never taken *this type* of test before, failure to read the instructions *extremely carefully* may lower your score.

1. You will read a brief story. Assume that all the information presented in the story is definitely *accurate and true*. Read the story carefully. You may refer back to the story whenever you wish.

2. You will then read statements about the story. Answer them in numerical order. *Do not go back* to fill in answers or change answers. This will only distort your test score.

3. After you read carefully each statement, determine whether the statement is:
   a. "T": On the basis of the information presented in the story, the statement is *definitely true*.
   b. "F": On the basis of the information presented in the story, the statement is *definitely false*.
   c. "?": The statement *may* be true or false, but on the basis of the information presented in the story you cannot be definitely certain. If any part of a statement is doubtful, mark the statement "?."
   d. Indicate your answer by circling either "T," "F," or "?" opposite the statement.

*Reproduced by permission from W. Haney, *Communication and Organizational Behavior,* rev. ed., Richard D. Irwin, Inc., Homewood, Ill., 1967, pp. 185–186.

Sample Test—The Story

The only car parked in front of 619 Oak Street is a black one. The words "James M. Curley, M.D." are spelled in small gold letters across the front left door of that car.

Statements about the Story

1. The color of the car in front of 619 Oak Street is black.   (T)   F   ?

2. There is no lettering on the left front door of the car parked in front of 619 Oak Street.   T   (F)   ?

3. Someone is ill at 619 Oak Street.   T   F   (?)

4. The black car parked in front of 619 Oak Street belongs to James M. Curley.   T   F   (?)

Remember: Answer *only* on the basis of the information presented in the story. Refrain from answering as you think it *might* have happened. Answer each statement in numerical order. Do not go back to fill in or change answers.

The Story

A businessman had just turned off the lights in the store when a man appeared and demanded money. The owner opened the cash register. The contents of the cash register were scooped up, and the man sped away. A member of the police force was notified promptly.

Statements about Story

1. A man appeared after the owner had turned off his store lights.   T   F   ?

2. The robber was a man.   T   F   ?

3. The man who appeared did not demand money.   T   F   ?

4. The man who opened the cash register was the owner.   T   F   ?

5. The store owner scooped up the contents of the cash register and ran away.   T   F   ?

6. Someone opened a cash register.   T   F   ?

7. After the man who demanded money scooped up the contents of the cash register, he ran away.   T   F   ?

8. While the cash register contained money, the story does not state how much.   T   F   ?

9. The robber demanded money of the owner.   T   F   ?

10. The robber opened the cash register.   T   F   ?

11. After the store lights were turned off, a man appeared.   T   F   ?

12. The robber did not take the money with him.   T   F   ?

13. The robber did not demand money of the owner.   T   F   ?

14. The owner opened the cash register.   T   F   ?

15. The age of the store owner was not revealed in the story.   T   F   ?

16. Taking the contents of the cash register with him, the man ran out of the store.   T   F   ?

17. The story concerns a series of events in which only three persons are referred to: the owner of the store, a man who demanded money, and a member of the police force.   T   F   ?

18. The following events were included in the story: someone demanded money, a cash register was opened, its contents were scooped up, and a man dashed out of the store.   T   F   ?

What's Her Name?

Try to untangle the following riddle:

A man went for a walk one day and met a friend whom he had not seen, or heard from, or heard of in ten years. After an exchange of greetings, the man said, "Is this your little girl?" and the friend replied, "Yes, I got married about six years ago."

The man then asked the child, "What is your name?" and the little girl replied, "Same as my mommy's."

"Oh," said the man, "then it must be Margaret."

If the man did not know whom his friend had married, how could he know the child's name?

The Nine Dots

Objective: Draw a line through all nine dots.
Restrictions:
1. Start with your pencil on any one of the dots.
2. Draw four and only four straight lines without removing your pencil from the page.
3. You may cross lines but you may not repeat them, i.e., trace back on them.

Laboratory Groups

Picture Makers:

1. Illustrate with diagrams, pictures, or any other nonverbal means the effects of hidden assumptions on interpersonal behavior.

or

2. Illustrate nonverbally how unanswerable questions may lead to communication difficulties.

or

3. Illustrate nonverbally the IFD disease (idealization, frustration, demoralization). You may want to cut out pictures from magazines and make posters or collages to represent each phase of the disease.

Forum Discussion:

1. Why do you think people have difficulty discovering and/or admitting hidden assumptions? What kind of hidden assumptions are at work in this class to make learning more difficult?

or

2. Discuss the need to ask answerable questions.

or

3. Discuss the use of the scientific method in our everyday life. You will need to define the scientific method and show whether it can be applied in everyday situations and whether it should be applied. Show what happens when the scientific method is not used, or is used. You may want to discuss what sort of situations benefit most from the use of the scientific process and which situations in your opinion may not.

or

4. Imagine an important event that took place in your community. How do you find out about it? What are your sources of information, generally? How dependable are they? What are their limitations? In your opinion, what would be the best way to find out what *really* happened? Is it ever possible to know what *really* happens? Why or why not? Does it mean we can never believe anything or anyone? When do we decide (and how do we decide) that a source is reliable and the degree of its reliability? Is it important to find out?

or

5. How is the IFD disease related to the scientific method?

Role Players:

1. Role-play a situation in which failure to ask answerable questions resulted in communication difficulties. A situation in which it is important for someone to find out some information might be appropriate. Show how the kind of questions asked will determine the kind of information you get.

or

2. Using alter egos or other hidden assumption devices (see Suggestions for Work in Small

Groups, p. 212), role-play a situation in which failure to identify hidden assumptions led to communication difficulties.

or

3. Role-play a situation in which one person makes specific assumptions about an event and acts in a particular way as a result of the assumptions. Role-play the same situation, but this time the person makes a different assumption about the event. Show how his behavior is changed. Two acts might be indicated.

Observers:

1. Watch especially for the kind of inferences or assumptions among group members which tended to interfere with good communication. Were members aware of their assumptions? How did they indicate their awareness? Did members pay attention to each other's assumptions and try to clarify them? Did they watch feedback from each other in order to interpret other members' messages? Comment also on the communication patterns and flow. (Who talked to whom, and how much?)

2. Observe the kind of questions asked in the group. Were they mostly answerable (capable of being answered through observations in the empirical world) or were they unanswerable (not capable of being answered through observations in the empirical world)?

    Notice what happens when a group member gives a suggestion. What happens to the suggestion? Is it noticed at all? Is it accepted by the group? How rapidly? Is it accepted as it is? Is it modified? Or is it overtly rejected? What happens to the person who made the suggestion as a result of the group reaction to it? Does the person whose ideas are accepted make more suggestions? Does the person whose ideas are rejected stop making suggestions and keep quiet? Does the person whose ideas are not commented upon try to force them onto the group, or does he withdraw from the interaction?

Feedback Blank Four

1. Rate the productivity of this session for you.

   1   2   3   4   5   6   7   8   9   10

   Not productive   Highly productive

2. Rate how you think the rest of the class felt about the productivity of this session.

   1   2   3   4   5   6   7   8   9   10

   Not productive   Highly productive

   Comments:

3. Were there any examples of unanswerable questions asked in your group?

4. What kind of insights did you get from the exercises this week (session)?

5. Comment on your listening to the lectures so far.

6. Other comments, questions, criticisms, suggestions, etc.

Personal Improvement Blank Four

1. Recall a recent decision you made—decision of some significance. Analyze as far as you can the assumptions that went into making the decision.

2. What kind of assumptions are you aware of, in yourself as well as in other students, when you attend this class?

3. Cite examples of unanswerable questions from your own experience. Why are they unanswerable? What consequences did they have on communication?

4. Can you identify a recent instance in your experience when failure to ask an appropriate question resulted in confused communication? Describe the instance.

Assignment One

News Clippings

For this assignment you will compare a newspaper story of a current event and an editorial from the same newspaper in terms of the amount of factual statements, inferences, and judgments found in the two clippings.

Step 1: Cut out a newspaper story on any current event (about 500 words). Underline in red all the reports of factual information (statements that are capable of verification through observations). Underline in blue all the statements of inferences (statements made about the unknown on the basis of the known). Underline in green all the statements of judgments (expressions of values).

Step 2: Cut out an editorial (about 500 words) and underline in red the statements of factual information, in blue the statements of inferences, and in green the statements of judgments.

Step 3: Write a brief paper to explain what you discovered when you compared the two clippings in terms of the *amount* of facts, inferences, and judgments. What conclusions do you draw? Hand in your clippings with the completed assignment.

Assignment Two

Slanting

''A youth and a man were killed and three teen-agers were seriously injured early today in two accidents.''
   Write:
1. A report of these accidents, inventing names and places.

2. A slanted report for a newspaper campaigning against juvenile delinquency. Be sure to use only factual statements, as in the report above, letting your reader make his own inferences and judgments. The facts must be the same as in the first story.

3. A slanted report for a newspaper highly critical of the local city administration. Again, use factual statements only, and the facts must be the same as those presented in the first story. Only the slant should differ.

Assignment Three

Recommendations

Write a one page paper using judgments and inferences in the following way:
1. Report heavily slanted *against* persons or organizations you like.

2. Report heavily slanted *in favor* of persons or organizations you dislike.

For example, imagine that your fraternity, or any club you belong to, is a subversive organization and report the facts about its activities and members upon which unfavorable inferences could be made by people suspecting the organization to be subversive. What is innocent to someone knowing the real purpose of the organization might appear very suspicious to a person not knowing the organization and ready to suspect subversive activities.

Or imagine that one of your most disagreeable neighbors has been offered a job 2,000 miles away, and write a *factual* letter of recommendation to help him get the job. Don't invent anything, just tell what the neighbor is like with a positive slant.

CHAPTER 5 MEANING AND COMMUNICATION— WORDS DON'T MEAN, PEOPLE MEAN

The text outlines two fallacies of meaning: first, that words actually have meaning, and second, that a word has only one meaning. The exercises and activities in the laboratory section will help our investigation of these two faulty assumptions about words and meaning. The shifting meanings of our descriptions of our friends in the Irregular Conjugation—the Conjugation of Adjectives—can lead to all sorts of additional games we can play with our language. It is also possible to develop your own vocabulary and grammar in your search for a language which will not be understood by everyone, but will be your own special means of communicating with your closest friends.

This chapter will begin our most serious use of communication cases to demonstrate the potential for communication breakdowns in our society. Not only does the subject matter of a case help us understand the problems of our communication, but we should pay attention to how our group works together to discuss the case.

Because we believe that the case method of learning is valuable in communication laboratory work, we have included the following material: first, How Groups Solve Case Problems and second, Notes on Discussing Cases. These will help you work on the cases and also make you more understanding of your own involvement in the groups discussing the cases in the laboratory.

How Groups Solve Case Problems*

A group will generally tend to go through several stages to arrive at a satisfactory solution in discussing a case.

Stage 1: The stage of condemnation and aggressive evaluation.

Participants take sides; tend to put the blame for the communication breakdowns on one person or another—usually in relation to their own biases about the kind of people involved in the case.

The tendency at this stage is to oversimplify the situation by blaming.

Stage 2: The stage of frustration and rejection.

Participants complain that they do not have enough data to solve the problem. They do not feel they are given enough information to come to a solution.

The discovery that we all must make decisions most of our lives based on fragmentary or incomplete evidence is an important experience.

Stage 3: The stage of widening perceptions.

Participants will begin to ask more probing questions and try to discover how the people in the case view the situation.

Analysis of the past history and other pressures acting on the people in the case is involved.

*Eugene Rebstock, "General Semantics Training through Case Analysis," *ETC,* 1963, vol. 20, no. 3.

Stage 4: The stage of alternative solutions and resolutions.
Participants come up with thoughtful considerations of possible solutions.

Solutions grow out of the complexities of the situation and are proposed with a feeling for the consequences of actions growing out of the case.

Notes on Discussing Cases

1. A case initiates discussion in the following areas:

   a. Details of the case and their relationships.

   b. Inferences that are drawn by the participants in the discussion concerning why the event occurred. Also, inferences about motivation of the people involved in the case itself.

   c. Illustrations and examples from personal experiences are brought up by participants in the discussion.

   d. Expressions of feelings about the actions and assertions in the case.

2. What can be analyzed in a case:

   a. The content of the sender's message.
   What was said? Do we have all that was said?

   b. The kind of message that was sent.
   Was it written, oral, or both? Was it simple, clear, or ambiguous? What made it simple, clear, or ambiguous? What does this have to do with the way the situation developed?

   c. The setting of the communication situation.
   Where did the incident take place—office, home, or face to face? What kind of situation was it? Were people tense, relaxed, formal, or informal?

   d. The sender.
   What status does he have, and does this affect the communication? If so, how? What assumptions does the sender have toward the situation? What attitudes, opinions, or feelings? What kind of person is he?

   e. The receiver.
   Same questions as those asked about the sender. In addition, what is his response to the sender's message, and how does this affect the communication?

   f. Outside pressures.
   Did the situation occur in an environment which provided certain rules and regulations that governed the sender and the receiver? Was the message sent directly, or was it received through intermediaries?

What's in a Name?

Juliet, of the Capulet family, addressed Romeo:

Tis but thy name that is my enemy;
Thou art thyself though, not a Montague.
What's Montague? It is nor hand, nor foot,
Nor arm, nor face, nor any other part
Belonging to a man. O! be some other name;
What's in a name? that which we call a rose
By any other name would smell as sweet;
So Romeo would, were he not Romeo call'd,
Retain that dear perfection which he owes
Without that title.

What implications can you draw from this situation about communication? Are there examples like these now? Are labels and names very important in our world today? Can you find examples from your own experience?

Irregular Conjugation—the Conjugation of Adjectives

Bertrand Russell on a British Broadcasting Company radio program called the "Brain Trust" gave the following "conjugation of adjectives."

I am firm.

You are obstinate.

He is pig-headed.

The *New Statesman and Nation,* quoting the above as a model, offered prizes to readers who sent in the best conjugated adjectives of this kind. Here are some of the published entries:

I am sparkling. You are unusually attractive. He is drunk.

I am righteously indignant. You are annoyed. He is making a fuss about nothing.

I am fastidious. You are fussy. He is an old woman.

I am a creative writer. You have a journalistic flair. He is a prosperous hack.

I am beautiful. You have quite good features. She is not bad looking, if you like that type.

I daydream. You are an escapist. He ought to see a psychiatrist.

I have about me something of the subtle, haunting, mysterious fragrance of the Orient. You rather overdo it, dear. She stinks.

Conjugate in a similar way the following statements:

I am stocky.

I am slender.

I love music.

I don't believe in excessive savings.

I believe in the new morality.

I live in a fantasy world.

I need plenty of sleep.

I believe in honesty being the best policy.

I am a casual housekeeper.

Who Understood You?

Think back over the last few years or so since you have been relatively mature and aware of your relationships with others and try to determine the one person who understood you better than anyone else did. It is not necessary that the person understood you for a very long period of time or that he still understands you now. It is only necessary that you feel that for some period of time this individual understood you better than anyone else has. Try to determine what it was about yourself, the other person, the situation, or any combination of these that made this understanding take place.

Jot down a few notes so that you will be prepared to speak next class session. The discussion will be informal and all students will be expected to take part for a few minutes.

Let's Define

If you were compiling a dictionary and had before you only the following sentences, what definition would you write for the word "chabation"? Do not try to find a one-word synonym, but write out a ten- to twenty-word *definition*. A definition should tell what general category the object can be put into and how this object differs from other objects that might also be put into the same general category.

1. A chabation is an extremely useful instrument.

2. Most people own a chabation and all college students must have at least one if not more.

3. A chabation is not expected to last forever.

4. A chabation is not only needed for math problems but also for English themes.

5. You will probably use a chabation to complete this exercise.

Definition: A chabation is

What's the Context?

Here are some simple statements, the context of which is given upside down beneath each statement. Before reading the context, write down your immediate response to the statement. For example:

Statement: He can't even add two and two.

Response: He is pretty stupid.

Context: He is only two months old.

1. He never studies at school.

He can't because of the noise, so he goes to the public library.

2. She never stays in the dorm for the weekend.

Her mother is very ill, and she must go home every chance she gets.

3. Of course you may spend your summer in Europe, honey.

Your sister gets a fur coat, your brother gets to go around the world, and I am going to the moon!

Laboratory Groups

Picture Makers:

1. Illustrate nonverbally how a communication problem could occur when people have different meanings for the words they use.

or

2. Illustrate nonverbally that meanings are not fixed—they change as experiences change and they change as times change.

or

3. Illustrate nonverbally all the meanings that come to your mind when you hear the words: home, book, school, civil rights, freedom, dissent, love, warmth, happiness, and wealth.

Forum Discussion:

1. Discuss the idea that there is more room for misunderstanding when people speak in general and vague terms than in specific terms. Why? (Give examples.)

2. Discuss the idea that "words don't mean, people mean." What are the implications of this idea for human communication?

3. Are meanings culture-bound? That is, are there some meanings that are more agreed upon in some cultures than others? Why and how does this happen?

4. Have one group member make a controversial statement about some current event. Then ask him to define his terms. He will then use more words to do this. Ask him to define some of the other words he used to define his first word. He will again use more words. Ask him again to define the new words, and so on, until he runs out of definitions or patience.

   What happened in the process? What feelings do you think the person you questioned had? Can he comment himself on his feelings? Why did he run out of definitions? Are there certain words that we just do not know how to define even though "we know what they mean"? Is it possible that "what they mean" is different from one person to another? How do we know if we mean the same things if we cannot give the definition? How do we know that we do mean the same thing when we do give a definition since we are simply using more words that may themselves not be understood in the same way by all?

Role Players:

Role-play a situation in which people misunderstood each other's words and how the misunderstanding could have been prevented. Stay away from obvious examples.

Observers:

This observing exercise focuses on group members' participation in any group activity. As an observer you will be assigned one particular group member to observe. There should thus be as many observers as there are group participants.

It would be desirable that the group members sit in a circle and that the observers sit on the outside of the circle, also forming a circle. Each observer will observe the group member who sits in front of him.

Observer Recording Sheet

Name of the participant you observed: _____

Your name: _____

Give the participant you observed one of the following ratings for each of the following recorded criteria:

5—superior, 4—excellent, 3—good, 2—below average, 1—poor

Criteria: Rating

Attitude: Objectivity, open mindedness, willingness to change views in light of   _____
new information or evidence.

Knowledge: Information on the problems.   _____

Thinking: Ability to analyze and reason about the problems.   _____

Listening: Ability to understand and interpret views of others.   _____

Speaking: Ability to communicate ideas clearly and effectively. Willingness to   _____
participate.

*Consideration
for others:* Tact, cooperation, evenness of contribution (not talking too much or   _____
too little).

General criticism or other comments:

When the group has completed their discussion or presentation to the class, the observer should go and talk for about ten minutes with the group member he observed. The observer should share with the group member what he observed and how he evaluated the group member. The observer should explain the basis for his judgments and talk about the group member's behavior in the group in a constructive manner. This interaction should not be a monologue on the part of the observer, but a dialogue between two people, in an effort to understand communicative behavior.

Case One: The Car and the Kids*

"I only figured that any kid who was messing around like that deserved some kind of punishment."

John and Patricia Conley were apparently no more, no less perplexed by the generation gap than any other parents of a teen-age girl. Julie, their sixteen-year-old daughter, was a good student, reliable, known for her quick smile and friendly manner. She rarely caused her parents any great problems, though they had long since given up trying to make sense out of the exuberant and slang-filled speech she constantly used.

Julie was an only child and her parents were often quite restrictive as to where she went and who she went with. Julie naturally complained occasionally, but there were never any major problems until one warm June evening.

School had just been dismissed for the summer and Julie was given the family car for the evening to go to a girlfriend's party. She was given careful instructions that she was to be home by 12 o'clock.

The all-girl party was a success, and the happy teen-agers were so engrossed in talk that the hours slipped by quickly. Someone finally pointed out that it was almost 1 A.M. Julie gasped with surprise and quickly told her hostess that she had to leave. Several of her friends quickly asked for rides home. Julie knew she was already late so why would a few extra minutes matter?

As she drove down the street toward the first girl's house, one of the other girls in the car spotted two boys she knew walking down the street and asked Julie to stop to give them a ride. Julie knew neither of them but stopped anyway to pick them up. At the next intersection Julie's car was hit broadside by a man who failed to stop at the traffic light. No one was hurt, but the car was inoperable. Police, after questioning all of them took Julie home in a squad car. Both worried parents came running out of the house to see what had happened. In the turmoil of Julie's excited efforts to explain, all her father heard was "We were riding around with a couple of guys and some old man hit us." Visions of his daughter roaming the streets late at night in a car with boys she didn't even know combined with the built up tensions in Mr. Conley, and he vented his anger by slapping Julie so hard she fell to the pavement. The patrolman attempted to intervene and Mr. Conley hit him, breaking his nose.

Julie spent ten days in the hospital with a concussion, the officer needed emergency treatment, and Mr. Conley was fined $300 and given a suspended sentence for striking an officer of the law. It was months before father and daughter could even begin to talk to each other without anger and three years later, there is still bitterness between them.

Some Questions to Ask about the Case

1. Who was the sender and who the receiver of the fateful communication?

2. What effect did the time, place, and circumstances have on Mr. Conley's actions?

3. Did Julie's choice of words have any effect on Mr. Conley's actions?

*Handbook for Teachers of Speech, by Bobby Patton, The University of Kansas, 1970. Reproduced by permission of the author.

4. What effects did the emotions of both Julie and her father have?

5. Were both Julie and her father attempting to communicate? Were they listening to each other?

6. What roles do values play in this incident? What are the possible differences in orientation for Mr. Conley and Julie?

7. Was the "punishment" related by Mr. Conley more to what Julie did or what she said?

8. How do Julie and her father perceive each other? What are their differences in orientations? Does the generation gap have any effect?

9. Did Mr. Conley show any sensitivity to Julie's needs?

10. How could this incident have been prevented?

11. What sort of interference was there on the communication channel?

12. Was Mr. Conley reacting logically or emotionally to the content of what Julie said?

13. Did Mr. Conley's perception of himself and/or Julie color his judgment?

Case Two: The Skate Exchange

You are a member of the Parent-Teacher Association. You and several other parents discussed the problem of children outgrowing skates and the expense involved. A plan was worked out to establish a skate exchange. When it was presented to the Association the plan was met with enthusiasm and immediate approval. You were appointed to chair a committee and work out the details.

The committee decided to invite all children, whose skates were in good condition but too small, to bring their skates to school at which time they would be given a dated receipt. At a specified date, all who had brought skates could return to pick a pair that would suit them, if there were any, and take the skates at 50 cents for the service. At the end of the week, all or anyone else could come to select from what was left at 50 cents. There was to be no profit on the arrangement for anyone. The entire project was to be manned by members of the committee.

When the committee reported its plan to the Association, the plan was approved and the committee received thanks from the Association. At first, things went very well. Skates were brought in in large numbers, and many children got skates back that fitted and were serviceable. In several weeks, however, the complaints began to roll in from parents whose children contributed skates but could not find substitute ones in return.

You are at the exchange now, and Mr. Johnston has come in in a fury. He accuses you of making a fancy profit on the deal while he contributed a $15 pair of skates and got nothing in return.

What are you going to say to Mr. Johnston?

Case Three: Mary Jones

Mary Jones is working for Dr. Calley and Dr. Casey. Among other duties she has charge of instruments and preparations of injections. The doctors operate in a small county hospital with limited surgery facilities.

Shortly after coming on the job, Mary Jones discovers that sterile techniques are not being observed. The very busy doctors reuse instruments and syringes and don't pay attention to scrub techniques. After a week, Mary is completely frustrated in her attempts to maintain the kind of regime she has learned and practiced for three years before coming to work with the doctors. She is also concerned that her failure to maintain the techniques will some day have serious consequences although she is not aware that there has been any difficulty in the past.

New residents of the small community where they plan to make their home, Mary Jones and her husband both need to work to support their three young children. The county hospital is about the only medical facility for miles around.

What are the real problems here, and how might they be solved?

Feedback Blank Five

1. Rate the productivity of this session's work for you.

1   2   3   4   5   6   7   8   9   10

Not productive   Very productive

2. Rate how you think the rest of the class felt about the productivity of this session's work.

1   2   3   4   5   6   7   8   9   10

Not productive   Very productive

Comments:

3. Did anything you remember interfere with good communication in your group? Anything which held back understanding or working with each other effectively?

4. Did you observe anyone in your group who was silent (or nearly so)?

5. Any examples of communication difficulties created by different use of the same words by different group members?

6. Other comments, questions, criticisms, suggestions, etc.

Personal Improvement Blank Five

1. Give at least two examples from your own experience when someone used a word that meant something to one person and something else to another. Show the confusion that resulted.

2. If "words don't mean, people mean," what is the use of dictionaries? Do you think words do have a "correct" meaning, or a "right" meaning?

3. Can words be made to mean anything an individual wants them to mean? What limitations must we place on extreme individualized meaning? Why?

Assignment One

Definition

1. Scientists use the concept of operational definition in their work. What is the difference between an operational definition and a dictionary definition?

2. Make up a list of words and see if you can find operational definitions and dictionary definitions for each. How do the definitions differ? What types of words have the greatest differences in definitions?

3. Try writing an operational definition for some nonsense word. Then, try to use the word in its various forms in sentences. Make a variety of sentences.

Assignment Two

Mini Language

In many social groups, there is a standard miniature language that is different from the overall language. There are special meanings to common words, and there are new and invented words for special circumstances, events, or objects. On your own campus or in your own work group, there are probably several pet phrases and words in use. Observe your surroundings and see if you can identify and define these phrases and terms. Are there some you don't understand? What do you think could cause this? Are there words you use with friends that perhaps others can't understand? What do you think causes this, and how does it affect communication between you and your friends? Between you and those who can't understand?

Assignment Three

Connotations

Choose a word which might connote something controversial. For example, "president," or "freedom." Write down what the words mean to you.

Then add information (other words) to the word you chose. For example, "college president," or "president of General Motors," or "President of the United States," or "freedom of speech," or "freedom to peaceably assemble." Write down what each phrase means to you.

Then interview several people on your campus (students, faculty members, staff members, and administrators) and have them tell you their meanings for the word alone, then their meanings for the phrases.

Write a short paper on this topic in which you will compare the meanings stimulated by the words. Do they differ significantly? Are any of them similar to your meanings? Compare the meanings elicited by the phrases. Are they more nearly alike than the meanings elicited by the words alone? What conclusions do you draw from this exercise?

Assignment Four

Interpretations

There are many real-life situations on a college campus or in an organization when communication breaks down because of some differences in interpretation of a rule, a regulation, etc.

In your school, many student activities are under the supervision of faculty and/or administration. Seek out an event or a situation in which such a difference of interpretation of a rule or regulation has caused some problem. Interview the people involved and ask them what their interpretation of the regulation is.

Write a brief discussion for the class in which you will (1) trace the origins of the regulation (or whatever triggered the problem) and the various stages it went through before it got passed on to the students, (2) report the results of your interview about people's interpretations of the regulation, and (3) suggest a course of action designed to alleviate or solve the problem.

Assignment Five

Making Up Words

Make up a word, an adjective, preferably, or an adverb, and decide what you want it to mean. For example, the word "campy" will mean "cool," "neat," "far out," or "great." Then use this newly coined word over and over again as if it were the latest slang and as if it were used and accepted by everyone else. If people ask you what the word means, tell them (but don't tell them you made it up). See how long it will take for the word to be used by other people besides yourself. Who will start using it first, and how slowly or fast does it spread?

When you have some data on the frequency of its use by people around you, report to the class what you have found. If after a while no one uses the word, report this finding too. Then consider with the class what you would have to do to make this word a widely used word on campus. Enlist the help of the class and try out the suggestions made.

CHAPTER 6 LANGUAGE AND COMMUNICATION—
BEYOND OUR WILDEST DREAMS

Class activities about relationships can give rise to much discussion of how we choose those with whom we will share our feelings and our thoughts. In the book *Future Shock,* one of the points made by author Toffler is that our acceleration of living today is making it more and more difficult to establish relationships, and that in the future it will be even more difficult. If that is the case, and we add to our difficulties our uncertain use of language, the future may look pretty drab. The laboratory exercises are designed to help us look at our use of stereotypes as shortcuts toward making the human contacts which we must do on such short notice. Stereotypes help us put people and events into neat packages—with words. If the empirical world does not fit those word packages, then we have our own form of "future shock" when we discover that our language and our empirical (real) world are not coming out the same.

Besides the laboratory exercises, there are in this laboratory manual chapter a large number of very simple and quick assignments about our language. If we are curious about our "labeling" habits, it is possible to see many of them in action in the assignments in this chapter.

If the laboratory activities of Role Players, Forum Discussion, etc. are used, it should be particularly noted that the Observers have a very involved task to observe the group functions and assign role behaviors to the people who have participated in the planning sessions. A recording sheet outlines some very useful categories of individual roles (or functions) which may be observed in any group. Observers in other settings or other exercises may want to note the group functions categories in this exercise and make use of them at other times than in the laboratory period for this chapter.

Relationships

Everyone is talking about "relationships." Young people are accused of jumping into relationships irresponsibly. What is a "relationship"? What role does communication play in building a "relationship"? How do you avoid a breakdown in communication which ultimately results in jeopardizing a "relationship"? Do you and those with whom you share a "relationship" play by rules? If so, what are some of the rules? Do you have "relationships" with friends?

Keeping your answers to the above in mind, what do you think are the differences in your "relationships" with the following people?

1. A fellow student of the opposite sex

2. A fellow student of the same sex

3. A male professor

4. A female professor

5. A dean

6. The kids you went to high school with who do not go to college

7. Your parents

8. Your rich aunt (or a rich relative, or a rich friend of the family)

9. Your drinking uncle

10. The man who interviews you for a job

Why are there these differences? Can you generalize about "relationships" from these ideas?

Lovers' Quarrel

You have just had a serious quarrel with your boy (girl) friend. As a result, you won't be having your usual date this weekend. The quarrel was over the amount of control that your parents exert over your relationship—specific gripes were exchanged about your parents' involvement in your affairs.

You are now faced with explaining to the people around you, who will probably ask, why you will not be having your usual date this weekend. How will you explain the situation to:

1. Your best friend

2. His (or her) best friend

3. Your roommate

4. Your parents

5. Your meddling aunt

Can you make some generalizations about the levels of abstraction that you will use in your explanations to these different people? With which people do you use the most abstract language, the least abstract language? Why?

What Is the Level?

I. Starting with the one at the lowest level of abstraction, arrange the following statements in order of increasing higher levels of abstraction.

1. I like driving better than flying

2. I like Rambler cars

3. I like American cars better than English cars

4. I like my Rambler classic four-door sedan

5. I like to travel

1. Joe keeps all our household appliances in working condition

2. Joe is a mechanical genius

3. Joe is very handy with tools

4. Joe is 100 percent real American boy

5. Yesterday, Joe replaced a burned-out condenser in the radio

6. Joe is an awfully useful person to have around

7. Joe keeps that radio in working condition

II. Make up your own series of statements and arrange them in order of increasingly higher levels of abstraction.

Laboratory Groups

Picture Makers:

1. Illustrate with pictures or any other nonverbal means, the meanings that come to your mind when you hear the words: house, book, school, civil rights, dissent, freedom, love, happiness. Can the illustrations you give be ordered along an empirical-symbolic continuum?

or

2. Select several objects and illustrate nonverbally as many categories these objects can be placed into that you can think of. See if you can order the categories in some fashion (the more specific—empirically oriented—to the more general—symbolically oriented—perhaps).

or

3. Illustrate nonverbally as many examples of symbols that are particularly respected and protected in our society that you can think of. For example, a Bible, the flag, a draft card, a uniform. Try to indicate in your illustrations the various groups of people for whom the particular symbol chosen is meaningful. Another way to look at the question is to figure what symbols are meaningful to young people, midde-aged people, upper-class people, army veterans, teachers, etc.

Forum Discussion:

Your instructor may assign any of the following topics:

1. Select a field (journalism, physics, biology, psychology, political science, etc.) and find out what ideas have revolutionized that particular field. How often did it happen? What were the consequences?

   You may want to leave the classroom as a group to interview a specialist in the field who might help you determine the important turning points in the development of his field.

2. Discuss the idea that there is more room for misunderstanding when people speak at high levels of abstraction. Why?

3. Do you listen to yourself? How much? Why? Can you talk yourself into things? Do you talk to yourself aloud (in private)? How much does this affect your attitudes?

   It was demonstrated in Nazi Germany that the saying of hateful words by people who did not even believe them seemed to heighten that emotion. What do you think this means in relation to today's "generation gap"?

   How many of what we call "problems" are real, and how many are simply talked about and believed to be problems simply because people *talk* about them as problems?

   For example, have you ever felt odd because you got along fine with your parents and you know "you are not supposed to" since the "generation gap" is assumed to be everywhere? When you discuss with friends who have difficulty with their parents, do you feel somewhat hesitant to admit you don't have that kind of problem? Is it at all possible that the "generation gap" is only a verbal myth that most people subscribe to in the abstract but that has little empirical validity?

4. It is said that the slow learner operates on a low level of abstraction while a mentally ill person operates on a high level of abstraction. What does this mean? Do levels of abstraction have a definite relationship with "sanity"? Which person, the slow learner or the mentally ill, would you expect to be the "sanest"? Why? Which person would you expect to communicate with the greatest accuracy?

   How do you usually cope with friends whose behavior is based on a totally unrealistic and unchecked verbal world? Do you feel responsible to help them acquire a more realistic view of the situation, or do you feel it is their problem and their business? Why do you think anyone bothers to help a mentally ill person who is not harmful to anyone?

5. "If language is not correct, then what is said is not what is meant; if what is said is not what is meant, then what ought to be done remains undone; if this remains undone, morals and art will deteriorate; if morals and art deteriorate, justice goes astray! and if justice goes astray, the people will stand about in helpless confusion" (Confucius).

   What do you think is meant by this quotation? Do you think that it can possibly be relevant today? How? Give specific examples. Perhaps from our social and political ills.

6. "Words, like glasses, obscure everything that they do not make clear" (Joseph Joubert).

   How do words obscure or clarify? Is this due to the nature of words themselves? What is it due to? How obscure or clear is your own answer?

7. "The real enemy of mankind is delusion inside the heads of so-called normal people . . . delusion means the nonsense we talk to ourselves and believe. . . . These are dangerous delusions because they are not known by those who hold them to be delusions" (Edmund Taylor).

   What kind of language do you use to talk yourself into something? Do you hold hidden assumptions which do not match reality? Why do you continue to make these assumptions? Are there things you cling to and want to believe that perhaps are not accurate, that perhaps are delusions?

8. "For evil, then as well as for good, words make us the human beings we actually are. Deprived of language we should be as dogs or monkeys. Possessing language, we are men and women able to persevere in crime no less than in heroic virtue, capable of intellectual achievements beyond the scope of any animal, but at the same time capable of systematic silliness and stupidity such as no dumb beast could ever dream of" (Aldous Huxley).

   What do you think is meant by the above quotation? Do you think language is really all that important? Why or why not?

Role Players:

1. Role-play a situation in which failure to look appropriately for similarities and differences resulted in communication difficulties.

or

2. Role-play a situation in which symbolic behavior created communication difficulties. Show how it could have been prevented. Two acts might be indicated.

or

3. You are a male college student, and your hair is shoulder length, usually combed and clean. You wear jeans and boots most of the time. Peace signs are sewn to your clothes. You are not a political radical and have never participated in violent demonstrations of any kind. Actually you feel very strongly against violence in any form. You do believe some things are wrong with the "system."

You are a middle-aged, middle-class father. You have worked very hard for what you have and believe in hard work and education to "get ahead." You made a lot of sacrifices, financially and otherwise to provide for your family and for the education of your children. You feel that "longhaired hippies" are bums, radical, no good, and that all they want is to destroy what you worked so hard to get.

Imagine now, that these two people meet somewhere, sometime. What will the conversation be like? Will they see each other as persons or through the stereotyped appearance? How should the young man behave to make the older man understand he is not a "hippie-bum"? How should the older man behave to make the other understand he is not necessarily narrow-minded?

Role-play the encounter.

You can do the same thing by choosing an encounter between two people belonging to two opposite groups which hold strong prejudices against each other.

Observers:

At this stage of the class development, students should be able to make quite sophisticated observations on communication behavior in the small laboratory groups. In order to aid them in making and recording these observations, the following material has been gathered and should be used by students when called upon to make observations on group communication behavior. Not all this material is to be used at any one time. Students should read it through carefully first, then decide which part they will use to help them in their observations.

A sample recording sheet based on the information presented here is included on p. 281.

Additional observations on the points covered in this unit can be made if students are assigned to observe the small groups during any of the activities chosen for this session.

How empirical are the members of the group you observed? When ideas are suggested, are they specific or at a high level of abstraction? Keep track of high-level abstraction terms exchanged. Do group members make an effort to clarify them or have them clarified?

Observe the nonverbal behavior of group members. Can you tell when someone gets ready to talk? How? What cues does he give? Do other members get the cues? Are efforts made by group members to include the more quiet members? What is actually done, and how do the quieter members respond to these attempts to include them in the conversation? Were there instances of categorizing or stereotyping in the group? How did it manifest itself? How did the members respond to it?

Group Functions Recording Sheet

DIRECTIONS: For each member place a check mark in the column representing the roles that he has played most often in the group so far. Include yourself.

Roles or Functions	Members' Names					
Group-task Roles						
Initiator contributor						
Information seeker						
Information giver						
Coordinator						
Evaluator						
Summarizer						
Group-maintenance Roles						
Encourager						
Harmonizer						
Gatekeeper						
Standard setter						
Follower						
Self-oriented Roles						
Blocker						
Recognition seeker						
Dominator						
Avoider						

Feedback Blank Six

1. Rate the productivity of this session's work for you.

            1   2   3   4   5   6   7   8   9   10

   Not productive   Very productive

2. Rate how you think the rest of the class felt about the productivity of this session's work.

            1   2   3   4   5   6   7   8   9   10

   Not productive   Very productive

   Comments:

3. How satisfied are you with your group discussion? Why?

4. How I feel about the way the observers have been functioning:
   a. Generally favorable   _____
   b. Generally unfavorable   _____
   Please check: I have been an observer   _____
                     I have not been an observer _____

5. Do you ever suffer from the IFD disease in this class?

6. Other comments, questions, criticisms, suggestions, etc.

Personal Improvement Blank Six

1. Describe the recent behavior of a person you know who is primarily "word oriented" (symbolically oriented) and the behavior of a person you know who is primarily "fact oriented" (empirically oriented). What are the consequences of their behavior in their communication with other people?

2. What is meant by the concept of feedback? How does feedback work in the communication process? What purposes does it serve?

3. Give a couple of examples of oververbalized behavior (talking too much) you have observed recently in yourself or in others. What were some of the effects of this behavior?

4. Give two illustrations of stereotyping behavior you noticed recently.

5. Can you report an example of failure to notice differences that had an effect on your communication?

6. Briefly state what you feel are the most important concepts touched on so far in this course—most useful to you and most applicable to your communication.

Assignment One

Stereotyping

1. How is the grading system most widely used in today's schools related to stereotyping? How do you react to such statements as "He is an 'A' student" or "He is a 'D' student"? What do they mean? What are the consequences of such statements?

2. Think of a specific stereotype that you may have about a particular group (e.g., religious, ethnic, or political). Try to explain how the stereotype developed and how it influences your behavior toward the members of the group. Be specific in describing the effects of the stereotype on your behavior.

3. Is it possible to treat an individual "as an individual regardless of classification"? Defend your answer. Use examples from your experience if possible.

4. List some attitudes you have held, or still hold, which you now consider to be stereotypes. How were they formed? Why? What has made you perceive them as stereotypes?

5. Stereotyped attitudes are frequently influential in determining communication behavior. Cite examples. In what way do stereotypes help and/or hinder your communication?

Assignment Two

Language of Advertising

Analyze the language of advertising.

Take a particular magazine that caters to a certain kind of reader and compare the advertisers' language to the advertisers' language of another magazine catering to a different kind of reader (e.g., *Playboy* versus *Good Housekeeping*). What kinds of variations do you find in their particular language? What are some of the assumptions made by the advertisers? How do the various types of language used in these advertisements affect your personal response to the products being advertised?

Advertisements usually give information about a product and also give affective and symbolic meanings. The latter is seen when the ad seeks to make the consumer identify the product with something beyond the product itself. For example, linking a mouthwash with social success.

Select ten different ad slogans and separate the information about the product from the affective and symbolic meaning.

For example:

"You will enjoy this different tomato juice made from aristocrat tomatoes."

Information about the product	Affective and symbolic meaning
Tomato juice is made from tomatoes.	Because you have sophisticated and discriminating taste you will prefer tomato juice made from superior, exclusive tomatoes. An average person may not notice the difference, but you will. To drink our own tomato juice is to symbolize your aristocratic taste.

Assignment Three

Language Behaviors

1. What do you think is meant by "First we look, then we name, and only then do we see" (Lippmann)?

    Do you agree with this idea? Defend your stand in your own words.

2. Identify an area in which you exhibit somewhat dogmatic and rigid behaviors. Analyze what you feel might account for such behaviors. Analyze the responses they elicit from others toward you. What kind of person would you be without these behaviors? Would life and communication be simpler or more complex?

3. People sometimes talk about punishing children who use dirty language by washing out their mouths with soap. Is this ever actually done? Comment on the reactions or thoughts involved among those who use this method of control over their children's language.

Assignment Four

Dirty Books

A few years ago, a Denver father noticed a book that his daughter had brought home from high school. It was a collection of poems by E. E. Cummings. Leafing through the book, he came across some "pornographic poems." He complained to the Denver schools and their response was to withdraw this book from circulation in school libraries. A great reaction came from the Denver chapter of the American Civil Liberties Union, which claimed this constituted "censorship." The Denver Public School head librarian issued a statement saying that, in the best interest of the students and in keeping with the requests of parents, they were practicing "book selection." A letter in the *Denver Post* from members of the English Department of the University of Denver noted that no matter whether you called something "mass murder" or "the final solution to the Jewish problem," the results were the same.

    Discuss the sanity of how the words that were used described the circumstances of the situation. What would you recommend should have happened? How would you have described it? Which word aroused the most emotion? What effects might this have had on the behavior of those involved?

Assignment Five

Beyond Content

How can you go beyond what people say and listen to what people mean? What sort of distance is there between what is said and what is meant? When you argue with another person, how much of the problem is a "people problem," and how much is a "content problem"?

CHAPTER 7 REDUCING INTRAPERSONAL BARRIERS—NO EASY WAY

The triad exercise where one person acts as a recommender and another as a questioner to the person with a problem has many variations. It can be an extremely useful way to look at our own relations with the techniques of questions and giving advice. It is particularly useful to write down the reactions you have, and a set of sheets is made out for that purpose. You have a chance to see how near your expectations have come toward being realized.

The "either-or" slogans in the assignment section relate to our looking at the world with that kind of attitude that everything can be neatly divided into us-them, black-white, rich-poor, bad-good, etc. You will discover that much of the impact made by slogans on people is dependent on that kind of simple either-or logic—slogans must be brief, catchy, and must tell us exactly where the sloganeer stands in a minimum of words.

Some of the general semantics devices, or the scientific attitude described in Chapter 7, may be of some use to the person trying to analyze mass movements or the impact of demagogues or some kinds of leaders. Activities involving the meaningless expressions which somehow captivate us as voters and as consumers are included in this chapter and also in the Chapter 5 exercises on meaning.

Observers in the laboratory are asked to look especially at the use of feedback by persons in the groups. Feedback is a very important concept and will keep recurring in these discussions and exercises just as it has in the use of the Feedback Blank provided in each laboratory manual chapter.

The Consultation Process*

Instructions to the Person (P) with the Problem

Choose a conflict situation on which you would like some help. It should be important to you and something you have thought a good deal about. It should be a situation you really want to do something about. You will have about ten minutes to tell about it, about twenty minutes to discuss it, and ten minutes with each of the other members of your triad.

Join freely and genuinely in the discussion—first with the person designated R, then with the person designated Q. Try to get help from them. Test their suggestions and explore their ideas. Try to give them a real understanding of your situation.

Note if your feelings change. If they do, at what point during the discussion does the change occur? Try to see if there is any relationship between your changes of feelings and what Q or R do.

*Adapted from National Training Laboratories materials.

Instructions to the Recommender (R)

1. Listen thoughtfully to the conflict situation as presented.

2. Respond with any of the following attempts to help:
   a. *Recall* and describe a similar experience you or someone you know or read about has dealt with. Tell what was done to improve the situation. If *P* does not accept or seem to hear and you still see it as a good solution, try to explain further.
   b. *Recommend,* in order, the steps you would take if you were in his situation. If *P* does not accept some of these, make other proposals until you hit on something he finds helpful.

Instructions to the Questioner (Q)

1. Listen thoughtfully to the conflict situation as presented.

2. Your task is, by *raising questions,* to help *P* diagnose his own difficulty. Refrain from giving any advice or citing any experience of your own or of others. Keep probing to bring about new angles. Keep responsibility for the answers on *P* himself. You will have succeeded if you enable him to redefine his situation, seeing the difficulty as due to rather different factors than those he originally presented.

Consultation Process Feedback

Person with the Problem

1. How did you feel during the consulting process?

2. What did he (she) do that helped?
   a. The recommender:

   b. The questioner:

3. What did he (she) do that did *not* help?
   a. The recommender:

   b. The questioner:

4. What did the consultants do that helped me define my problem?

5. Ideally, what would you have liked to have happen?

Consultation Process Feedback

Recommender

1. How did you feel during the consulting process?

2. What did you do that seemed helpful?

3. What did you do that seemed *not* to be helpful?

4. What did you do that helped the person describe and define his problem?

5. Ideally, what would you have liked to have happen?

Consultation Process Feedback

Questioner

1. How did you feel during the consulting process?

2. What did you do that seemed helpful?

3. What did you do that did *not* seem helpful?

4. What did you do that helped the person describe and define his problem?

5. Ideally, what would you have liked to have seen happen?

Words Without Meaning

If writing is communication, every phrase should convey a message to the reader. Unfortunately some combinations of words are meaningless.

A thesaurus of these nothing statements was made by the Royal Canadian Air Force to warn its writers against fuzzy phrases. It was popularized by a U.S. Public Health Service official who circulated it among government employees and businessmen.

The thirty words involved are listed in three columns. When a writer wants to use a meaningless phrase, he selects at random a three-digit number and then uses the corresponding words from the three columns. For example, 257 produces "systematized logistical projection," which has the ring of absolute authority and means absolutely nothing.

	A	B	C
0	Integrated	Management	Options
1	Total	Organizational	Flexibility
2	Systematized	Monitored	Capability
3	Parallel	Reciprocal	Mobility
4	Functional	Digital	Programming
5	Responsive	Logistical	Concept
6	Optional	Transitional	Time-phase
7	Synchronized	Incremental	Projection
8	Compatible	Third-generation	Hardware
9	Balanced	Policy	Contingency

Your instructor may ask you to get into small groups to devise a series of these meaningless phrases and to write sentences or paragraphs to incorporate them.

Laboratory Groups

Picture Makers:

1. Illustrate nonverbally one or more of the extensional devices.

or

2. Illustrate with pictures without words some of the following:
   education, liberty, democracy, communism, hot, beautiful, pain, truth, racism, groovy, straight, equality.

or

3. Illustrate your expectations of how you hope your communication will improve as a result of taking a course such as this one.

Forum Discussion:

1. Discuss how the Forum Discussion, Picture Makers, Role Players, or Observers could be improved.

or

2. How might the extensional devices be helpful in your work, studies, social life, etc.? How can an appropriate use of these devices be of help to you in your daily life?

or

3. Discuss the relationship between the process of abstraction and the extensional devices.

NOTE: Many of the assignments which appear in this workbook can be used as Forum Discussion questions.

Role Players:

1. Role-play a situation in which a communication breakdown is created by polarization.

2. Role-play a situation where empirical behavior and/or symbolic behavior are exhibited *inappropriately.* Show what the consequences are.

3. Role-play a situation in which failure to apply the extensional devices led to communication difficulties. Show how communication could have been improved by their use.

Observers:

Use the following check list to record your observations of the group members' communicative behaviors.

1. *Group atmosphere:* How friendly, congenial, cooperative, and good humored group members acted toward one another.

2. *Conflict:* How much dissension or conflict (overt or covert) did you notice? Note the events that triggered the conflict, how members reacted to it (what they actually did in the face of conflict), and what effects it had on group members' communicative behaviors.

3. *Communication breakdowns:* Were there any instances when group members did not understand each other? Were there instances when one or several group members tried to get their ideas across but could not? What prevented them from being understood? (Was the breakdown mostly their own fault—inarticulate, off the subject, or confused, or was it mostly the fault of other members—lack of listening or disinterest?)

4. *Barriers reduction:* Did anyone make use of the barriers-reducing techniques mentioned in the text (Chapter 7)? What effects did these attempts have on the group functioning?

5. *Feedback:* Did group members make good use of feedback? Were they able to give as well as to receive feedback from each other?

Case One

The Bob Lee Case

Bob Lee was taking a difficult, required course during his junior year at Strivemore University. Bob needed a B average to keep his scholarship, but no matter how hard he studied, he could only get C's and D's on the weekly tests that would form the major part of his grade in the course. The professor curved the grades of the thirty students in the class and Bob just could not seem to come out on the top of the curve.

After the fourth test, Bob was complaining about the situation to a fraternity brother who also was in the class. The brother sized him up and decided that since Bob was a good guy and part of the group; he'd give him the inside dope on the course. He swore Bob to secrecy and then told him the whole story. It seemed that the professor didn't correct his own papers but used a graduate-student grader. The grader had found a new way to work his way through college. He had arranged, through a star football player in the class, to provide cram sessions before each test based on the key the professor gave him. He "tutored" nine of Bob's classmates at the rate of $5 per test or $10 if the student wanted the answers to memorize. So for just "five or ten bucks" a week, Bob could join the group and his problem would be solved.

Bob had a little money saved from his summer job, but he wasn't immediately ready to invest it in an A. Wasn't the whole thing unethical? Shouldn't the professor be told? But then again, what if his fraternity brother or the football player were expelled? Still, what about the students at the bottom of the curve?

All these questions and more went through Bob's mind. He had to decide soon or it would be too late to save his grade.

If you were Bob, what would you do? Why? Try to get a consensus from your group. Have one member report your decision to the rest of the class.

Case Two

The Fair Housing Case

The problem You are the advisory and investigatory board for your local community which determines whether or not a specific case involving alleged racial discrimination should be brought to court under the Fair Housing Act in your state. The board employs its own investigator.

The section of the act with which you are presently concerned reads: "It shall be an unlawful discriminatory practice . . . for any person to . . . refuse to sell, transfer, assign, rent, lease, sublease, finance, or otherwise deny or withhold commercial housing from any person because of race, color, religion, ancestry, or national origin of any prospective owner, occupant, or user of such commercial housing."

Greg Stephen and John Moore have filed a case with your board alleging that Mr. Genove has unlawfully discriminated against them. They state that they are students at the university. They are Negroes. They arranged by telephone, answering an ad in the local paper, to rent an apartment owned by Mr. Genove. The apartment is part of a four-unit apartment house. They sent a check for the first month's rent on an upstairs apartment. The check was cashed by Mr. Genove. He wrote them a letter which stated they could rent the apartment for a full year if they so desired. Mr. Genove did not know that the boys were Negroes.

The boys stated that they arrived at the university on the day before registration for the fall semester. They called Mr. Genove, and he delivered the keys to the apartment. Mr. Genove seemed "surprised" that the boys were Negroes. He gave them the keys, however, and stated at the time that he hoped they would find the apartment comfortable and that they would "decide to stay."

One week later, the boys were served notice by registered mail that Mr. Genove was starting eviction proceedings and that they had two weeks to vacate the apartment. They phoned Mr. Genove to ask him why they were being evicted. Mr. Genove replied, "My attorney advised me not to discuss the case."

Additional information The board's investigation disclosed the following:

1. Mr. Genove and his attorney, in conference with the board, claimed absolutely no discrimination basis for asking the boys to move.

2. Mr. Genove showed the board a note from one of his renters in the apartment units, complaining that the boys had staged a "wild party the night they moved in, with people tramping up and down the stairs until 3 A.M. and noise like a wild orgy or something."

In talking with the boys, the board discovered:

1. They claim not to have had a "wild" or noisy party. They state that on the night in question

they had asked two of their friends over and that they had watched television and had played cards until 12:30 A.M.

2. The boys claim that while they were moving in, they overheard the complaining renter say to another occupant: "I am going to do something about them."

3. The complaining renter refused to talk to the board, stating that he did not want to be bothered by a lot of "silly" questions.

4. The only other occupant of the building who was home the night in question stated that she had heard the boys "laughing" late in the evening but did not consider it "excessive noise."

5. Mr. Genove has stated that the complaining renter was an old, retired man who had been renting from Mr. Genove for fourteen years.

What should the board do?

Case Three

The Harassed Professor*

After the departmental level, the next natural area for students to exert pressure is on the individual faculty member whom they classify as irrelevant, or unfair, or guilty of poor teaching. Suppose you are a professor designated by student activists as irrelevant and that during your first class, fall semester, about six or eight students began a systematic disruption of your lectures. You give them the time to state their disenchantment with the grading system, with the organization of the class, with the lack of relevant issues to be discussed, even with the immorality of the war in Vietnam, although this is irrelevant to the class content.

As you meet your class for the second and third sessions, you realize the hecklers are there to stay, and they are making it impossible for you to conduct the class as you wish. You have about two hundred students in your class and since you won't have the class roster for another week, you have no idea who the disrupters are. At the end of the third session, you hear mutterings from a dozen or so students who are tired of the disruptions and are threatening to do something to the hecklers. If any teaching is to be done, the classroom interruptions must be stopped.

What are you going to do about the situation?

*Josiah S. Dilley, *Higher Education: Participants Confronted,* Wm. C. Brown, Dubuque, Iowa, 1970, p. 51. Reproduced by permission of the publisher.

Feedback Blank Seven

1. Rate the productivity of this session's work for you.

                1   2   3   4   5   6   7   8   9   10

Not productive   Very productive

2. Rate how you think the class felt about the productivity of this session's work.

                1   2   3   4   5   6   7   8   9   10

Not productive   Very productive

Comments:

3. List those members of the class or of your group with whom communication is easy for you. Can you speculate why?

4. List those members of the class or of your group with whom you find it difficult to communicate. Why?

5. At this point, how comfortable or at ease do you feel in this class?

6. Did you notice anyone left out in your group? Do you think anyone else noticed? Was anything done about it? What? What was the response of the person left out?

Personal Improvement Blank Seven

1. Give your own definition at present of communication.

2. How can you help influence the symbolic world around you to make communication with others more effective?

3. Briefly cite what you feel are the most important concepts touched on so far in this course (most useful to you, most applicable to your communication).

Assignment One

Polarization

It is said that the easiest way to slide through life is to believe everything or to deny everything. How do you react to this idea? Do you detect any polarization? Explain your answer.

Assignment Two

Letter to the Editor

Clip some "letters to the editor" from your school paper or from a local paper. Analyze the language used and what it tells you about the sender of the letter. Generalize your reactions to the techniques employed.

Write a paper to explain your findings and your reactions. Be sure to include all the clippings you analyzed.

Assignment Three

Group Report

As a group project, attend some public function. Everyone in the group is to observe the event.

Each one of you is to write a short report on what each one of you "saw." Compare the reports. Are there differences in them? What accounts for the differences? Are there similarities? What accounts for the similarities? Write a one- to two-page paper in which you will explain your answers. Include the report itself.

Assignment Four

Either-Or

Identify as many examples as you can of the allness or polarization types of statements in radio or television advertising. Include them in your scrapbook.

Think of either-or slogans such as "My country—right or wrong," "America—love it or leave it," "You're either for me or against me." Write a short paper in which you explain what might be other possible alternatives to the choices suggested by the slogans. Try to recall other either-or slogans that you are familiar with.

Assignment Five

Madmen

Zorba, in *Zorba the Greek*, told his young boss that he was too reserved and needed a "little bit of madness." Do you? Do your friends? From this notion, can you derive any advice for success in communication?

Chapter 8 SELF-CONCEPT, ROLES, AND BEHAVIOR—WHO AM I?

Groups working on the Agree/Disagree lists have an interesting set of activities to observe. When the student has written down his own response to the agree/disagree choices, he has made a personal commitment. When, following that, he must expose his personal preference to the group, another set of factors becomes involved. Very few of us can argue from an entirely objective view—that is, we are not very good at keeping our personal feelings out of our public statements. Another way of putting it: we seem to feel that everything we say or write is so much a part of our own self that we get uptight when somebody asks a question about what it was we wrote. Watch your own activities in ego-involving commitment to points of view as your group discusses the items about groups.

This should be a good time for role-playing groups to adopt a role-reversal type of performance. Many kinds of organizations have used this technique in their attempts to increase human understanding. It works like this: the parent may take the part of the son or daughter in a role-playing situation while the youngster takes the role of the parent. They carry on a dialogue as if each were the other person. This is similar to a "mirror technique," but has the advantage of both persons being forced to analyze their own behaviors and those of the other person so they can be role-played effectively.

Agree/Disagree List on Groups

1. Agree or disagree with each statement on groups. Record (A) if you agree, (D) if you disagree on the left-hand column. Do this first by yourself.

2. You will now discuss each statement with the other members of the small group you will be placed in and reach a consensus for each of the statements.

   Record in the right-hand column the letters A (for agree) or D (for disagree) when the group has reached a consensus on the items. This means that the decision for each item *must* be agreed upon by each member before it becomes a part of the group decision. Consensus is difficult to reach. Therefore not every answer will meet with everyone's approval. Try, as a group, to make each answer one with which *all group members* can at least partially agree. Here are some guidelines to use in reaching consensus:

   a. Avoid arguing for your own individual judgments. Approach the task on the basis of logic.

   b. Avoid changing your mind *only* in order to reach agreement and avoid conflict. Support only solutions with which you are able to agree somewhat at least.

   c. Avoid "conflict-reducing" techniques, such as majority vote, averaging, or "trading" in reaching your decisions.

   d. View differences of opinion as helpful rather than a hindrance in decision-making.

1. A primary concern of all group members should be to establish an atmosphere where all feel free to express their feelings.

2. In a group with a strong leader, an individual is able to achieve greater personal security than in leaderless groups.

3. There are often occasions when an individual who is part of a working group should do what he thinks is right regardless of what the group has decided to do.

4. It is sometimes necessary to use autocratic methods to obtain democratic objectives.

5. Generally there comes a time when a democratic group method must be abandoned in order to solve practical problems.

6. In the long run, it is more important to use democratic methods than to achieve specific results by other means.

7. Sometimes it is necessary to change people in the direction you yourself think is right, even when they object.

8. It is sometimes necessary to ignore the feelings of others in order to reach a group decision.

9. When the leader is doing his best, one should not openly criticize or find fault with his conduct.

10. Most any job that can be done by a committee can be done better by having one individual responsible for it.

11. Democracy has no place in a military organization, an air task force, or an infantry squad, when in battle.

12. By the time the average person has reached maturity, it is almost impossible for him to increase his skills in group participation.

13. Much time is wasted in talk when everybody in the group has to be considered before making the decision.

14. In a group that really wants to get something accomplished, the leader should exercise friendly but firm control.

15. If someone does not like the way a meeting is going, he should say so and try to do something about it even though he is not the chairman.

16. When two group members cannot seem to get along, the best thing to do is to ignore the difficulty and carry on.

17. The best atmosphere to work for in a group is one where the personal thoughts and feelings of group members are kept to themselves.

Laboratory Groups

Picture Makers:

1. Illustrate nonverbally the effects of self-concepts on communicative behavior.

or

2. Illustrate nonverbally a situation in which a person experiences role-conflict and how this affects his communication.

Forum Discussion:

1. Discuss the idea that self-concept is the product of interaction and communication with others.

or

2. Some people maintain a self-concept that does not correspond with what they know to be the judgment of others who know them. What are the possible sources for this discrepancy?

Role Players:

Role-play a situation in which communication difficulties occurred because of discrepancies between the self-concept of an individual and the images others have of him.

or

Role-play a situation in which an individual has to interact with different people who all have a different image, and thus expectations, of him.

Observers:

For this observing assignment, observer will select a group in which two or more members are well known to him. During the group planning, the observer will observe primarily those members he knows well. The behavior of other group members will be noted only when it is related to that of the members he is observing.

The observer will analyze the roles he sees his "friends" play in the group. Are they playing leadership roles or follower roles? Are they playing a devil's advocate role? Are they the "jokers" in the group? Are they dominating or submissive? Are they "experts" on the subject, etc.? The observer will then try to compare the roles as he observed them played in the group with the roles he sees his "friends" play outside class.

Instead of reporting to the whole class the results of his observations, the observer will meet with the members he observed after the performances, for five to ten minutes, and share with them the results of his observations.

Case: The Citizen of the Year

"Well, gentlemen," said the chairman of the Community Club, "That does it! We've selected our 'Citizen of the Year.'"

"And a close race it was, too," said Al Martin. "People were saying it was going to be close, but I never figured. . . ."

"By the way, Al," the committee chairman broke in, "I want you to see that all three candidates are at the Community Club dinner Thursday night. I don't care how you get them there, but they all should come."

"You mean you want all three candidates rather than just the winner?"

"That's right, Al. I've been thinking. With the selection being as close as it was, I really think we ought to mention all three candidates—even though, of course, only one will receive the award." The other committee members nodded in agreement. "We've never done this before, but it will be good to have a change in format."

The committee began to break up, and Al sighed. Well he would see what he could do.

Next morning, while getting the mail, Al met Jim Farnsworth, one of the candidates. After a few pleasantries Al commented, "By the way, Jim, the annual Citizen's Award Dinner is coming up Thursday night, and I've been asked by the committee to let you know that we want you to be *sure* and be there. Okay?"

"Of course," said Jim, "Wouldn't miss it for the world."

"Good. Glad to hear that. Should be quite a night for you," Al said with a smile.

Later that day, Al ran into Bill Nichols. "Bill, good to see you again. I've been looking all over for you. The Community Club committee wanted me to check to be sure you were coming to the Annual Citizen's Award Dinner. I assume you are planning to be there."

"Well," drawled Bill, "hadn't figured. . . ."

"Say!" Al exclaimed, "I don't think you're going to want to miss this one. You know what I mean?"

Bill began to smile slowly. "Well, since you put it that way, I guess I had better give it some reconsideration. Sure, Al, I'll be there."

"Fine, fine," Al replied. "See you there."

That evening, Al called Francis Van Rookle. "Francis," Al said when he heard the "Hello" on the other end, "I've been wanting to call and let you know that I hope you are planning to attend the Citizen's Award Dinner. Should be quite an event this year. And, of course, always the usual surprises," said Al laughing.

"Why, yes," Francis replied. "Certainly should be able to make it."

"Very good," said Al. "And by the way, if you can make it a few minutes early, the committee and I would surely appreciate it. See you then, Fran. Bye."

Thursday night arrived, and the Community Center was packed for the big event. The program began. The mayor's speech and then the awards. The Community Club chairman stepped to the stage.

"Ladies and gentlemen," the chairman began, "I would like now to present this year's annual Citizen Award to. . . ."

Three chairs began to scrape, and slowly three men began to rise. . . .

Feedback Blank Eight

1. Rate the productivity of this session's work for you.

                             1   2   3   4   5   6   7   8   9   10

   Not productive   Very productive

2. Rate how you think the rest of the class felt about the productivity of this session's work.

                             1   2   3   4   5   6   7   8   9   10

   Not productive   Very productive

   Comments:

3. In relation to this week's lecture, were you assigned a role you did not like in your group activity? If people assign "identities" to you, what effect does this have on your reactions?

4. Did you enjoy working with your group? Why or why not?

5. Other comments, criticisms, questions, suggestions, etc.

NAME _____

DATE _____ SECTION _____

Personal Improvement Blank Eight

1. Analyze your patterns of communication when you are with your peers, with persons of higher status, and with persons of lower status than yours.

2. Is there any conflict between your role as a college student and your role as a son or daughter?

3. Describe a situation in which you have been under pressure to fill two or more conflicting roles. How did you resolve the conflict? Would you say the resolution was successful, unsuccessful, or somewhere in between?

Assignment One

Group Expectations

There are many times when you feel confused and dissatisfied with what happens in the groups you belong to. You may have some idealized picture in your mind of the type of group member you would like to be. This assignment is designed to give you an opportunity to express your feelings about such matters. Briefly complete the following statements on this page.

1. Things I would like to *understand* better about the groups I work in or associate with.

2. Things I would like to learn *how to do* better in groups.

3. *Feelings* I have in groups which I would like to change or improve.

Assignment Two

Self-concept

It was said in your text (Chapter 8) that in arriving at a conception of self, every person sees himself in relation to others. Can you explain in brief what is meant by the statement? What other factors play a part in helping a person arrive at a conception of himself?

Assignment Three

Changing Self-concept

What aspects of the self-concept are particularly difficult to change? How do we protect our self-concept? What do we protect it from? Why do we feel the need to protect it? Rather than answering these questions in the abstract, use yourself as a concrete example. Write your comments.

Assignment Four

Reference Groups

Reference groups help us determine whether we are performing our roles successfully. Can you give examples from your own experience that would support this statement?

Assignment Five

Teacher Evaluation

1. What would you like your instructor to know about you in order to evaluate you fairly? Write your answer in the space provided below.

2. Look at what you just wrote, and try to figure out how much of it you said because you thought your instructor would want to read it, or because it would look good, and how much of it represents a real and honest expression of what you believe is important for him to know if he is to evaluate you fairly. Write your answers in the space provided below.

Assignment Six

Movie Analysis

Write a short analysis of a current movie in terms of the problem of self and society. Do not just tell the plot of the movie. Analyze its implications in terms of the concepts mentioned in this chapter.

CHAPTER 9 ATTITUDES, BELIEFS, AND VALUES— WHO SHOULD I BE?

Another Agree/Disagree list is provided this section of the laboratory—this time focusing on the qualities of leadership. Again you can observe the group's responses to the items in the list and gain some insight into members' attitudes about leadership and human nature. You can also go one step further and observe the group as it interacts and thus gain some additional insight into how groups operate.

The recommendation for the laboratory activities is to include a *scramble,* or an open-choice activity session. At times the structure of Role Players, Forum Discussion, Picture Makers, and Observers has been considered *too structured* but the fact that students move from one activity to another, and often with different groups of students working together, tends to optimize the opportunities for learning. This session is a deliberate break from the structure of a laboratory session and will give you a chance to find out how the class responds to lack of structure for one session. How much do the expectations of others have to do with the choice you make in this exercise?

Agree/Disagree List on Leadership and Group Process

A. What is your opinion on the statements listed below? Give your first reactions, and check each statement indicating whether you agree or disagree. Record the letter A if you agree, D if you disagree.
B. Break up into groups of six or seven students and reach a consensus on each of the statements. Record in the right-hand column the letters A for agree, or D for disagree when the group has reached a consensus for the item.

Individual (A) (D)		Group Consensus (A) (D)
____ ____	1. The primary job of the leader is to bring about change in others.	____ ____
____ ____	2. The most effective leader is the one who can maintain a pleasant emotional climate at all times.	____ ____
____ ____	3. Discipline of the over-talkative member is the responsibility of the group leader.	____ ____
____ ____	4. Leadership is a set of functions which are distributed within the group.	____ ____
____ ____	5. Very little progress can be made unless every member of the group feels a personal responsibility for leadership.	____ ____

_____ _____ 6. Most committee assignments would be better carried out _____ _____
by one person with the will to act.

_____ _____ 7. If leadership is effective, the group members will have few _____ _____
feelings of dependency toward the leader.

_____ _____ 8. Unless a group is pushed by its leader, it will make little _____ _____
progress.

_____ _____ 9. In discussion, it is more important for the leader to know _____ _____
a lot about the topic than about discussion methods.

_____ _____ 10. An authoritarian leader is better than one who lets the _____ _____
group function without any control.

_____ _____ 11. It is impossible to be absolutely impartial in discussion. _____ _____

_____ _____ 12. Most discussion groups will make progress if given enough _____ _____
time.

_____ _____ 13. The effective discussion leader should never take a stand _____ _____
in opposition to the group.

_____ _____ 14. Summarizing is the most important single task of the _____ _____
discussion leader.

Interpersonal Perception*

Procedure

Form a dyad with some person you do not know well or at all but would like to get to know. Each dyad will spend ten minutes discussing politics without discussing *political parties*. Try to get to know as much about that person by discussing politics as you are able to. After ten minutes, answer the following questions:

A.

1. What is the other person's name?

2. What political party do you think the other person supports?

3. What position do you think the other person supports concerning the social welfare system—maintain it as it is, diminish it, eliminate it, or expand it?

4. Do you think the other person is a member of a fraternity or sorority?

5. What do you think the other person's major is?

6. What do you think the other person's academic classification is?

7. What type of record album do you think this person would buy: classical, jazz, acid rock or soul rock?

*From *The Handbook for Teachers of Speech,* by Bobby Patton, The University of Kansas, 1970, pp. 20–22. Reproduced by permission of the author.

8. Do you think the other person would like to get to know you better, say have a Coke together after class?

9. List three adjectives which you think describe the way the other person is feeling now.

10. List three adjectives which you think best describe the other person's personality.

11. Which of the above questions do you think you answered correctly about the other person?

B.

1. What is your name?

2. What political party do you support?

3. What position do you take concerning the social welfare system—maintain it as it is, diminish it, eliminate it, or expand it?

4. Are you a member of a fraternity or sorority?

5. What is your major?

6. What is your academic classification?

7. What kind of record album would you buy: classical, jazz, acid rock, soul rock?

8. Would you like to get to know the other person better, say have a Coke together after class?

9. List three adjectives which best describe the way you are feeling now.

10. List three adjectives which best describe your personality.

11. Which of the above questions do you think the other person answered correctly about you?

Laboratory Groups

Scramble

This week, the nature of these laboratory groups will be left up to you in what the authors call a "scramble."

You choose your own group. You choose your own activity (Picture Makers, Forum Discussion, Role Players, or Observers). The only limitation is that you must end up with at least one Picture Makers, one Forum Discussion, one Role Players, and one Observers groups.

Topics will be any concept developed so far in the course. Try not to duplicate past performances but to develop new insights into the formulations of this course.

The observers may want to watch for the kind of communication patterns and techniques developed by people in selecting a group to work with. How quickly did they develop a "group feeling"? How were leaders chosen? After the group got under way, did you feel various individuals reacted to this kind of structure for the class? In what way?

Feedback Blank Nine

1. Rate the productivity of this session's work for you.

                        1   2   3   4   5   6   7   8   9   10

   Not productive   Very productive

2. Rate how you think the rest of the class felt about this session's productivity.

                        1   2   3   4   5   6   7   8   9   10

   Not productive   Very productive

   Comments:

3. Did you observe anyone who was silent in your group? How many people? Was anything done to bring them out and encourage them to participate more?

4. How useful is this feedback for you? Can it be made more useful to you? How?

5. How would you feel about meeting with the same students in a group for a few weeks? You would change activities but would remain with the same group of people.

6. What are your reactions to the "scramble" this week? What criteria did you use in selecting the group you were in?

Personal Improvement Blank Nine

1. You have certain attitudes regarding going to college and education in general. What would it take for your attitudes to be radically changed?

2. Can you cite an example of an attitude you held for a long time which subsequently changed? Why did it change? What made it change?

3. Can you identify some values that you have which are in conflict with one another? How do you feel about these discrepancies?

Assignment One

Trace an Attitude*

Think about an attitude you have today about something. Try to trace it back to its origin. Think of what your attitude toward that thing was when you were first confronted with it. And then try to find out all the things that have influenced that attitude as years passed until the attitude finally became the one you now hold.

Make a few notes to bring to class. You will be encouraged at the next class meeting to share with the rest of the class your comments about the topic.

Reference to the material about assumptive sets in Chapter 4 in your text might be useful.

Assignment Two

Attitude Measurement A

Go to the library and browse through the literature on attitude measurement. Select one attitude scale. Write a short paper in which you describe the scale and explain in what type of research it has been used. Tell what its advantages and disadvantages are, and explain how the authors of the scale made sure that it measures what it is supposed to measure.

Assignment Three

Attitude Measurement B

Write a description of the values and attitudes of a particular group of people you are familiar with but which differs from a group you identify with.

Assignment Four

Consultant on Race Relations

Imagine the President of the United States appointed you Chief Consultant on Race Relations. Your task is to draft a report in which you will advise the President on how to ease the tensions between the various ethnic groups in this country. Obviously there is no simple or pat solution.

Outline the kinds of things you would want to include in your report to the President.

*Charles Rossiter, Jr., "Personalizing the Basic Course," *The Speech Teacher,* 1971, vol. 20, no. 1, pp. 61–62. Reproduced by permission of the author and the publisher.

Assignment Five

Die-hard Values

Some values are more important (salient) to us than others. Some, we are willing to change fairly easily, some less easily. There are some values we feel extremely committed to, either because of our upbringing or because of the various teachings (religious, social) we have been exposed to very early in our life.

   If you were to identify the one value that holds the greatest importance in your life, the one value that you would not change under any circumstances, what would that value be? Can you explain why it is so important to you?

CHAPTER 10 COMMUNICATION IN GROUPS— THREE'S A CROWD

The group activity known as the NASA Exercise has become very popular with many different training groups. It is not only timely—with its suggestion that we are moon travelers—but it also has a very well-defined set of answers based on expert testimony. Comparisons of individual and group choices provide an interesting topic of class discussion.

Other activities in this chapter are designed to give us experience in recognizing task functions and process functions in groups. The Observers instructions and checklist in Chapter 6 of the laboratory manual may prove interesting to you at this session (see p. 280).

The assignments include those which require your taking a few minutes to think about how you react to people in the groups you are in. When you try to think about the groups you belong to, don't let the term be too strictly defined for you. In other words, you have associations with many groups which are not usually considered groups in the formal sense because they don't elect officers and call meetings. Whom do you meet for coffee or a Coke? What same collection of people do you see very often informally, but with enough purpose to consider yourselves a group?

NASA Exercise Individual Worksheet

Instructions

You are a member of a space crew originally scheduled to rendezvous with a mother ship on the lighted surface of the moon. Due to mechanical difficulties however, your ship was forced to land at a spot some 200 miles from the rendezvous point. During landing, much of the equipment aboard was damaged, and, since survival depends on reaching the mother ship, the most critical items available must be chosen for the 200-mile trip. Below are listed the fifteen items left intact and undamaged after landing. Your task is to rank order them in terms of their importance to your crew in allowing them to reach the rendezvous point. Place the number 1 by the most important item, the number 2 by the second most important, and so on, through number 15, the least important. You have ten minutes to complete this phase of the exercise.

_____ Box of matches

_____ Food concentrate

_____ 50 feet of nylon rope

_____ Parachute silk

_____ Portable heating unit

_____ Two .45 caliber pistols

_____ One case dehydrated Pet milk

_____ Two 100-pound tanks of oxygen

_____ Stellar map (of the moon's constellation)

_____ Life raft

_____ Magnetic compass

_____ 5 gallons of water

_____ Signal flares

_____ First-aid kit containing injection needles

_____ Solar-powered FM receiver-transmitter

NASA Exercise Group Worksheet

Instructions

This is an exercise in group decision making. Your group is to employ the method of *group consensus* in reaching its decision. This means that the prediction for each of the 15 survival items *must* be agreed upon by each group member before it becomes a part of the group decision. Consensus is difficult to reach. Therefore not every ranking will meet with everyone's complete approval. Try as a group to make each ranking one with which all group members can at least *partially* agree. Here are some guides to use in reaching consensus:

1. Avoid *arguing* for your own individual judgments. Approach the task on the basis of logic.

2. Avoid changing your mind *only* in order to reach agreement and avoid conflict. Support only solutions with which you are able to agree at least somewhat.

3. Avoid "conflict reducing" techniques such as majority vote, or trading in reaching your decision.

4. View differences of opinion as helpful rather than as a hindrance in decision making.

_____ Box of matches

_____ Food concentrate

_____ 50 feet of nylon rope

_____ Parachute silk

_____ Portable heating unit

_____ Two .45 caliber pistols

_____ One case dehydrated Pet milk

_____ Two 100-pound tanks of oxygen

_____ Stellar map (of moon's constellation)

_____ Life raft

_____ Magnetic compass

_____ 5 gallons of water

_____ Signal flares

_____ First-aid kit containing injection needles

_____ Solar-powered FM receiver-transmitter

NASA Exercise Direction Sheet for Scoring

A group member will assume the responsibility for directing the scoring.
  Individuals will:

1. Score the net difference between their answers and the correct answers given by the instructor. For example, if your answer was 9 and the correct answer was 12, the net difference is 3. Three becomes the score for that particular item. If your answer is 12 and the correct answer is 9, your score for that item will be 3.

2. Total all item scores to obtain your individual score.

3. The member responsible for directing the scoring will then total all individual scores and divide that number by the number of participants to obtain the average of individual scores.

4. The member in charge of the group worksheet will then score the group worksheet in the same fashion individual scores were obtained.

5. The group consensus score and the average of individual scores will then be given to the instructor who will record them on the board. The range of individual scores in the group will also be given to the instructor. The range should consist of the lowest and the highest individual scores.

Ratings

 0–20 Excellent

20–30 Good

30–40 Average

40–50 Fair

Over 50 Poor

Group Problem-solving Exercise

Problem-solving Task Instructions

Pretend that lutts and mipps represent a new way of measuring distance, and that dars, wors, and mirs represent a new way of measuring time. A man drives from town A through town B and town C, to town D. The task of your group is to determine how many wors the entire trip took. You have twenty minutes for this task. Do *not* choose a formal leader.

You will be given cards containing information related to the task of the group. You may share this information orally, but you must keep the cards in your hands throughout the exercise.

Problem-solving Task Reactions Form

Fill out this form *individually* where the instructor will tell you to.
1. Whose participation was most helpful in the group's accomplishment of the task?_____

   _____

   What did he or she do that was helpful?

2. Whose participation seemed to hinder the group's accomplishment of the task?_____

   _____

   What did he or she do that seemed to hinder?

3. What feelings or reactions did you experience during the problem-solving exercise? If possible, tell what behavior evoked a feeling response on your part.

4. What role(s) did you play in the group as it worked on the task?

5. What was the atmosphere of the group like? Friendly, cooperative, cold, impersonal, business-like?

When class discussion is over, group members are encouraged to share the reactions recorded on this page with one another.

Man Bought a Horse

A man bought a horse for $60 and sold it for $70. He then bought that same horse back again for $80 and sold it for $90. How much money did the man make in the horse-trading business?

1. Solve the above problem *individually* first. Record your answer in the space provided below.

2. Your instructor will then OK you to break up in groups of six or seven students. You will then try to arrive at a consensus on the right answer to the above problem. Record the group answer in the space provided below.

Individual Answer   Group Answer

Laboratory Groups

Picture Makers:

Illustrate the various interpersonal needs that group members bring with them when they participate in group discussions. In a series of diagrams or pictures, show the effects of these needs upon group communication.

Forum Discussion:

Discuss some of the norms that have developed in this class and their implications for communication and learning.

or

What kind of assumptions do you have about leadership? About small groups? How do these assumptions affect your behavior in groups in general, and in this class in particular?

Role Players:

Role-play a group in which dysfunctional behavior is exhibited to a large extent. It can be a committee meeting, a family situation, an informal gathering of friends. Then role-play the same group showing the various functional roles that can be played by group members.

or

Role-play several short group situations in which the various interpersonal needs are exhibited. Show how they affect group process.

Observers:

1. What behaviors in the group seemed to be oriented more toward meeting individual members' needs rather than helping the group to accomplish the task at hand? (Examples of dysfunctional behaviors: dominating the discussion, cutting off others, horsing around, not listening, being overly aggressive, nitpicking, avoiding responsibility, smoothing over arguments, withdrawing, doing something unrelated to the task at hand, digressing excessively, etc.)
   Who did it? What exactly did he/she do?

What effects did this kind of behavior have on the group as a whole?

2. What behaviors in the group appeared to be aimed toward helping the group members to interact with one another effectively? (Examples: keeping members involved, harmonizing disagreements, reinforcing good contributions, relieving tension, encouraging cooperation, friendly and supportive contributions, etc.)
   Who did it? What exactly did he/she do?

   What effects did this type of behavior have on the group as a whole?

3. What behaviors in the group were focused on attempting to accomplish the group's task? (Examples: getting things started, sharing information, organizing, giving opinions, clarifying, summarizing, checking out consensus, keeping the group on the task, etc.)
   Who did it? What did he/she do?

   What effects did these behaviors have on the group as a whole?

Feedback Blank Ten

1. Rate the productivity of this session's work for you.

                    1   2   3   4   5   6   7   8   9   10

   Not productive   Very productive

2. Rate how you think the rest of the class felt about the productivity of this session's work.

                    1   2   3   4   5   6   7   8   9   10

   Not productive   Very productive

   Comments:

3. Did your group seem to spend most of its time on task (getting the job done) or on process (maintaining open interaction, taking care of feelings, etc.)?

   Task _____   Process _____   Even _____   Couldn't tell _____

   Comments:

4. Do you find it useful to have a chapter on group communication? Why or why not?

5. Did you have communication difficulties in your group as a result of differing interpersonal needs among the group members?

6. Other comments, criticisms, questions, suggestions, etc.

NAME _____

DATE _____ SECTION _____

Personal Improvement Blank Ten

1. What did you learn from watching the group interactions during our last laboratory session? About other group members? About group functioning?

2. Think about the groups you belong to. Can you assign reasons for your belonging to some or most of them?

3. Comments, questions, etc.

Assignment One

Choosing

Select a group of which you are a member or which you can readily observe. The group should comprise at lease six members but should not be so large as to be difficult to observe.

1. List what you consider to be six of the most relevant or basic factors characteristic of the group.

2. In terms of your own observations up to this point, describe the attraction and repulsion patterns in the group as you perceive them. Make a sociometric sketch of the informal social network based on your perception.

3. Now using a simple questionnaire as a means of ascertaining the members' actual choices, determine the attraction and repulsion patterns present in the group. Make a sociometric sketch showing the informal social network based on the members' choices. The questions you may ask:

   a. Which three members in the group would you most like to work on a class project with?

   b. Which three members would you most like to invite to a party?

   c. Which three members would you least like to work with?

   d. Which three members would you least like to invite to a party?

4. What differences, if any, appear when 2 and 3 are compared? How do you account for these differences?
   Write a short paper summarizing your findings and be prepared to present them in front of the whole class. In your class presentation, names should be changed if you wish to preserve the anonymity of the group members you observed.

Assignment Two

Honesty

How do you feel about the advantages and potential dangers of honesty about interpersonal relationships in group situations?

Assignment Three

Leadership

Do you feel that groups have to have an authoritarian leader to get things done? Why or why not? Do you think that such leadership has any effect on group morale? What kind of effect?

Assignment Four

Competition

1. It is often asserted that competition stimulates individuals and groups to their greatest achievements. In your experience, is this true for a competitive system of grades?

2. Under which conditions are people more likely to compete and under which conditions are they more likely to cooperate with one another? Can you give examples to illustrate your comments?

Assignment Five

Conformity

Can you identify the kind of situations in which you are more likely to conform and those situations in which you are more likely to resist conformity? What are the differences between these situations?

CHAPTER 11 INTERPERSONAL TASK AND PROCESS—WE THINK AND WE FEEL

Following the last chapter's activities with groups, the exercises in this chapter give you additional chance to see yourself and others in a competitive and cooperative setting. In either case, you will continue to be aware of the effects of the task/process relationship in our dealings with others.

You have undoubtedly been playing competitive games (Monopoly, card games, tennis, baseball, etc.) for many years. The idea that two contestants can work out a maximum possibility of gain is part of the logical system called game theory. It is not our intention to involve you in the classical zero-sum strategies, etc., but rather we hope you will become interested in the fact that the behaviors we see around us are repeated often enough to form a whole category of communication games people play.

Building Towers: An Intergroup Competition Exercise*

Tower Observers' Role

1. You are to observe and record significant behaviors of members of your group during the construction, judging, and reaction phases of this exercise.

2. You will give a brief, oral report of your observations of the group after the reactions to the judging.

3. Remember that feedback is more effective when it is specific, nonevaluative, focused on modifiable behaviors, and checked to insure accuracy.

What the group did
During construction:

During judging:

*Adapted from J. William Pfeiffer and John E. Jones, *A Handbook of Structured Experiences for Human Relations Training,* vol. III, University Associates Press, Iowa City, 1971, pp. 22–26.

Reacting to the judging:

What individuals did
During construction:

During judging:

Reacting to the judging:

Tower Judges' Role

1. The judges select a winning tower according to the following criteria: height, aesthetic appeal, and sturdiness. You are *not* to evaluate the towers on other criteria, such as how well the groups worked together.

2. The judges decide the relative weight given to the three criteria. You may or may not announce your weighting procedure.

3. The judges decide whether their decision making is public or private.

4. Your major consideration should be fairness, not trying to make your group win.

5. You should remain uninvolved during the construction phase, observing only.

Criterion	Judge	Group				
		1	2	3	4	5
Height (Weight _____)	1					
	2					
	3					
	4					
	5					
Aesthetic appeal (Weight _____)	1					
	2					
	3					
	4					
	5					
Sturdiness (Weight _____)	1					
	2					
	3					
	4					
	5					

Win as Much as You Can*

Tally Sheet

DIRECTIONS: For ten successive rounds you and your partner will choose either an "X" or a "Y". The pay-off for each round is dependent upon the pattern of choices made in your cluster:

4 X's:	Lose $1 each
3 X's:	Win $1 each
1 Y:	Lose $3
2 X's:	Win $2 each
2 Y's:	Lose $2 each
1 X:	Win $3
3 Y's:	Lose $1 each
4 Y's:	Win $1 each

STRATEGY: You are to confer with your partner on each round and make a *joint decision.* Before rounds 5, 8, and 10, you confer with the other dyads in your cluster.

*Adapted from J. William Pfeiffer and John E. Jones, *A Handbook of Structured Experiences for Human Relations Training,* vol. II, University Associates Press, Iowa City, 1970, pp. 66–70.

Round	Strategy		Choice	$ Won	$ Lost	$ Balance	
	Time allowed	Confer with					
1	2 min	Partner					
2	1 min	Partner					
3	1 min	Partner					
4	1 min	Partner					
5	3 min + 1 min	Cluster Partner					Bonus Round: Pay-off is multiplied by 3
6	1 min	Partner					
7	1 min	Partner					
8	3 min + 1 min	Cluster Partner					Bonus Round: Pay-off is multiplied by 5
9	1 min	Partner					
10	3 min + 1 min	Cluster Partner					Bonus Round: Pay-off is multiplied by 10

Laboratory Groups

Picture Makers:

Illustrate nonverbally the internal reactions of different people taking part in a group discussion.

or

Illustrate nonverbally some formulations from the lecture or Chapter 11 in your text which you consider important in communication with others.

Forum Discussion:

Can you identify some of the most common games played in the classroom by students and instructors? What purposes do these games have?

Role Players:

In a series of short acts, role-play a highly task-oriented group, a highly process oriented group, and then some combination of the two.

or

Role-play what happens during periods of phatic communion. Then role-play a situation in which one of the participants does not follow the rules of phatic communion.

Observers:

In your opinion, was the group you observed more task oriented, more process oriented, or a combination? What did group members do that made you characterize them as you did?

Can you recall the instances of small talk during the group planning? How much of the group planning was actually spent in small talk? What effect did that small talk have on the group interaction?

Do you think group members were satisfied with the way their group operated? On what do you base your answer?

Feedback Blank Eleven

1. Rate the productivity of this session's work for you.

                             1   2   3   4   5   6   7   8   9   10

    Not productive   Very productive

2. Rate how you think the rest of the class felt about the productivity of this session's work.

                             1   2   3   4   5   6   7   8   9   10

    Not productive   Very productive

    Comments:

3. Did you notice any defensive behavior in yourself or in other members of your group? How was it expressed? What seemed to trigger it?

4. How would you like it if the observers reported to the group itself after the activities, rather than presenting a report to the whole class about your group process?

5. What kind of behaviors on the part of the group members seemed to foster an atmosphere in the group that made you feel comfortable?

6. What kind of role did you play in your group this session?

Personal Improvement Blank Eleven

1. Identify one or several games you play with people (games in the sense discussed in Chapter 11 in your text). Analyze the reasons why you might be playing them and the responses they elicit in the people you communicate with.

2. Analyze a recent incident in which you took part when a fairly serious conflict arose. What was its impact on interpersonal relationships? How did *you* react to it? Was your reaction typical of the way you generally respond to conflict?

Assignment One

Loneliness

Have you ever been in a crowded room and felt alone? Have you ever talked to somebody for a while and felt that absolutely nothing that was said made any sense?

How would you describe these situations? What do you and your friends do to overcome the feeling of loneliness? What prescriptions would you give to an incoming freshman at your school to help him overcome loneliness? What skills would he have to have?

Assignment Two

Games

Games are often considered as barriers toward "authentic" relationships. Do you feel that the games we play in our communication with one another are always unhealthy? Can we have "authentic" relationships with everyone, all the time? Should we?

Assignment Three

Consumer Games

Have you ever been "had" in a business transaction, or deceived by unethical advertising? Recall such instances in a written report.

CHAPTER 12 NONVERBAL COMMUNICATION— THE SOUNDS OF SILENCE

Before we go into the exercises in *listening* (the next chapter) we should be involved in the process of *watching*. There is much to be learned from one another in the nonverbal communication we exchange. How tuned are we to it? Do we belong to the school of thought which believes that the only time there is any communication is when we are making noises at each other or sending squiggles through the mail?

Laboratory exercises are designed to give us some practice in identifying more than the words we use as a part of our communication. The assignments are an integral part of the recognition of that dimension of our association which we seldom acknowledge to ourselves, and even more seldom talk to anyone else about—our nonverbal communicative system.

Cooperative Squares

Instructions to Participants: Each of the five envelopes (A, B, C, D, and E) contains pieces for forming squares. When the signal is given to begin, distribute the envelopes so each person has one. Each person is then to empty the contents of his envelope in front of him.

Next, start forming squares in the group, one square to each person, each person making his own square, following these three simple rules:

1. No member of the group may speak to another member.

2. No member may take a piece of a square from another member, or in any way signal that he wants it.

3. Any member may give one or several of his pieces to another member.

The task will not be complete until each member of the group has in front of him a completed square of the same size as those held by the others.

REMEMBER: *You may give, but you cannot take.*

Laboratory Groups

Picture Makers:

Produce a diagram or drawing with a minimum of verbal explanations to illustrate some facets of silence.

or

Illustrate nonverbally a situation in which a communication breakdown occurs because of a misunderstanding about silences.

Forum Discussion:

What are some of the misinterpretations about silences we should be aware of in evaluating other people's behaviors?

or

Discuss different types of silences. During your discussion in front of the class you will deliberately convey one thing with the words you are saying and quite the opposite through your paralanguage. See if the class catches on to what you are doing and if they can decipher both messages you are sending.

Role Players:

Demonstrate some kinds of silences and their possible consequences on communication.

or

Role-play a situation in which several members of an audience are exhibiting different kinds of silences in responding to a speaker.

or

Demonstrate with the use of alter egos a situation in which two or more people can use silences on each other to respond agreeably or disagreeably.

Observers:

Watch especially for silences during the planning session. Can you interpret them? What kind of nonverbal clues did you get from the members' postures, attitudes, gestures, etc.?

Comment on the seating arrangement during the group planning and its performance (for Forum Discussion especially). Was the seating arrangement related in any way to the verbal participation of the group members?

During the performances, did the group live up to its responsibility to the audience and appear to be aware of and make use of the nonverbal feedback they received?

Feedback Blank Twelve

This feedback blank is somewhat different from the previous ones. Please read the directions before filling the form out.

  DIRECTIONS: Below are two sets of statements. You are to rank order the items in each set from 1 (most like) to 10 (least like) what the meeting was like. Use this procedure: rank 1 first, then 10, then 2, then 9, alternating toward the middle.

The session was like this:

_____ There was much warmth and friendliness

_____ There was a lot of aggressive behavior

_____ People were uninterested and uninvolved

_____ People tried to dominate and take over

_____ We were in need of help

_____ Much of the conversation was irrelevant

_____ We were strictly task oriented

_____ The members of the group were very polite

_____ There was a lot of underlying irritation

_____ We worked on our process problems

My behavior was like this:

_____ I was warm and friendly to some

_____ I did not participate much

_____ I concentrated on the job

_____ I tried to get everyone involved

_____ I took over the leadership

_____ I was polite to all group members

_____ My suggestions were frequently off the point

_____ I was a follower

_____ I was irritated

_____ I was eager and aggressive

Comments:

Personal Improvement Blank Twelve

1. Do you find it useful to have a unit on silence in this course? Why?

2. Do you have difficulties dealing with silence? What silences are easy or difficult to cope with in your experience? Describe the situations specifically.

3. If a person intrudes in your group, and you do not wish to tell him to leave too directly, what nonverbal means will you use to make him leave?

Assignment One

Space Design

How may the way a house is designed affect the nature of family relationships? Use examples from your own experience to answer this question.

Assignment Two

Interview

If there is any way for you to meet an architect, interview him, and ask him how he sees the relationships between space and space design and its effects on communicative behavior. Use the notes you take during your interview to make a report to the class.

Assignment Three

Group Observation

Select any small group (not more than twelve members) on the campus holding its regular meeting. Secure permission to attend the meeting and observe the group. Make a chart representing the seating arrangement and observe exclusively the nonverbal behavior of the group members. Observe their postures, gestures, facial expressions, who they look at, how they look at each other, etc. Take notes and later summarize your findings in a short paper you will present to the class.

CHAPTER 13 LISTENING—IS ANYONE THERE?

The exercise in repeating what the other person said before you can make your own statement (Listening Exercise) is a technique developed by Dr. Carl Rogers and has occupied many an hour of frustration for the participants. It is not easy to repeat statements others make, even when we put them in our own words. When group members make long speeches, it becomes nearly impossible to synthesize the speech and its meaning. We are really not accustomed to repeating the statements of others, and for that reason the referee is suggested to help remind us that the rules of the game call for getting approval of a repeated statement before we can make our own contribution to the discussion.

A recurring question being asked by some educators and many teachers of listening is "Why is listening not taught in school?" With the emphasis we have placed on the skills of reading and writing, both the speaking and the listening skills have been sorely neglected. It is important to consider that the skill involved in all these activities (reading, writing, speaking, and listening) is not simply a mechanical or physical skill—these are higher cognitive functions which require not only motor coordination but, especially in listening, the most sophisticated organizational and logical functioning the human brain is capable of. For that reason, the activities in this laboratory on listening are involved with these higher functions of intellectual and emotional exchanges, as well as the consideration of speaking loudly and distinctly. Our belief is that if nonsense is enunciated clearly, it does not become any less nonsense, and if lies are shouted, they do not take on any measure of truth with the added volume.

Listening Exercise

Instructions to Participants

Your task consists of discussing any one of the topics you will find on p. 370 in this workbook. However, you must follow these rules:

Before each group member can speak, he must first summarize *in his own words* and without notes what the member who spoke just before him has said, to that member's satisfaction.

If the summary is felt to be incorrect or incomplete by anyone in the group, the referee will help clear up any misunderstanding.

When someone else summarizes what you have said, do not be too easily satisfied just for the sake of continuing the discussion.

Instructions to Referees

1. Read the instructions to participants and find out what topic your group will discuss.

2. Your job is:
   a. To make sure that members stick to the rules throughout their discussion. They cannot

speak *unless* they have summarized what the previous speaker has said to that speaker's satisfaction.

b. If you or anyone in the group think the summary is incorrect or incomplete, you must interrupt and help clear up the misunderstanding.

Topics for Discussion

Group A: Are student activists justified in taking over campus buildings?

Group B: Premarital sex relations—acceptable or not?

Group C: Grades should be totally eliminated in college. Why or why not?
What other alternatives do we have to evaluate students' work?

Group D: Your task as a group is to rank the following statements that might describe the characteristics of an effective group. To do this, place a 1 in front of the statement that is the most important characteristic of an effective group, place a 2 in front of the next most important characteristic, etc. Place a 12 in front of the statement least descriptive of an effective group.

You must work on this task as a group. You may organize for work in any way you wish, as long as you work as a total group.

_____ There is a healthy competitiveness among members

_____ Everyone sticks closely to the point

_____ Members perform leadership functions

_____ The group avoids conflict situations

_____ Each member gives and receives feedback

_____ The leader suggests a plan for each group meeting

_____ Aggression is openly expressed

_____ Informal subgroups develop spontaneously

_____ Members freely express negative feelings

_____ The goals of the group are explicitly formulated

_____ Information is freely shared among members

_____ Members' feelings are considered when tasks are performed

Laboratory Groups

Picture Makers:

Illustrate in a diagram the relationships you see between silence, listening, and feedback.

or

Illustrate nonverbally the feelings experienced by a speaker who is not being listened to.

Forum Discussion:

What relationships do you perceive between the concepts of silence, listening, and feedback?

or

"Communication is a reciprocal process." Do you agree with this statement? Why or why not?

Role Players:

Role-play a situation related to what you consider an extremely important principle of communication discussed this term in this class.

or

Role-play a situation in which one of the participants does not listen to the other(s) and show how this affects their communication. This may be a family situation, a class situation, or any situation you have encountered in real life.

Observers:

Pay particular attention to how group members listen to one another. How can you tell when they are listening and when they are not? What do they do to reveal their listening or absence of listening? Who seems to be listened to most of the time? Are there any members in the group who are not listened to? How did you notice? How would you characterize the behavior of those members in the group who are not listened to? Were the group members sensitive to the way other members reacted to what they were saying? Did they make it easy for others to listen to them? From what you observed in this group, how would you describe the kind of behaviors which make it easy to listen to someone and the kind of behaviors which make it hard to listen to someone?

Feedback Blank Thirteen

This feedback blank is designed to provide you with an opportunity to evaluate the course as a whole.

1. Rate on a ten-point scale how productive this course has been for you.

   1 2 3 4 5 6 7 8 9 10

   Unproductive   Very productive

   Comments:

2. What aspects of the class seemed of *most* value to you? Why?

3. What aspects of the class seemed of *least* value to you? Why?

4. Did you feel free to participate in class? Why or why not?

5. Did you feel the class was interesting and challenging? Why or why not?

6. What are your reactions to the assignments? What did you like or dislike about them? How helpful were they for your understanding of the course material?

7. What are your reactions to the laboratory part of the course? How helpful was the laboratory for your understanding of the material?

8. What are your reactions to the textbook used in the class and to the other reading assignments, if any?

9. After this course, do you feel you would like to take another course in the field of communication? Why or why not?

10. Do you have any other comments, criticisms, questions, suggestions, etc.?

Assignment One

A Listening Course

As was pointed out in Chapter 13 of your text, few listening courses are part of the regular curriculum in high schools or colleges. Assuming you believe that such courses would be beneficial to the students, write a newspaper article in which you will advocate the creation of such courses.

Assignment Two

Interview

Interview a member of a profession in which a great amount of time is spent talking and listening to people (doctor, lawyer, psychiatrist, social worker, teacher, executive, administrator, policeman, etc.). In the course of your interview you will try to find out that person's view on the importance of listening in his job, the kinds of problems that result from poor listening in his profession, and some of the ways he overcomes these problems, etc. Take notes and then report your findings to the class.

INDEX